Frommer's®
Grand Canyon National Park

8th Edition

by Shane Christensen

WILEY

John Wiley & Sons, Inc.

Published by:

JOHN WILEY & SONS, INC.

111 River St.
Hoboken, NJ 07030-5774

ISBN 978-1-118-11804-7 (paper); ISBN 978-1-118-22455-7 (ebk);
ISBN 978-1-118-26265-8 (ebk); ISBN 978-1-118-23819-6 (ebk)

Editor: Anuja Madar
Production Editor: Lindsay Beineke
Cartographer: Andrew Murphy
Photo Editor: Richard Fox
Production by Wiley Indianapolis Composition Services

Front cover photo: Grand Canyon National Park: Steep rugged cliffs above the Colorado River at sunset, Toroweap ©Gary Crabbe / AGE Fotostock, Inc.

For information on our other products and services or to obtain technical support, please contact our Customer Care Department within the U.S. at 877/762-2974, outside the U.S. at 317/572-3993 or fax 317/572-4002.

Wiley also publishes its books in a variety of electronic formats. Some content that appears in print may not be available in electronic formats.

Manufactured in the United States of America

5   4   3   2   1

CONTENTS

8 GRAND CANYON NATIONAL PARK IN DEPTH 163

Index 201

LIST OF MAPS

ABOUT THE AUTHOR

Shane Christensen, a California native, has written extensively for Frommer's in the United States, Europe, and South America. He is also the author of *Frommer's Dubai* and a co-author of *Frommer's Mexico.*

HOW TO CONTACT US

In researching this book, we discovered many wonderful places—hotels, restaurants, shops, and more. We're sure you'll find others. Please tell us about them, so we can share the information with your fellow travelers in upcoming editions. If you were disappointed with a recommendation, we'd love to know that, too. Please write to:

Frommer's Grand Canyon National Park, 8th Edition
John Wiley & Sons, Inc. • 111 River St. • Hoboken, NJ 07030-5774

ADVISORY & DISCLAIMER

Travel information can change quickly and unexpectedly, and we strongly advise you to confirm important details locally before traveling, including information on visas, health and safety, traffic and transport, accommodations, shopping, and eating out. We also encourage you to stay alert while traveling and to remain aware of your surroundings. Avoid civil disturbances, and keep a close eye on cameras, purses, wallets, and other valuables.

While we have endeavored to ensure that the information contained within this guide is accurate and up-to-date at the time of publication, we make no representations or warranties with respect to the accuracy or completeness of the contents of this work and specifically disclaim all warranties, including without limitation warranties of fitness for a particular purpose. We accept no responsibility or liability for any inaccuracy or errors or omissions, or for any inconvenience, loss, damage, costs, or expenses of any nature whatsoever incurred or suffered by anyone as a result of any advice or information contained in this guide.

The inclusion of a company, organization, or website in this guide as a service provider and/or potential source of further information does not mean that we endorse them or the information they provide. Be aware that information provided through some websites may be unreliable and can change without notice. Neither the publisher nor author shall be liable for any damages arising herefrom.

FROMMER'S STAR RATINGS, ICONS & ABBREVIATIONS

Every hotel, restaurant, and attraction listing in this guide has been ranked for quality, value, service, amenities, and special features using a **star-rating system.** In country, state, and regional guides, we also rate towns and regions to help you narrow down your choices and budget your time accordingly. Hotels and restaurants are rated on a scale of zero (recommended) to three stars (exceptional). Attractions, shopping, nightlife, towns, and regions are rated according to the following scale: zero stars (recommended), one star (highly recommended), two stars (very highly recommended), and three stars (must-see).

In addition to the star-rating system, we also use **seven feature icons** that point you to the great deals, in-the-know advice, and unique experiences that separate travelers from tourists. Throughout the book, look for:

special finds—those places only insiders know about

fun facts—details that make travelers more informed and their trips more fun

kids—best bets for kids and advice for the whole family

special moments—those experiences that memories are made of

overrated—places or experiences not worth your time or money

insider tips—great ways to save time and money

great values—where to get the best deals

The following **abbreviations** are used for credit cards:

AE	American Express	DISC	Discover	V	Visa
DC	Diners Club	MC	MasterCard		

TRAVEL RESOURCES AT FROMMERS.COM

Frommer's travel resources don't end with this guide. Frommer's website, **www.frommers.com,** has travel information on more than 4,000 destinations. We update features regularly, giving you access to the most current trip-planning information and the best airfare, lodging, and car-rental bargains. You can also listen to podcasts, connect with other Frommers.com members through our active-reader forums, share your travel photos, read blogs from guidebook editors and fellow travelers, and much more.

WELCOME TO THE GRAND CANYON

I t was after completing one of my first hikes in the Grand Canyon years ago, as I stood at the rim and gazed at the majestic painting living before me, that I really began to appreciate its wonder. With time, that sense of wonder grew more vivid, and my connection to the canyon more personal. I even felt the canyon move me in the way religion moves fervent believers. During those first visits, I couldn't quite explain why. Here was a destination so quintessentially American, and yet very much for all the world; a place that is so human, and yet it transcends the human experience by billions of years. Only after working on this book have I come to understand all those things that, for me, make the canyon not just a beautiful place, but a spiritual one.

Each time I've returned to stand on the edge of time, I've been awed by the terraced buttes and mesas rising thousands of feet from the canyon floor and dividing the many side canyons. Early cartographers and geologists noticed similarities between these pinnacles and some of the greatest works done by human hands. Clarence Edward Dutton, who scouted the canyon for the U.S. Geological Survey in 1880 and 1881, referred to them as temples and named them after Eastern deities such as Brahma, Vishnu, and Shiva. François Matthes, who drew a topographical map of the canyon in 1902, continued the tradition by naming Wotans Throne, Krishna Temple, and other landmarks.

The temples not only inspire reverence, but also tell the grandest of stories. Half of earth's history is represented in the canyon's rocks. The oldest and deepest rock layer, the Vishnu Formation, began forming 2 billion years ago, before aerobic life forms even existed.

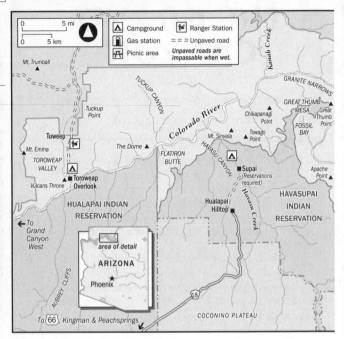

The different layers of sedimentary rock that piled up atop the Vishnu tell of landscapes that changed like dreams. They speak of mountains that really did move before eroding into nothingness, of oceans that poured forth across the land before receding, of deserts, swamps, and rivers the size of the Mississippi—all where the canyon is now. The fossils in these layers illustrate the very evolution of life. A descent into the canyon is quite literally a walk back in time.

Many of evolution's latest products—more than 1,500 plant and 400 animal species—exist at the canyon today. If you include the upper reaches of the Kaibab Plateau (on the canyon's North Rim), this small patch of Northern Arizona encompasses many diverse zones of biological life (associated plants and animals that fall into distinct bands or communities). In fact, climbing from the canyon floor to the top of the North Rim is like traveling from Mexico to Alaska in terms of the biological life you'll see.

The species come in every shape, size, and temperament, ranging from tiny ant lions on the canyon floor to 1,000-pound elk

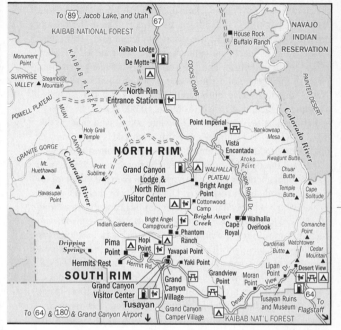

roaming the rims. And for every species, there is a story within the story. Take the Douglas fir, for example. Once part of a forest that covered both rims and much of the canyon, this tree has endured since the last ice age on shady, north-facing slopes beneath the South Rim—long after the sun-baked rim itself became inhospitably hot.

As much as I like the stories, I also enjoy the unexplained mysteries. The web of ecological cause and effect among the canyon's species is too complicated for any mortal to untangle. It leaves endless questions to ponder, such as, "Why does the agave bloom only once every 20-odd years?" Similarly, the canyon's rocks withhold as much as they tell. More than a billion years passed between the time the Vishnu Schist formed and the Tapeats Sandstone was deposited atop it—a gap in the geological record commonly referred to as the Great Unconformity. Other gaps—or unconformities, as they're called—exist between other layers. And river gravels that would have explained how the canyon was cut have long since washed away.

There's a fascinating human history here, too. The more time I spend inside the canyon, the better I hope to understand the first people who dwelt there. A number of tribes have lived in or around the canyon, and the Navajo, Havasupai, Kaibab Paiute, Hopi, Zuni, and Hualapai tribes still inhabit the region. Before Europeans arrived, they awakened to the colors of the canyon, made their clothes from its plants and animals, smelled it, touched it, tasted it, and felt it underfoot. The Hopi still regard the canyon as their place of emergence and the source to which their dead return. Native Americans have left behind more than 4,000 archaeological sites and artifacts that may be as old as 10,000 years.

I also reflect on some of the first white people who came to this mystical place. The canyon moved them to take extraordinary, if not always productive, actions. I think about the prospectors who clambered through the canyon in search of precious minerals, and then wonder about the ones who stayed here even after their mines proved unprofitable. I wish I could have met icons such as Georgie White, who began her illustrious river-running career by *swimming* 60 miles down the Colorado River in the western canyon, and Mary E. Jane Colter, the brilliant architect who aspired to create buildings that blended with the landscape, going so far as to grow plants out of the stone roof at the Lookout Studio (p. 53). I'd still like to meet David Brower, who, as the Sierra Club's executive director, helped nix a proposal to dam the Colorado River inside the Grand Canyon. He did so by running full-page ads in the *New York Times* that compared damming the canyon to flooding the Sistine Chapel.

Theodore Roosevelt also belongs in this group. During his 1903 visit, the canyon moved him to say, "Leave it as it is. You cannot improve on it. The ages have been at work on it, and man can only mar it. What you can do is to keep it for your children, your children's children … as the one great sight which every American … should see." That wasn't just talk. He backed up his words, using the Antiquities Act to declare the Grand Canyon a National Monument in 1908. Congress established Grand Canyon National Park in 1919. I imagine that President Obama, during his 2009 summer visit to the Grand Canyon with his wife and daughters, strongly identified with President Roosevelt's counsel.

Although most visit the park for recreational reasons, the canyon has a daunting, even ominous side. Everyone must negotiate for survival. One look at a river guide's clenched jaw as he or she rows into Lava Rapids will remind you that the canyon exacts a heavy price for mistakes. The most common error is to underestimate it. Try to escape, and it becomes a prison 10 miles wide (on average) and 277 miles long, with walls 4,000 feet high. The canyon's menace, for me, is part of its allure—a reminder of man's insignificance when measured against nature's greatest accomplishments.

Clearly, you can suffer here, but reward is everywhere. It's in the spectrum of colors: The Colorado River, filled with runoff from the Painted Desert, runs blood red beneath slopes of orange Hakatai Shale. Cactus flowers explode in pinks, yellows, and reds, while lichens paint rocks orange, green, and gray, creating art more striking than in any gallery. It's in the shapes, too—the spires, amphitheaters, temples, and ramps—and in the shadows that bend across them before lifting like mist. It's in the myriad organisms and their individual struggles for survival. Most of all, it's in the constancy of the river, which reminds us that, in time, all things move forward, wash away, and return to the earth.

CURRENT PARK PROJECTS

The first decade of the new millennium led to modernizing the South Rim, including constructing a new visitor center, expanding the free shuttle system and the number of parking spaces, and developing "greenway trails," paths specifically for cyclists and walkers that lessen the impact of motorized traffic.

The Grand Canyon Visitor Center is encircled by four large parking lots and a shuttle bus transit center. The excellent park film *Grand Canyon: A Journey of Wonder* runs for free every 20 minutes at the new theater adjacent to the visitor center. The visitor center also offers trip-planning tools to help visitors organize their time, and the new Science on a Sphere enclosure shows "The Canyon World," a short presentation of 1.8 billion years of canyon history projected outside of a 6-foot diameter sphere.

Visitors can now ride the park's shuttle bus system around Grand Canyon Village, to all Hermit Road and Yavapai overlooks, and to Yaki Point. A free shuttle from Grand Canyon Village to Tusayan operates in high season as well. More lanes have been opened for cars at the South Entrance, significantly limiting the long lines of the past. New parking lots have opened throughout the South Rim, reducing traffic and bottlenecks.

Bicycles can now be rented from the visitor center (except in winter). A building for the bike rental facility, as well as a limited food service facility, should be completed by summer 2012. Hermit Road has been completely repaved, and the greenway trail has been extended to Hermits Rest. There's also a new paved bike and pedestrian trail extending from the Grand Canyon Visitor Center to the South Kaibab trail head. Another bike trail will be completed by late spring 2012 connecting the visitor center and Tusayan.

Also new on the South Rim, the Trail of Time is a 1.3-mile section of paved rim trail between Verkamp's Visitor Center and

Yavapai Point, in which each meter (think of a large step) represents 1 million years of time. Visitors can touch rocks along the walk from each of the canyon layers as they learn about its geologic history.

In order to reduce litter in the area, plastics in the waste system, and greenhouse gas emissions, Grand Canyon National Park has installed free water bottle filling stations throughout the park (on both the South Rim and North Rim), including at: Hermits Rest, Bright Angel trail head, Verkamp's Visitor Center, the General Store at Market Plaza, Grand Canyon Visitor Center, South Kaibab trail head, Desert View Visitor Center, and the General Store at Desert View. On the South Rim, the park concessionaire Xanterra is now operating buses powered by natural gas.

THE best OF THE GRAND CANYON

Choosing the best part of the Grand Canyon is like naming what's most endearing about your true love. However, I've done my best to isolate a few of the most memorable places.

o **Most Dramatic Rim View: Lipan Point** (on Desert View Dr., South Rim). Above a sweeping curve in the river and with views far downstream to the west, Lipan Point is the most dramatic and easily accessible place from which to view the canyon. It's also a superb spot to watch the sunset. The **Unkar Delta,** one of the park's archaeologically richest areas, is visible directly below the overlook. See "Desert View Drive" in chapter 3. (That said, all of the points overlooking the Colorado River along the rim offer dramatic views. These include Pima, Mohave, Hopi, Moran, Lipan, Desert View, and several unnamed pull-offs.)

o **Best Scenic Drive: Desert View Drive** (South Rim). You'll see more of the canyon on this route than on either of the canyon's other two main drives (Cape Royal and Hermit roads). From the western overlooks, behold the monuments of the central canyon; the eastern overlooks have far-ranging views of the Marble Platform (p. 48) and the canyon's northeast end. Along the way, stop at the 825-year-old Tusayan Ruin and Museum (p. 31), which was once occupied by the Ancestral Puebloans. The Watchtower (p. 44), a historic edifice fashioned after towers built by the Ancestral Puebloans, is a perfect place to finish the drive. See "Desert View Drive" in chapter 3.

o **Best Place to Picnic: Vista Encantada** (on the North Rim's Cape Royal Rd.). This picnic area has canyon views and provides a convenient stopping point when you're visiting Cape

Royal Road's overlooks. You'll find few tables on the South Rim, so you'll need to be more creative there. If the weather's calm, pack a light lunch and walk along one of the rim trails until you find a bench or smooth rock on which to picnic. (If the weather's inclement, skip the picnic.) See "North Rim: Cape Royal Drive" in chapter 3.

o **Best Bike Ride: Hermit Road in summer** (South Rim). During high season, when this road is closed to most private vehicles, motorized traffic consists mostly of the occasional shuttle bus. Between shuttles, you'll often have the gently rolling road, and some of its overlooks, to yourself. A 2.8-mile paved greenway trail allows bicyclists to move off the road and closer to the rim from Monument Creek Vista almost to Hermits Rest. This is among the world's most scenic bike rides, and bicycle rentals are now available at the Grand Canyon Visitor Center. See "Other Sports & Activities" in chapter 4.

o **Best Rim Walk: Trail of Time** (South Rim). This 1.3-mile trail along the rim between Verkamp's Visitor Center and Yavapai Point affords great views along with an education in geology. See and touch rocks from each of the canyon's layers as you walk along a path in which each meter represents a million years of history. See "Trails on the South Rim" in chapter 4.

o **Best Day Hike Below the Rim: Plateau Point Trail** (accessible via the Bright Angel Trail on the South Rim). With views 1,300 feet down to the Colorado River, Plateau Point is a prime destination for fit, well-prepared day hikers. The hardest part of this 12.2-mile round-trip is on **Bright Angel Trail,** which descends 4.6 miles and 3,060 vertical feet from Grand Canyon Village to Indian Garden. The trail head for the Plateau Point Trail is a half-mile west of Indian Garden on the Tonto Trail. From there, it's a smooth and relatively level stroll to the overlook. This is an especially tough hike in summer, when you may not want to venture farther than Indian Garden. See "Corridor Trails" under "Trails on the South Rim" in chapter 4.

o **Best Corridor Trail: North Kaibab Trail** (North Rim). For those backpacking into the canyon for the first time, this is a scenic, less-crowded alternative to the South Rim corridor trails. During its 14-mile, 5,850-vertical-foot descent from rim to river, the trail passes through vegetation ranging from spruce-fir forest to Sonoran Desert cacti. **Cottonwood Campground** (p. 81) lies halfway down. The trail ends near **Phantom Ranch** (p. 110), the only lodging inside the canyon within the park boundaries. See "Corridor Trails" under "Trails on the North Rim" in chapter 4.

○ **Best Active Vacation: Oar-powered raft trips.** On these trips, expensive and worth it, you'll negotiate thrilling rapids on the Colorado River. Between rapids, though, rafts move slowly and quietly enough to reveal the canyon's subtle magic. During stops, hikers have access to some of the prettiest spots anywhere. See "Other Sports & Activities" in chapter 4.

○ **Best Historic Hotel: El Tovar** (Grand Canyon Village; ☎ 928/638-2631). Made of Oregon pine, this grand 1905 hotel rises darkly above Grand Canyon Village on the South Rim. Inside, dim lighting accentuates the hunting-lodge feel; guest rooms feature classic American furnishings. By far the park's most upscale hotel, El Tovar received a significant face-lift for its 100th anniversary. You don't need to be a guest to enjoy the hotel, and the elegant rim-view restaurant is one of the area's finest places to dine. See p. 106.

○ **Best Hotel Near the Park: Best Western Grand Canyon Squire Inn** (Tusayan; ☎ 800/622-6966 or 928/638-2681). Just a mile outside the park, this Best Western offers many of the amenities generally associated with big-city resorts. Here, you'll find the town's best dining (in the elegant Coronado Room), its liveliest watering hole (downstairs, in the sports bar that locals call "the Squire"), and its only bowling alley and arcade. The deluxe rooms in the main building are great for families. See p. 133.

○ **Best B&B: Inn at 410** (Flagstaff; ☎ 800/774-2008 or 928/774-0088). Your journey doesn't end at the door of this inn. Inside, each elegantly decorated room evokes a different setting. One celebrates the cowboy way of life; another recalls a 19th-century French garden; a third is fashioned after a music conservatory. See p. 124.

○ **Best RV Park: Kaibab Camper Village** (Jacob Lake; ☎ 928/643-7804). Old-growth ponderosas and views of Jacob Lake make this RV park, about 45 miles from the North Rim entrance, the best in the area—now it even has showers. Tent camping is possible here, too. Supplies are available at the nearby store and gas station. See p. 100.

○ **Best Campground: North Rim Campground** (☎ 877/444-6777). The campsites along Transept Canyon's rim have lovely views accented by ponderosa pines. The trees shade the sites, which are far enough apart to afford privacy. For hikers, the Transept Trail begins just a few yards away. See p. 73. On the South Rim, try **Desert View Campground** (p. 94).

○ **Best Expensive Restaurant: Cottage Place** (Flagstaff; ☎ 928/774-8431). The quiet serenity of Flagstaff's most elegant restaurant is ideal for special occasions; it's a wonderful spot to peacefully celebrate your vacation to the Southwest. Original art decorates three rose-colored rooms, where soft conversations emanate from candlelit tables. Chateaubriand for two is chef-owner Frank Branham's signature dish. See p. 127.

o **Best Moderately Priced Restaurant: Pine Country Restaurant** (Williams; 𝄢 928/635-9718). The pie here is so good that many locals order dessert first. Most of the straightforward dinner entrees—baked chicken, pork chops, and fried shrimp—go for less than $15. See p. 142.

o **Best Inexpensive Restaurant: Black Bean Burrito Bar & Salsa Co.** (Flagstaff; 𝄢 928/779-9905). Get a burrito as heavy as a hand weight—at a price that makes it feel like a handout. The food is ready within seconds, making this a great place to get a quick fix after a long day. See p. 130.

o **Best Bar in the Park: El Tovar deck** (𝄢 928/638-2631). It's hard to imagine a more inspirational view of the South Rim than that from El Tovar Hotel's deck. A draft beer come sunset could be the defining moment in your quest to better know the canyon. Light meals are offered as well. See p. 113.

o **Best Bar Outside the Park: Cuvée 928** (Flagstaff; 𝄢 928/214-9463). As wine bars gain in popularity around Flagstaff, this one has emerged as the most spirited, with a terrific selection of California and international wines. Cuvée, popular with locals and singles, offers an excellent selection of light dishes and opens onto Flagstaff's festive Heritage Square. See p. 129.

o **Best Place to Watch the Sunset: Grand Canyon Lodge's westernmost deck.** While the sun disappears behind the pines along the rim, soak up the colors on the horizon sitting in a comfortable chair, sipping a beverage from the nearby saloon. After the sun sets, cozy up beside the huge outdoor fireplace on the lodge's eastern deck. See p. 111. For unobstructed views, go to Lipan Point on the South Rim (p. 44) or Cape Royal on the North Rim (p. 46).

o **Best Accessible Backcountry Destination: Havasu Creek's waterfalls.** Surrounded by Havasu Canyon's red-rock walls, these turquoise falls seem to pour forth from the heavens into the Grand Canyon's cauldron. Travertine dams the creek in places, forming seductive swimming holes. The 10-mile hike from Hualapai Hilltop eases you into this area, home of the Havasupai people. See "Havasu Canyon & Supai" in chapter 7.

o **Best Area Museum: Museum of Northern Arizona** (Flagstaff; 𝄢 928/774-5213). This museum has one of the most extensive Native American art collections in the country. Functional and striking, the artifacts are compellingly displayed in exhibits that illuminate the close relationship between the indigenous people and the Colorado Plateau land. There's no better place to begin learning about the area. See p. 122.

o **Best Place to Escape the Crowds: More than a half-mile from any parking lot or shuttle stop.** The vast majority of park visitors seldom venture farther than this. If you do, you'll find quiet and solitude. This is especially the case on the North Rim, which gets far fewer visitors than the South Rim.

PLANNING YOUR TRIP TO GRAND CANYON NATIONAL PARK

As with any trip, a little preparation is essential before you start your journey to the Grand Canyon. This chapter provides a variety of planning tools, including information on how to get there; tips on accommodations; and quick, on the ground resources. Unless you're coming through Utah, it's generally easier to get to the South Rim than the North Rim, and there are many more tourist services available on the south side. The North Rim, open only in the warmer months, makes up in serenity what it lacks in conveniences. There are far fewer people here during the peak summer months, and the views of the canyon are equally spectacular. The best way to get to the Grand Canyon and then to move around the rims is by car (or by shuttle bus on the South Rim), although keep in mind that the drive from one rim to the other is about 200 miles.

GETTING THERE

Las Vegas and Phoenix are the closest major cities to the North and South rims, respectively. You can save money by flying into these cities, but they're too far from the canyon to stay. Flagstaff, Williams, and Tusayan (all in Arizona) and Kanab (in Utah) are better choices for lodging near the Grand Canyon.

By Plane

Many travelers fly into **Phoenix Sky Harbor International Airport** (PHX; ✆ **602/273-3300;** http://skyharbor.com), 220 miles from the South Rim, or **Las Vegas McCarran International Airport** (LAS; ✆ **702/261-5211;** www.mccarran.com), 263 miles from the North Rim. Most major airlines serve both airports, and it's easier to get a direct flight into these than into Flagstaff.

To land closer to the canyon, **US Airways** (✆ **800/428-4322;** www.usairways.com) offers daily jet service ($220 and up for a round-trip) from Phoenix to **Flagstaff Pulliam Airport** (**FLG**) (✆ **928/556-1234**), roughly 80 miles from the park. Closer still is **Grand Canyon National Park Airport** (GCN; ✆ **928/638-2446**) in Tusayan, 5 miles from the park's south entrance.

Grand Canyon Scenic Airlines (✆ **800/634-6801;** www.scenic.com) and **Grand Canyon Airlines** (✆ **866/235-9422;** www.grandcanyonairlines.com) offer daily service between Grand Canyon National Park Airport and Boulder City (BLD), Nevada (30 min. south of Las Vegas). The cost for these flights, which often include air tours of the canyon, is about $200 one-way. **Vision Air** (✆ **800/256-8767;** www.visionholidays.com) serves Grand Canyon National Park Airport from **North Las Vegas Airport** (✆ **702/261-3806**).

To find out which airlines travel to the Grand Canyon, see "Airline Websites," p. 27.

By Car

Major rental-car companies with offices in Arizona and Las Vegas include **Avis** (✆ **800/331-1212;** www.avis.com), **Budget** (✆ **800/527-0700;** www.budget.com), **Dollar** (✆ **800/800-4000;** www.dollar.com), **Hertz** (✆ **800/654-3131;** www.hertz.com), **National** (✆ **800/227-7368;** www.nationalcar.com), and **Thrifty** (✆ **800/367-2277;** www.thrifty.com).

Tip: Many of the Forest Service roads leading to remote areas on the rims are impassable in wet weather. During monsoon season, these roads can become too muddy or slippery to negotiate. In winter, there's no snow removal. People using these roads should be aware that they could be stranded indefinitely by heavy snowfall, rain, or other factors.

By Train

Amtrak (✆ **800/872-7245** or 928/774-8679 for station information only; www.amtrak.com) regularly stops in downtown Flagstaff, where lodging, rental cars, and connecting bus service are available. You can take the train from Albuquerque to Flagstaff for about $75 one-way (unreserved coach fare). The one-way fare from L.A. to Flagstaff is about $60. Amtrak also serves Williams, where connecting rail service (on the historic, lively **Grand Canyon Railway;** p. 137) is available. The one-way fare from L.A. to Williams is also about $60.

By Bus

Arizona Shuttle (© 800/888-2749; www.arizonashuttle.com) provides bus service between both Flagstaff and Williams and Grand Canyon National Park for $35 each way (prices include entry fee and are discounted if booked online).

By RV

Cruise America (© 800/327-7799; www.cruiseamerica.com) rents RVs nationwide and has offices in Phoenix, Flagstaff, and Las Vegas. Daily rates range from $70 to $150 (depending on the season) for a 25-foot, C-class motor home, which gets 8 to 10 miles per gallon on a 40-gallon tank. Thirty-foot motor homes go for $10 more per night. There is a 3-day rental minimum, plus a charge of 32¢ per mile. When making reservations at a campground, make sure that your RV meets its regulations; some sites don't allow larger RVs.

GETTING AROUND

When heading to the South Rim, it's easiest to park at a designated parking spot and then take a free shuttle from there. The Grand Canyon Visitor Center has four large parking lots. Grand Canyon Village also has a number of lots; refer to the park's free newspaper, The Guide, available at all park entrances, for a map of parking locations. Three shuttle routes serve Grand Canyon Village, the Grand Canyon Visitor Center, Mather Point, Yavapai Point, Yaki Point, and Hermit Road. Shuttles run year-round in Grand Canyon Village and from March to November on Hermit Road. When shuttles are in service, Hermit Road and Yaki Point (including the South Kaibab trail head) are closed to private vehicles.

By Car

If you're visiting from abroad and plan to rent a car in the United States, keep in mind that foreign driver's licenses are usually recognized in the U.S., but you may want to consider obtaining an international driver's license.

Taxes are already included in the printed price for gasoline. One U.S. gallon equals 3.8 liters or .85 imperial gallons. It is less expensive to buy gasoline in the gateway cities than along the highway or at the Grand Canyon itself.

International visitors should note that insurance and taxes are almost never included in quoted rental-car rates in the U.S. Be sure to ask your rental agency about additional fees for these. They can add a significant cost to your car rental.

By Train

International visitors can buy a **USA Rail Pass,** good for 15, 30, or 45 days of unlimited travel on **Amtrak** (© **800/USA-RAIL** in the U.S. or Canada; © **001/215-856-7953** outside the U.S.; www.amtrak.com). The pass is available online or through many overseas travel agents. See Amtrak's website for the cost of travel within the western, eastern, or northwestern United States. Reservations are generally required and should be made as early as possible. Regional rail passes are also available. The closest Amtrak station to the Grand Canyon is in Flagstaff, and there is also a historic railway that links Williams directly to the Grand Canyon's South Rim.

By Bus

Greyhound (© **800/231-2222** in the U.S.; © **001/214/849-8100** outside the U.S. with toll-free access; www.greyhound.com) is the sole nationwide bus line. International visitors can obtain information about the **Greyhound North American Discovery Pass.** The pass, which offers unlimited travel and stopovers in the U.S. and Canada, can be obtained outside the United States from travel agents or through www.discoverypass.com.

Daily shuttle service between the North and South rims (and to Marble Canyon/Lees Ferry) is available from mid-May to mid-October on the **Trans-Canyon Shuttle** (© **928/638-2820;** www.trans-canyonshuttle.com). This is the only way to travel between the two rims besides hiking or driving, and the trip takes 4½ hours. The fare is $80 one-way, $150 round-trip, for all ages. Reservations required.

TIPS ON ACCOMMODATIONS

Lodging inside the Grand Canyon is managed by park concessionaires that offer hotel and motel options that are generally well-kept and economical. The most upscale, and expensive, accommodations inside the park are found at the El Tovar hotel. Lodges inside the park typically need to be booked months in advance, especially for the high season. The nearest accommodations outside the South Rim are found in Tusayan, which is conveniently located but lacking in character. The gateway towns of Flagstaff, Williams, and Kanab offer a wider range of independent and chain hotels, motels, and bed-and-breakfasts for all budgets.

[FastFACTS] GRAND CANYON

Area Codes   The area code for northern Arizona is 928 and for southern Utah it's 435.

Business Hours   Business hours vary depending on the season, but are generally 9am to 6pm.

Car Rental   See "By Car" under "Getting There," earlier in this chapter.

Disabled Travelers   The steep, rocky trails below the rim pose problems for travelers with certain disabilities. People with limited vision or mobility may be able to walk the **Bright Angel and North Kaibab trails** (p. 56 and 56, respectively), which are the canyon's smoothest. If you need to take a service animal on trails below the South Rim, check in at the Backcountry Information Office (© **928/6 38-7875**), located across the train tracks near Maswik Lodge on the South Rim. On the North Rim, check in at the Backcountry Office, located 12 miles south of the North Entrance (just north of the campground entrance). For details about the accessibility of park buildings and facilities, pick up the free *Accessibility Guide* at the Grand Canyon Visitor Center, Kolb Studio, Tusayan Ruin and Museum, the Desert View Information Center, or any of the park entrance stations.

All **shuttle buses** in the park are equipped with ramps and space to carry passengers in wheelchairs that are up to 30 inches wide and 48 inches long. Visitors can also indicate to the driver that they would like the bus to "kneel" to reduce the size of the step up to the front door when entering or exiting.

On the rims, many attractions are accessible to everyone. On the South Rim, **Desert View Drive** (p. 40) is an excellent activity. Four of its overlooks—Yaki, Grandview, Moran, and Desert View—are wheelchair accessible. The **Tusayan Ruin and Museum** (p. 31) is also accessible (ask for assistance at the information desk). At **Desert View** (p. 44), the bookstore and grocery store are accessible, but no designated seating is available at the snack bar. Along Desert View Drive, restrooms for the mobility impaired are at Yaki Point, Grandview Point, Tusayan Ruin and Museum, and Desert View (just east of Desert View General Store).

Hermit Road (p. 35) has been repaved, and although the drive is closed to most private cars when shuttles are running, travelers with disabilities can obtain **accessibility permits** for their vehicles at the park's entrance gates, Grand Canyon Visitor Center, Yavapai Geology Museum, Kolb Studio, Verkamp's, El Tovar's concierge desk, and the transportation desks at Bright Angel Lodge, Yavapai Lodge, and Maswik Lodge. On the drive itself, **Hopi Point, Pima Point, Maricopa Point,** and **Powell Memorial** (p. 37, 38, and 36, respectively) are all wheelchair accessible. The road also affords a number of nice "windshield views" from pullouts where one need not leave the car to see the canyon. To reach the gift shop at **Hermits Rest** (p. 39), you'll have to negotiate two 5-inch steps and a route that slopes gently sideways. Along Hermit Road there are wheelchair-accessible restrooms at Hopi Point and Hermits Rest. Despite having many historic buildings, most of **Grand Canyon Village** (p. 107) is wheelchair accessible. The notable exceptions are Kolb Studio and Lookout Studio. **Hopi House** (p. 52) is accessible only through a 29-inch-wide door on the building's canyon side. Also, some hallways in **Yavapai Lodge** (p. 108) are too narrow for wheelchairs. Wheelchair-accessible restrooms are at the Grand Canyon Visitor Center, Canyon Village Marketplace, Yavapai Geology Museum, El Tovar Hotel, Bright Angel Lodge, Mather Campground, and Maswik Lodge. Mather Campground has six sites for people with disabilities.

The **Grand Canyon Visitor Center** (p. 30), on the South Rim, is tailored for people with disabilities. Walkways and doorways are wheelchair accessible. **Mather Point** (p. 40) can be reached from the visitor center via a paved walkway, and a new wheelchair-accessible ramp takes visitors out to a point offering fantastic canyon views.

Those who have difficulty walking can usually negotiate the 1.5-mile-long rim trail between Bright Angel Lodge and Yavapai Point (except when icy). An additional half-mile from Yavapai Point is a doable distance to Mather Point. Wide and smooth, the new greenway has moderate grades—and stunning canyon views.

On the North Rim, most buildings are accessible. An accessible trail connecting Grand Canyon Lodge, its motel units, and the visitor center is under construction. The two most popular North Rim overlooks—**Point Imperial** and **Cape Royal** (p. 48 and 46, respectively)—are accessible, though neither has a designated parking space. **Grand Canyon Lodge** (p. 53) is accessible via a lift and a ramp, and the **North Rim Campground** (p. 98) has six accessible sites. Wheelchair-accessible restrooms are at the Backcountry Office (assistance required), Grand Canyon Lodge (assistance may be required), the North Rim Campground, and behind the visitor center.

Xanterra (✆ **928/638-2822**), with advance notice, can sometimes arrange for buses with lifts for its tours. The canyon's mule-trip operators accommodate people with certain disabilities, as do many river companies. **Western River Expeditions** (✆ **800/453-7450**; www.westernriver.com), **Arizona Raft Adventures** (✆ **800/786-7238**; www.azraft.com), **Grand Canyon Expeditions** (✆ **800/544-2691**; www.gcex.com), and **Canyon Explorations, Inc.** (✆ **800/654-0723**;

www.canyonx.com) are particularly accommodating to people with certain disabilities.

The National Park Service supplies U.S. citizens with permanent disabilities a free federal **Access Pass,** which can only be obtained in person at a national park. Good for a lifetime, the pass admits a car with four adults, and gets holders a half-off discount on some facilities and services, such as camping.

Doctors   Check with your hotel staff for help identifying local doctors.

Drinking Laws   The legal age for purchase and consumption of alcoholic beverages is 21; proof of age is required and often requested at bars, nightclubs, and restaurants, so it's always a good idea to bring ID when you go out. Do not carry open containers of alcohol in your car or any public area that isn't zoned for alcohol consumption. The police can fine you on the spot. Don't even think about driving while intoxicated.

Electricity   Like Canada, the United States uses 110 to 120 volts AC (60 cycles), compared to 220 to 240 volts AC (50 cycles) in most of Europe, Australia, and New Zealand. Downward converters that change 220–240 volts to 110–120 volts are difficult to find in the United States, so bring one with you.

Embassies & Consulates   All embassies are in the nation's capital, Washington, D.C. Some consulates are in major U.S. cities, and most nations have a mission to the United Nations in New York City. If your country isn't listed below, call for directory information in Washington, D.C. (✆ **202/555-1212**) or check **www.embassy.org/ embassies.**

The embassy of **Australia** is at 1601 Massachusetts Ave. NW, Washington, DC 20036 (✆ **202/797-3000;** www.usa.embassy.gov.au). Consulates are in New York City, Honolulu, Houston, Los Angeles, and San Francisco.

The embassy of **Canada** is at 501 Pennsylvania Ave. NW, Washington, DC 20001 (✆ **202/682-1740;** www.canadainternational.gc.ca/ washington). Canadian consulates are in Buffalo (New York), Detroit, Los Angeles, New York City, and Seattle.

The embassy of **Ireland** is at 2234 Massachusetts Ave. NW, Washington, DC 20008 (✆ **202/462-3939;** www.embassyofireland.org). Irish consulates are in Boston, Chicago, New York City, San Francisco, and other cities. See the website for a complete listing.

The embassy of **New Zealand** is at 37 Observatory Circle NW, Washington, DC 20008 (✆ **202/328-4800;** www.nzembassy.com). New Zealand consulates are in Los Angeles, Salt Lake City, San Francisco, and Seattle.

The embassy of the **United Kingdom** is at 3100 Massachusetts Ave. NW, Washington, DC 20008 (✆ **202/588-6500;** http://ukinusa.fco. gov.uk). British consulates are in Atlanta, Boston, Chicago, Cleveland, Houston, Los Angeles, New York City, San Francisco, and Seattle.

Emergencies   Dial ℂ **911** for emergencies requiring police, fire, or ambulance assistance.

Family Travel   The park's **Junior Ranger Program** will engage your kids. Register for it on the South Rim at the Grand Canyon Visitor Center, Verkamp's Visitor Center, or Tusayan Ruin and Museum, or on the North Rim at the North Rim Visitor Center. Your child will receive a *Junior Ranger Activity Book* outlining the needed steps to complete the Junior Ranger program (including attending a ranger-led program, completing educational puzzles, and picking up litter). When completed, bring the booklet back to any of the places listed above to obtain a Junior Ranger certificate and badge.

In summer, there are additional children's programs. For a complete listing of kids' activities, consult the park's free newspaper, *The Guide*, available at all park entrances.

Kids may also enjoy the following activities:

o **Look for deer.** At sunset, take a quiet walk in the grass along the train tracks by Grand Canyon Village, or watch a meadow along the entrance road on the North Rim. See how many deer you can count. But please don't feed or approach them.

o **Hike a rim trail.** If your kids are too young to make the steep descent into the canyon, take them walking along the canyon's rim. This gets them away from the car and into less crowded areas. On the South Rim, the rim trail from Grand Canyon Village to Mather Point is a nice option. On the North Rim, the Transept and Cliff Springs trails (p. 73 and 74) are fun for kids.

o **Go birding.** During the daytime, sit on the rim and watch raptors and ravens ride the thermals. See if you can identify eagles, hawks, or vultures—and perhaps even California condors. You'll also likely see swifts and swallows darting around the rim. Use the bird section under "The Fauna" in chapter 8 to help identify the different species.

o **Watch wranglers prepare mules for the trip into the canyon.** At 8am daily (9am in winter), wranglers bring mules to the corral on the South Rim (just west of Bright Angel Lodge). While the mules entertain the kids, the wranglers entertain adults with a humorous lecture on mule-ride protocol. A word of caution: Certain tourist-weary mules will bite when petted.

o **See the canyon on the big, big screen.** If the canyon fails to dazzle your young ones in person, show it to them on the 82-foot-high screen at the IMAX theater outside the park in Tusayan.

To locate accommodations, restaurants, and attractions that are particularly kid-friendly, refer to the "Kids" icon throughout this guide.

Gasoline   Please see "By Car" under "Getting Around," earlier in this chapter.

Health   Unless you're arriving from an area known to be suffering from an epidemic (particularly cholera or yellow fever), inoculations or vaccinations are not required for entry into the United States. During your visit to the Grand Canyon, it is helpful to keep the following in mind:

Bugs, Bites & Other Wildlife Concerns   The Grand Canyon offers a spectacular range of flora and fauna. It's important to keep wildlife wild—that means never approaching or feeding any animal and staying at least 300 yards away from larger animals. The National Park Service cautions that deer and elk can be aggressive and will defend their territory, and that even squirrels can bite, so don't feed them.

High-Altitude Hazards   The Grand Canyon rim's high elevation (approximately 7,000 ft.) can lead to altitude sickness, shortness of breath, fatigue, and even nausea. Be sure to drink plenty of water and take it easy, particularly when you first arrive to this elevation. Remember when hiking that climbing back out of the canyon is far more difficult at these elevations than descending into it, so pace yourself.

Sun/Elements/Extreme Weather Exposure   The Grand Canyon's intense sun, particularly in summer, can cause severe dehydration. Be sure to drink plenty of water, protect yourself from the sun, and avoid hiking into the canyon during the sweltering summer heat.

Internet & Wi-Fi   Wireless Internet access is increasingly available on the South Rim, including in the public areas of South Rim hotels, as well as in the Park Headquarters Building (open from 8am–5pm year-round). Free Wi-Fi should also be available in the Grand Canyon Visitor Center by early 2012. On the North Rim, the only place to get Internet (via free wireless connection) is at the General Store adjacent to the North Rim Campground. It's possible to access the Internet from one of the outdoor tables even after the store is closed.

Legal Aid   While driving, if you are pulled over for a minor infraction (such as speeding), never attempt to pay the fine directly to a police officer; this could be construed as attempted bribery, a much more serious crime. Pay fines by mail, or directly into the hands of the clerk of the court. If accused of a more serious offense, say and do nothing before consulting a lawyer. In the U.S., the burden is on the state to prove a person's guilt beyond a reasonable doubt, and everyone has the right to remain silent, whether he or she is suspected of a crime or actually arrested. Once arrested, a person can make one telephone call to a party of his or her choice. The international visitor should call his or her embassy or consulate.

Mail   At press time, domestic postage rates were 28¢ for a postcard and 44¢ for a letter. For international mail, a first-class letter of up to 1 ounce costs 98¢ (75¢ to Canada and 79¢ to Mexico); a first-class postcard costs the same as a letter. For more information go to **www. usps.com**.

If you aren't sure what your address will be in the United States, mail can be sent to you, in your name, c/o General Delivery at the main post office of the city or region where you expect to be. (Call ℂ **800/275-8777** for information on the nearest post office.) The addressee must pick up mail in person and must produce proof of identity (such as a driver's license or passport). Most post offices will hold mail for up to 1 month, and are open Monday to Friday from 8am to 6pm, and Saturday from 9am to 3pm.

Always include zip codes when mailing items in the U.S. If you don't know your zip code, visit www.usps.com/zip4.

Mobile Phones   There is reliable cellphone coverage on the Grand Canyon's South Rim. Coverage in Grand Canyon Village has greatly improved among most carriers, and there's typically good service between Maricopa Point and Yaki Point. However, cellphone coverage remains weak or nonexistent outside the South Rim, although some will be able to pick up a weak signal on the North Rim if they are located near the rim itself. Coverage does not generally exist within the canyon, so don't expect to use your phone on any hikes below the rim. A park ranger audio cellphone tour is available for free on the South Rim by dialing ℂ **928/225-2907.**

Money & Costs   Frommer's lists exact prices in the local currency. The currency conversions provided here for international visitors were correct at press time. However, rates fluctuate, so before departing consult a currency exchange website such as **www.oanda.com/ currency/converter** to check up-to-the-minute rates.

Most places of business accept credit cards, and ATMs are common throughout the gateway towns. There are only a couple ATMs within Grand Canyon National Park, however.

The two ATMs on the South Rim are at **Chase Bank,** in Market Plaza next to the Canyon Village Marketplace, and at **Maswik Lodge.** Both charge a $2 fee for non-Chase bank users. On the North Rim, an ATM is available at the **General Store** and in the **Roughrider Saloon** at Grand Canyon Lodge. Due to the limited availability of ATMs, it is best to make sure you have sufficient cash on you before arriving at the park.

THE VALUE OF THE U.S. DOLLAR VS. OTHER POPULAR CURRENCIES

US$	AUS$	CAN$	EURO (€)	NZ$	UK£
1.00	1.04	1.05	.75	1.31	1.65

WHAT THINGS COST IN THE GRAND CANYON

U.S.$

Prices in and around the Grand Canyon tend to be very reasonable compared with many destinations in the United States. The National Park Service mandates that its concessionaires keep prices down so ordinary citizens from across the United Sates and abroad can come enjoy this magnificent place without depleting their savings accounts. Prices are moderate at most lodging and dining facilities within the park and at many of the gateway towns listed in this book; an exception is Tusayan, which has expensive gas and food.

Taxi from Grand Canyon Village to Tusayan (1 or 2 adults)	10.00
Mule day trip to the Abyss	121.00
7-day park admission (per car)	25.00
Deluxe room at El Tovar Hotel (expensive)	273.00
West room at Yavapai Lodge (moderate)	114.00
Room at Hotel Weatherford (inexpensive)	89.00
Site at Grand Canyon Trailer Village	35.00
Three-course dinner for one without wine, moderate	20.00–30.00
Bottle of beer	5.00
Cup of coffee	1.50–3.00
1 gallon of gas	4.00
Admission to most museums	10.00

Credit cards are widely accepted in and around the Grand Canyon. Beware of hidden credit-card fees while traveling. International visitors should check with their credit or debit card issuer to see what fees, if any, will be charged for overseas transactions. Recent reform legislation in the U.S., for example, has curbed some exploitative lending practices. But many banks have responded by increasing fees in other areas, including fees for customers who use credit and debit cards while out of the country—even if those charges were made in U.S. dollars. Fees can amount to 3% or more of the purchase price. Check with your bank before departing to avoid any surprise charges on your statement.

For help with currency conversions, tip calculations, and more, download Frommer's convenient Travel Tools app for your mobile device. Go to www.frommers.com/go/mobile, and click on the Travel Tools icon.

Newspapers & Magazines   Pick up a copy of *The Guide* (there's one for both the South Rim and North Rim) at any entrance station to the Grand Canyon or online at www.nps.gov/grca/parknews/newspaper.htm. There's also a free online Trip Planner on the same site.

Packing   A wide-brimmed hat, sunglasses, and sunscreen are standard canyon equipment no matter the season. If you're planning to hike in cool weather, you'll be most comfortable in a water-resistant, breathable shell and several layers of insulating clothing, preferably made of polypropylene, polar fleece, or other fabrics that remain warm when wet. The shell-and-layers technique works especially well during spring and fall, when extreme temperature swings occur regularly. Even in summer, you'll want a shell and at least one insulating layer for cold nights or storms, especially on the North Rim.

For more helpful information on packing for your trip, download our convenient Travel Tools app for your mobile device. Go to www. frommers.com/go/mobile, and click on the Travel Tools icon.

Passports   Virtually every air traveler entering the U.S. is required to show a passport. All persons, including U.S. citizens, traveling by air between the United States and Canada, Mexico, Central and South America, the Caribbean, and Bermuda are required to present a valid passport. *Note:* U.S. and Canadian citizens entering the U.S. at land and sea ports of entry from within the western hemisphere must now also present a passport or other documents compliant with the Western Hemisphere Travel Initiative (WHTI; see www.getyouhome.gov for details). Children 15 and under may continue entering with only a U.S. birth certificate, or other proof of U.S. citizenship.

Australia   **Australian Passport Information Service** (© 131-232; www.passports.gov.au).

Canada   **Passport Office,** Department of Foreign Affairs and International Trade, Ottawa, ON K1A 0G3 (© 800/567-6868; www.ppt.gc.ca).

Ireland   **Passport Office,** Setanta Centre, Molesworth Street, Dublin 2 (© 01/671-1633; www.foreignaffairs.gov.ie).

New Zealand   **Passports Office,** Department of Internal Affairs, 47 Boulcott St., Wellington, 6011 (© 0800/225-050 in New Zealand or 04/474-8100; www.passports.govt.nz).

United Kingdom   Visit your nearest passport office, major post office, or travel agency, or contact the **Identity and Passport Service (IPS),** 89 Eccleston Sq., London, SW1V 1PN (© 0300/222-0000; www.ips.gov.uk).

United States   To find your regional passport office, check the U.S. State Department website (travel.state.gov/passport), or call the **National Passport Information Center** (📞 877/487-2778) for automated information.

Petrol/Gasoline   Please see "By Car" under "Getting Around," earlier in this chapter.

Safety   In 2001, two Arizona writers published a disconcertingly thick book detailing every known fatal accident within the canyon. *Over the Edge: Death in Grand Canyon* (Puma Press, Flagstaff, 2001) not only tells captivating stories but also serves as a handy reminder of what *not* to do here. (For starters, don't remove your hiking boots and run barefoot toward the river.) Below is a list of guidelines that will keep you from getting into *Over the Edge: Volume II.*

- **Exercise caution on the rims.** Every year, a handful of people fall to their deaths in the canyon. To minimize risk, don't blaze trails along the rim, where loose rocks make footing precarious. Use caution when taking photographs and when looking through your camcorder's viewfinder (unless you want your final footage aired on the nightly news). Be prepared for wind gusts, and keep an eye on your children.

- **Move away from rim overlooks during thunderstorms.** Get away from the rim during thunderstorms, where lightning frequently strikes and is extremely dangerous. On the rim, you may be the highest point—and, therefore, the best lightning rod—for miles around. Hair standing on end is a warning that an electric charge is building near you. If you hear thunder or see lighting, move as far away as possible from the rim and don't touch or cower under metal objects or tall trees. The safest place to be is inside a vehicle. If you are stuck out in the open, crouch down on the balls of your feet to minimize your contact with the ground until the lightning has passed.

- **Wear sunscreen and protective clothing.** Even during winter, the Arizona sun can singe unsuspecting tourists. To protect your skin and cool your body, wear long-sleeved white shirts, wide-brimmed hats, sunglasses, and high-SPF sunscreen.

- **Choose a reasonable destination for day hikes.** Although most park visitors quickly recognize the danger of falling into the canyon, they don't always perceive the danger of walking into it. Every year, the canyon's backcountry rangers respond to hundreds of emergency calls, most of them on the corridor trails (Bright Angel, North Kaibab, and South Kaibab). Day hikers are lured deep into the canyon by the ease of the descent, the sight of other hikers continuing downward, and, sometimes, the goal of reaching the river. As they descend into the canyon's hotter climes in late morning, temperatures climb doubly fast. By the time they turn around, it's too late. They are hot, fatigued, and literally in too deep. When hiking in the canyon, particularly during the summer months, pick a reasonable destination, and don't hesitate to turn back early.

o **Don't hike midday during hot weather.** Hiking when it is hotter than 100°F (38°C) will cause you to sweat out fluids faster than your body can absorb them, no matter how much you drink. For this reason, hiking in extreme heat is inherently dangerous. Think twice before you hike into the canyon during summer.

o **Yield to mules** If you encounter mules, step off the trail on the uphill side and wait for instructions from the wranglers. This protects you, the riders, and the mules.

o **Drink and eat regularly when hiking** During a full day of hiking, plan to drink more than 1 gallon of water; on the hottest days, make it more than 2. Consume both water and electrolyte-replacement drinks such as Gatorade. Also, remember that eating carbohydrate-rich, salty foods is as important as drinking. If you consume large amounts of water without food, you can quickly develop an electrolyte imbalance, which can result in unconsciousness or even death.

Senior Travel   Senior discounts are available for the National Park entrance fee, most museums, and many hotels.

Smoking   All hotel rooms, restaurants, bars, and public areas are nonsmoking within Grand Canyon National Park.

Taxes   The United States has no value-added tax (VAT) or other indirect tax at the national level. Every state, county, and city may levy its own local tax on all purchases, including hotel and restaurant checks and airline tickets. These taxes will not appear on price tags. Arizona sales tax is 6.6%. The hotel tax in the Grand Canyon area is 7.74%.

Telephones   Many convenience groceries and packaging services sell **prepaid calling cards** in denominations up to $50. Many public pay phones at airports now accept American Express, MasterCard, and Visa. **Local calls** made from most pay phones cost either 25¢ or 35¢. Most long-distance and international calls can be dialed directly from any phone. **To make calls within the United States and to Canada,** dial 1 followed by the area code and the seven-digit number. **For other international calls,** dial 011 followed by the country code, city code, and the number you are calling.

Calls to area codes **800, 888, 877,** and **866** are toll-free. However, calls to area codes **700** and **900** (chat lines, bulletin boards, "dating" services, and so on) can be expensive—charges of 95¢ to $3 or more per minute. Some numbers have minimum charges that can run $15 or more.

For **reversed-charge or collect calls,** and for person-to-person calls, dial the number 0 then the area code and number; an operator will come on the line, and you should specify whether you are calling collect, person-to-person, or both. If your operator-assisted call is international, ask for the overseas operator.

For **directory assistance** ("Information"), dial 411 for local numbers and national numbers in the U.S. and Canada. For dedicated long-distance information, dial 1, then the appropriate area code plus 555-1212.

Time The continental United States is divided into **four time zones:** Eastern Standard Time (EST), Central Standard Time (CST), Mountain Standard Time (MST), and Pacific Standard Time (PST). Alaska and Hawaii have their own zones. For example, when it's 9am in Los Angeles (PST), it's 7am in Honolulu (HST), 10am in Denver (MST), 11am in Chicago (CST), noon in New York City (EST), 5pm in London (GMT), and 2am the next day in Sydney.

Daylight saving time (summer time) is in effect from 1am on the second Sunday in March to 1am on the first Sunday in November, except in Arizona, Hawaii, the U.S. Virgin Islands, and Puerto Rico. Daylight saving time moves the clock 1 hour ahead of standard time.

For help with time translations, and more, download our convenient Travel Tools app for your mobile device. Go to www.frommers.com/go/mobile and click on the Travel Tools icon.

Tipping In hotels, tip **bellhops** at least $1 per bag ($2–$3 if you have a lot of luggage) and tip the **chamber staff** $1 to $2 per day (more if you've left a big mess for him or her to clean up). Tip the **doorman** or **concierge** only if he or she has provided you with some specific service (for example, calling a cab for you or obtaining difficult-to-get theater tickets). Tip the **valet-parking attendant** $1 every time you get your car.

In restaurants, bars, and nightclubs, tip **service staff** and **bartenders** 15% to 20% of the check, tip **checkroom attendants** $1 per garment, and tip **valet-parking attendants** $1 per vehicle.

As for other service personnel, tip **cab drivers** 15% of the fare; tip **skycaps** at airports at least $1 per bag ($2–$3 if you have a lot of luggage); and tip **hairdressers** and **barbers** 15% to 20%.

For help with tip calculations, currency conversions, and more, download our convenient Travel Tools app for your mobile device. Go to www.frommers.com/go/mobile and click on the Travel Tools icon.

Toilets You won't find public toilets or "restrooms" on the streets in most U.S. cities but they can be found in hotel lobbies, bars, restaurants, museums, department stores, railway and bus stations, and service stations. Large hotels and fast-food restaurants are often the best bet for clean facilities. Restaurants and bars in resorts or heavily visited areas may reserve their restrooms for patrons.

VAT See "Taxes" earlier in this section.

Visas The U.S. State Department has a **Visa Waiver Program (VWP)** allowing citizens of the following countries to enter the United States without a visa for stays of up to 90 days: Andorra, Australia,

Austria, Belgium, Brunei, Czech Republic, Denmark, Estonia, Finland, France, Germany, Greece, Hungary, Iceland, Ireland, Italy, Japan, Latvia, Liechtenstein, Lithuania, Luxembourg, Malta, Monaco, the Netherlands, New Zealand, Norway, Portugal, San Marino, Singapore, Slovakia, Slovenia, South Korea, Spain, Sweden, Switzerland, and the United Kingdom. (***Note:*** This list was accurate at press time; for the most up-to-date list of countries in the VWP, consult http://travel. state.gov/visa.) Even though a visa isn't necessary, in an effort to help U.S. officials check travelers against terror watch lists before they arrive at U.S. borders, visitors from VWP countries must register online through the Electronic System for Travel Authorization (ESTA) before boarding a plane or a boat to the U.S. Travelers must complete an electronic application providing basic personal and travel eligibility information. The Department of Homeland Security recommends filling out the form at least 3 days before traveling. Authorizations will be valid for up to 2 years or until the traveler's passport expires, whichever comes first. Currently, there is one US$14 fee for the online application. Existing ESTA registrations remain valid through their expiration dates. ***Note:*** Any passport issued on or after October 26, 2006, by a VWP country must be an **e-Passport** for VWP travelers to be eligible to enter the U.S. without a visa. Citizens of these nations also need to present a round-trip air or cruise ticket upon arrival. E-Passports contain computer chips capable of storing biometric information, such as the required digital photograph of the holder. If your passport doesn't have this feature, you can still travel without a visa if the valid passport was issued before October 26, 2005, and includes a machine-readable zone, or if the valid passport was issued between October 26, 2005, and October 25, 2006, and includes a digital photograph. For more information, go to **http://travel.state. gov/visa.** Canadian citizens may enter the United States without visas, but will need to show passports and proof of residence.

Citizens of all other countries must have (1) a valid passport that expires at least 6 months later than the scheduled end of their visit to the U.S., and (2) a tourist visa.

For information about U.S. visas, go to **http://travel.state.gov** and click on "Visas." Or go to one of the following websites:

Australian citizens can obtain up-to-date visa information from the **U.S. Embassy Canberra,** Moonah Place, Yarralumla, ACT 2600 ((*C* **02/6214-5600**), or by checking the U.S. Diplomatic Mission's website at **http://canberra.usembassy.gov/visas.html.**

British subjects can obtain up-to-date visa information by calling the **U.S. Embassy Visa Information Line** ((*C* **09042-450-100** from within the U.K. at £1.20 per minute; or *C* **866/382-3589** from within the U.S. at a flat rate of $16 and payable by credit card only) or by visiting the "Visas to the U.S." section of the American Embassy London's website at **http://london.usembassy.gov/visas.html.**

Irish citizens can obtain up-to-date visa information through the **U.S. Embassy Dublin,** 42 Elgin Rd., Ballsbridge, Dublin 4 (📞 **1580-47-VISA [8472]** from within the Republic of Ireland at €2.40 per minute; **http://dublin.usembassy.gov**).

Citizens of **New Zealand** can obtain up-to-date visa information by contacting the **U.S. Embassy New Zealand,** 29 Fitzherbert Terrace, Thorndon, Wellington (📞 **644/462-6000; http://newzealand. usembassy.gov**).

Visitor Information   Grand Canyon National Park distributes a free trip planner that should answer most of your questions. To get a copy and find out more information, call 📞 **928/638-7888,** or visit the park's website at www.nps.gov/grca.

AIRLINE WEBSITES
MAJOR AIRLINES

AEROMéxico
www.aeromexico.com

Air Canada
www.aircanada.com

Alaska Airlines/ Horizon Air
www.alaskaair.com

American Airlines
www.aa.com

British Airways
www.british-airways.com

Continental Airlines
www.continental.com

Delta Air Lines
www.delta.com

Hawaiian Airlines
www.hawaiianair.com

United Airlines
www.united.com

US Airways
www.usairways.com

BUDGET AIRLINES

Frontier Airlines
www.frontierairlines.com

Grand Canyon Airlines
www.grandcanyonairlines.com

Great Lakes Airlines
www.greatlakesav.com

JetBlue Airways
www.jetblue.com

Southwest Airlines
www.southwest.com

Spirit Airlines
www.spiritair.com

Sun Country Airlines
www.suncountry.com

WestJet
www.westjet.com

Vision Airlines
www.visionairlines.com

EXPLORING THE GRAND CANYON

One of the most enjoyable things to do at the canyon is also one of the simplest: Find a quiet place on the rim or off a trail and just sit for an hour or so. Feel the air rise, watch the shadows and light play across the monuments, and listen to the timeless hush. No matter how fast you drive or how far you walk, no matter how many photos you take or angles you see the canyon from, you'll never "do" the canyon. So relax and enjoy it.

THE BASICS
Access & Entry Points

The park has three gated entrances—two on the South Rim and one on the North Rim. The one that's most convenient from Flagstaff, Williams, and Phoenix is the park's **South Entrance Gate,** 1 mile north of Tusayan on Highway 64. Traffic occasionally backs up here during peak hours in high season (May–Sept). Many travelers from Flagstaff, as well as those from points east, prefer entering the South Rim area through its **East Entrance Gate,** near Desert View, 29 miles west of Cameron on Highway 64. From Flagstaff, the drive to the East Entrance is about 8 miles longer than to the South Entrance. There are seldom lines here.

The gate to the North Rim (210 highway miles away from the South Rim) isn't convenient to anywhere, except perhaps the small store, motel, and gas station at Jacob Lake, which is 30 miles north on Highway 67. The North Rim itself is 14 miles south of the gate. The closest real town is Fredonia, 71 miles north on Highway 89A. Visitors can also access parts of the park via Forest Service dirt roads.

Information Centers

Grand Canyon Visitor Center   The Grand Canyon Visitor Center, near Mather Point, has become the first stop for many visitors to the South Rim. The whole complex has the streamlined appearance of a modern mass-transit hub and continues to expand. Various kiosks provide basic information about tours, trails, overlooks, cycling, weather, ranger-guided programs, and other topics. The four large parking lots surrounding the visitor center accommodate up to 875 vehicles. Free shuttles connect the Information Plaza with Grand Canyon Village and the Kaibab Trail.

The Grand Canyon Visitor Center sits inside a long, glass-faced building. Here you'll find displays about the canyon, trip planning tools to help you decide how to spend your time in the park, and a ranger-staffed information desk. At one end of the visitor center is the Science on a Sphere enclosure presenting "The Canyon World," a short introduction to 1.8 billion years of canyon history projected on the outside of a 6-foot diameter sphere. From the other end of the visitor center you can enter the new theater, which shows the inspiring park film *Grand Canyon: A Journey of Wonder*. It's free and plays every 20 minutes. Adjacent to the visitor center are restrooms and Books and More, the large bookstore run by the Grand Canyon Association. The plaza outside the visitor center is a good place to learn about canyon flora—it's also a great place for kids to climb and explore. They can read a poem about the Grand Canyon, search the rocks for engravings of Grand Canyon birds, fossils, and animal tracks, and even pet the full-size granite sculpture of a mountain lion. The Grand Canyon Visitor Center is open daily 8am to 6pm in summer, and 8am to 5pm during the rest of the year.

Yavapai Geology Museum   Located a half-mile west of the Grand Canyon Visitor Center on Yavapai Point, this historic station has an observation room from which you can identify many of the central canyon's monuments. Rangers frequently lead interpretive programs here, and exhibits explain the region's geology, including how the canyon was formed. It's open daily from 8am to 8pm in summer, and from 8am to 6pm the rest of the year. (For more information, see "Desert View Drive," later in this chapter.)

Desert View Visitor Center   At this small visitor center 26 miles east of Grand Canyon Village, you can buy books from the Grand Canyon Association and get information about the canyon from park rangers. It's just inside the park's East Entrance, 29 miles west of Cameron on Highway 64. It's open daily from 9am to 6pm in summer, and daily from 9am to 5pm the rest of the year.

Tusayan Ruin and Museum This museum, 3 miles west of Desert View, has an information desk staffed by rangers, plus displays about the area's indigenous people including pottery, arrowheads, jewelry, and figurines. It's open daily from 9am to 5pm (closed Tues–Wed in winter). See p. 43.

Kolb Studio On the rim at the west end of Grand Canyon Village, Kolb Studio houses a small bookstore and an art gallery with free exhibits. It's open daily from 8am to 7pm in summer, and daily 8am to 6pm the rest of the year. See p. 52.

Verkamp's Visitor Center The park's newest visitor center lies within the century-old Verkamp's Curios building. It features displays depicting the canyon's history as well as a bookstore. It's open daily 8am to 8pm in summer, and 8am to 6pm the rest of the year. See p. 53.

North Rim Visitor Center This visitor center near Grand Canyon Lodge has a ranger desk with maps, trail information including water availability and weather conditions, and schedules for ranger programs, as well as a Grand Canyon Association bookstore. It's open daily 8am to 6pm from mid-May to mid-October, and after that from 9am to 4pm until the first snow closes the road.

Entrance Fees

Admission to Grand Canyon National Park costs $25 per private vehicle (includes all passengers) and $16 for adults (age 17 and older) on foot, bicycle, or motorcycle. The receipt is good for a week and includes both rims. Adults who enter the park in organized groups or on commercial tours usually pay about $8 each, though rates vary some.

SPECIAL DISCOUNTS & PASSES

Frequent visitors to National Park Service or other fee-charging federal sites will benefit from the **America the Beautiful–National Parks and Federal Recreational Lands Pass** ($80). Valid for 1 year from the date of purchase, the pass can be purchased at park entrance stations, Grand Canyon Association bookstores, the IMAX theater in Tusayan, or online at www. recreation.gov.

Also available from the National Park Service is a lifetime **Senior Pass** ($10) for U.S. citizens 62 and over, which admits the holder, free of charge, at all NPS sites. Another card, the **Access Pass,** is available for U.S. citizens with permanent disabilities. It's free, but must be obtained in person at the entrance gate or IMAX theater in Tusayan. Those who already have a **Golden Age** or **Golden Access** pass do not need to obtain these new passes.

Camping Fees

A site at **Mather Campground,** the South Rim's largest campground, costs $18 per night in high season (spaces are available for hikers without vehicles for $12). **Desert View Campground,** open mid-May to mid-October, costs $12 per site per night. And sites at **North Rim Campground,** also open mid-May to mid-October, cost $18 to $25 per night. At all three campgrounds, no more than two vehicles and six people can share a site. **Trailer Village,** an RV park on the South Rim, charges $35 per hookup for two people per night, plus $3 for each additional person over age 16. For more information, see chapter 5.

Park Rules & Regulations

The following list includes a set of rules established to protect both the park and its visitors (for more information, see the park's free publication, *The Guide*):

- **Bicycles** are allowed on all paved and unpaved park roads where motorized vehicles are permitted, and on the Greenway Trail. However, they are not allowed on hiking trails, including the Rim Trail. Bicyclists must obey all traffic regulations, and should ride single-file with the flow of traffic. On narrow Hermit Road, they should pull to the right shoulder and dismount when large vehicles are passing.
- It is **illegal to remove** any resource from the park. This covers anything from flowers to potsherds. Even seemingly useless articles such as bits of metal from the canyon's old mining operations have historical value to the park's users and are protected by law.
- Leashed **pets** are permitted on trails throughout the South Rim's developed areas, but not below the rim. The only exceptions are certified service animals.
- **Fires** are strictly prohibited except in the fire pits at North Rim, Desert View, and Mather campgrounds. In the backcountry, a small camp stove for cooking is acceptable.
- **Discharging weapons**—including guns, bows and arrows, crossbows, slingshots, and air pistols—is prohibited. So are all **fireworks.**
- If, by chance, you have a **hang glider** and are considering jumping into the canyon, forget it. It's illegal, and you'll be fined.

HOW TO SEE THE PARK IN SEVERAL DAYS

The itineraries below list some wonderful activities, all of which are described in detail later in the book. Remember, the rims are 210 highway miles apart.

If You Have 1 or 2 Days

ON THE SOUTH RIM   After stopping at the **Grand Canyon Visitor Center,** hike a short distance down the **Bright Angel Trail** in the morning. If the weather is hot or if you are not in top-notch condition, walk the **Trail of Time** between Yavapai Point and Verkamp's Visitor Center. Mid-day, attend a **ranger presentation,** for which times and locations are posted at the visitor centers. Later in the day, take the **Hermits Rest Route shuttle** along Hermit Road. From any of its stops, walk a short distance along the **Rim Trail** to quiet spots where you can savor the canyon. If possible, watch the sunset from **Hopi Point.**

The next morning, get an early start so that you can watch the sunrise from **Desert View** on the South Rim. On your way back to Grand Canyon Village, stop at the viewpoints along **Desert View Drive.** Most of them are open year-round and boast expansive views of the central and northeastern canyon. Upon returning to Grand Canyon Village, take a walking tour of the **historic buildings.** Then relax with an iced tea or cocktail on the veranda at **El Tovar Hotel's lounge.**

ON THE NORTH RIM   In the morning, after checking in at the **North Rim Visitor Center,** hike down the top of the **North Kaibab trail** to Coconino Overlook (less than a half-hour down) or Supai Tunnel (about an hour down). A less strenuous option is the short walk from Grand Canyon Lodge to Bright Angel Point. In the afternoon, drive down **Cape Royal Road.** After returning, buy a cold beverage at **Grand Canyon Lodge's Roughrider Saloon,** then sip it while sitting on the lodge's enormous, canyon-facing deck. After sunset, if the evening is calm, warm yourself by the fireplace here.

If you're an early riser, head to **Point Imperial** (the Grand Canyon's highest point) before dawn the next day to watch the sun rise. Or, consider **Cape Royal**—which affords brilliant views of the canyon's colors—if you don't want the sun in your eyes. Then take a walk on one of the rim trails—the **Transept Trail,** the **Uncle Jim Trail** (to Uncle Jim Point), or, my favorite, the **Widforss Trail** (to Widforss Point).

If You Have 3 or 4 Days

With 3 or 4 days at the canyon, a 3-day hike may be in order.

ON THE SOUTH RIM   Choose from the **Bright Angel, South Kaibab, Grandview, Hermit,** and **Rim trails.**

ON THE NORTH RIM   Try the **North Kaibab Trail** and two rim trails. Explore **Forest Service roads,** peer over the 3,000-foot vertical drop at **Toroweap Overlook,** or visit **Pipe Spring National Monument,** which memorializes the pioneering of the American Southwest. The North Rim has fewer diversions, so be prepared for deep relaxation on the third and fourth days.

ON BOTH RIMS   Consider riding a mule into the canyon, taking a ranger-led walk, or just sitting and reading on the porch at one of the canyon's peaceful lodges.

DRIVING TOURS

Driving in the Grand Canyon area can be a spectacle unto itself. Before listing specific itineraries, here are some general notes about driving in and around the national park.

The **South Rim** is easily accessible by car off Highway 64, which connects Williams and Cameron. Inside the park's southern gate, South Entrance Road diverges from Highway 64 and leads to **Grand Canyon Village.** A National Historic District, the village feels like a small town, with hotels, restaurants, shops, and a train depot. The loop road can be confusing, so take your time, watch carefully for signs, and use the village map in the park newspaper, *The Guide.*

Scenic drives hug the canyon rim on either side of the village. **Hermit Road** (closed to private vehicles during high season) traverses west for 7 miles from Grand Canyon Village to its terminus at Hermits Rest. **Desert View Drive** covers 25 miles between Grand Canyon Village and the Desert View overlook on the park's southeastern edge. The two scenic drives have numerous pull-offs with views of the canyon, some also with views of the river. The shuttle bus along Hermit Road makes nine stops on the way from Grand Canyon Village to Hermits Rest, and three stops on the way back.

Some 210 highway miles (4 driving hr.) separate the North Rim from the South Rim. On the way, **Highway 89A** crosses the **Colorado River** near the canyon's northeastern tip, where the river begins cutting down into the rocks of the Marble Platform. This is where the Grand Canyon begins. As you drive west from **Lees Ferry,** you'll see where rocks make a single fold along a fault line and rise more than 4,000 feet from the Marble Platform to the level of the Kaibab Plateau—the canyon's North Rim.

The **North Rim** stretches more than 1,000 feet above the busier South Rim. **Highway 67** travels south 44 miles from Highway 89A (at Jacob Lake) to where it dead-ends at Bright Angel Point, site of Grand Canyon Lodge. A 23-mile-long paved scenic drive spans from Highway 67 southeast to the tip of the Walhalla Plateau, a peninsula east of Bright Angel Point. This drive, which

Hermit Road & South Rim Trails

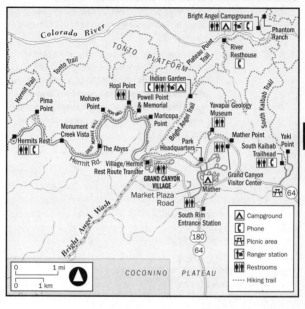

ends at Cape Royal, includes stops from which to view the eastern Grand Canyon. On this curvy road, signs appear quickly. Pay attention, as there aren't many places to turn around. The 3-mile-long spur road to Point Imperial, the Grand Canyon's highest point (8,803 ft.), forks to the northeast off this road.

The rims at the canyon's western end are lower, rockier, and more remote than those in the central canyon. Only a few roads cross these lands. The canyon ends abruptly at the **Grand Wash cliffs,** where the Colorado River flows out of the Grand Canyon and into Lake Mead. To drive from rim to rim around the western end of the canyon, cross the Colorado River at **Hoover Dam,** near Las Vegas.

DRIVING TOUR 1: HERMIT ROAD

START:	**Grand Canyon Village.**
FINISH:	**Hermits Rest.**
TIME:	**About 3 hours.**

HIGHLIGHTS:	**Closed to private cars (except vehicles carrying people with physical disabilities) from March 1 to November 30, the overlooks are quieter than those on Desert View Drive and afford excellent river views.**
DRAWBACKS:	**Occasional long waits for buses, which stop at nine points on the road to Hermits Rest and at only three points (Pima, Mohave, and Powell) on the return. The 7-mile-long road from Grand Canyon Village to Hermits Rest is open to private cars when shuttles aren't running. (The shuttles run Mar 1–Nov 30.)**

1 Trailviews 1 & 2

These viewpoints en route to Maricopa Point are great places from which to look back at **Grand Canyon Village.** Below the village, **Bright Angel Trail**'s switchbacks descend along a natural break in the cliffs. Erosion created this break along the **Bright Angel Fault,** one of many fault lines that crisscross the main canyon.

Looking north across the canyon, you'll see how the fault created two side canyons on opposite sides of the river. Runoff seeps into the cracks along fault lines, beginning the process of forming side canyons such as these. Indigenous humans and animals made the first footpaths through these side canyons. Below, **Indian Garden,** where the Havasupai people farmed for generations, is identifiable by the lush vegetation that grows around the spring there. Past Indian Garden, a trail leads straight out to the edge of **Tonto Platform,** where it dead-ends. This is not the Bright Angel Trail, but a spur known as **Plateau Point Trail.**

2 Maricopa Point

The **Orphan Mine,** southwest of here, produced some of the Southwest's richest uranium ore during the 1950s and 1960s. In fact, this land was once the center of the most exhaustive mining effort in the canyon. Workers removed half a million tons of ore for atomic energy use from 1956 until 1969, by which time mining here had ended.

3 Powell Memorial

Here you'll find a large memorial to Major John Wesley Powell, the one-armed Civil War veteran who is widely believed to have been the first non-native person to float through the canyon. In fact, the park was formally dedicated in 1920 at **Powell Point;** members of his family attended.

Funded in part by the Smithsonian Institution, Powell first drifted into the canyon on August 5, 1869. He and his eight-person crew portaged around rapids where the walls were gradual enough to allow it. In parts of the canyon's **Inner Gorge,** however, where the walls are too steep to climb, the men were forced to float blindly, in wooden boats, through some of the world's most dangerous waters.

Parts of the Inner Gorge are visible from here, but only a tiny stretch of the river can be seen. Where Powell saw the Inner Gorge's dark, steep rocks near the water, he thought not of their beauty but of the peril they represented. He called the gorge "our granite prison" and described his men "ever watching, ever peering ahead, for the narrow canyon is winding and the river is closed in … and what there may be below, we know not."

When the men stopped above what appeared to be another set of dangerous rapids after 3 weeks in the canyon, three of them left the expedition by walking out into what is now known as Separation Canyon, but were never seen again. The irony is that the expedition had already passed most of the worst rapids. The remaining crew negotiated the last of the white water and arrived at a small Mormon outpost. They brought with them the first records of the inner canyon's rocks, geography, and species. Powell later fleshed out these records into a lengthy diary, *The Exploration of the Colorado River and its Canyons.* The names of the three crew members who left at Separation Canyon do not appear on the monument.

4 Hopi Point ★

Because it projects far into the canyon, Hopi Point is the best place off Hermit Road to watch the sunset. It's also the Grand Canyon's most popular viewpoint. As the sun drops, its waning light plays across four of the canyon's loveliest temples. The flat mesa almost due north of the point is **Shiva Temple.** The temple southwest of it is **Osiris;** the one southeast of it is **Isis.** East of Isis is **Buddha Temple.**

Named for a destructive yet popular Hindu god, Shiva Temple was the site of a much-ballyhooed 1937 mission by a team of scientists from the American Museum of Natural History. Believing that the canyon isolated the forest atop Shiva Temple the same way ocean isolates the Galapagos Islands, the team set out to find species that had evolved differently from those on the rim. The press drummed up sensationalistic stories about the trip, even going so far as to hail it as a search for living dinosaurs.

Alas, the search didn't turn up any new species, let alone dinosaurs. Rather, it proved that cliffs and desert don't bar most species' movements. (The Colorado River poses a more significant barrier.) The most noteworthy discovery: an empty Kodak film box and soup cans deliberately left behind by canyon local Emery Kolb, who was upset when the expedition declined his offer to help. Kolb made the ascent himself, showing that the cliffs are hardly a barrier. *Note:* There are new vault toilets at Hopi Point.

5 Mohave Point ★

This is a great place from which to observe some of the Colorado River's most furious rapids. Farthest downstream, to your left, is **Hermit Rapids** (named after canyon pioneer Louis Boucher, considered "the hermit of Hermit Canyon" because, in the early 1900s, he made his home in the side canyons). Above Hermit Rapids, you can make out the top of the dangerous **Granite Rapids,** one of the steepest navigable rapids in the world. Just above Granite Rapids, the bottom of **Salt Creek Rapids** is visible. As you look at Hermit Creek Canyon and the rapids below it, you can easily visualize how flash floods washed rocks from the side canyon into the Colorado River, forming the natural dam that causes the rapids.

6 The Abyss

The walls in this side canyon—a deep bay cut into the South Rim by Monument Creek—fall a steep 2,600 feet to the base of the 335-million-year-old **Redwall Limestone layer.** The best way to appreciate these plunging walls is to follow the **Rim Trail** a few hundred yards west of the Abyss overlook, where the cliffs plummet most precipitously.

7 Monument Creek Vista

This is a new shuttle stop on the way to Hermits Rest that lets you access the new Greenway Trail. Cyclists can bring their bikes on the shuttle to this point, and then ride 2.8 miles (3.5km) along the greenway to Hermits Rest.

8 Pima Point ★

Three thousand feet below Pima Point—which offers a stunning view of the **Colorado River**—you can see some of the foundations and walls from the old **Hermit Camp,** a tourist destination built in 1912 by the same people who constructed the Santa Fe Railroad. Situated along Hermit Creek, the camp featured heavy-duty tents (each with a stove) and Native American rugs. An aerial tramway, used mostly to lower supplies, connected Pima Point with the camp below. It made the descent in roughly a half-hour.

To get to Hermit Camp, tourists traveled 51 miles by train from Williams to Grand Canyon Village, 9 miles by stage-coach from the village to the top of Hermit Trail's trail head, and 8 miles by mule to the camp. After the Park Service wrested control of Bright Angel Trail from Ralph Cameron in the 1920s, Phantom Ranch became a more popular tourist destination, and Hermit Camp closed its doors in 1930.

Hermit Trail, however, remains popular. North of the overlook, below the fin of rock known as **Cope Butte,** you can see it zigzagging down the blue-green **Bright Angel Shale layer,** which is 515 million years old.

During quiet moments here, listen carefully, and you should also hear the distant roar of **Granite Rapids.**

9 Hermits Rest ★

Before descending to Hermit Camp, tourists rested at this Mary Colter–designed building, built in 1914. Here, the renowned architect celebrated the hermit theme, making the building look as if an isolated mountain man had constructed it. It resembles a crude rock shelter, with stones heaped highest around the chimney. A large fireplace (not a bad place to warm up in winter) dominates the interior. Colter covered the ceiling above it with soot, so that the room has the look of a cave warmed by fire—much like the nearby Dripping Springs overhang where "the hermit of Hermit Canyon," Louis Boucher, once passed time.

Colter had a knack for creating perfect details. Note the anthropomorphic rock above the fireplace, the candelabra, and the lanterns. Some of the original hand-carved furniture is still here.

A snack bar sells candy, ice cream, chips, soda, sandwiches, and coffee. New vault toilets are near the shuttle bus stop, and there's also a water bottle filling station nearby.

Before leaving, take a last look at the canyon. The three-pronged temple across the canyon to the north is the **Tower of Ra,** named for the victorious Egyptian sun god. Seen from above, each prong points to a different set of rapids: the near arm to **Hermit Creek,** the middle to **Boucher Creek,** and the far one to **Crystal Creek**—waters that have triumphed over more than a few river guides.

START:	**Yavapai Point, about a mile east of Grand Canyon Village.**
FINISH:	**Desert View overlook, near the park's east entrance.**
TIME:	**About 4 hours.**
HIGHLIGHTS:	**Spectacular views of the central and northeastern canyon.**
DRAWBACKS:	**Sometimes closes temporarily in winter due to snow.**

Desert View Drive goes 2 miles on South Entrance Road, which links Tusayan and Grand Canyon Village. The remaining 23 miles are on the stretch of Highway 64 that links South Entrance Road and the Desert View overlook. An improved road system and new parking lots have enhanced this drive. The Yavapai and Mather overlooks are on South Entrance Road; the remaining seven stops, including six canyon overlooks and the Tusayan Ruin & Museum, are accessible from Highway 64.

1 Yavapai Geology Museum

Yavapai Point features some of the most expansive views both up and down the canyon. The historic observation station here features huge plate-glass windows overlooking the central canyon, and interpretive panels identifying virtually all the major landmarks. There are also exhibits that explain the canyon's formation and geology. The museum is open daily in summer from 8am to 8pm, and 8am to 6pm the rest of the year.

From here, you can spot at least five hiking trails. To the west, **Bright Angel Trail** can be seen descending to the lush Indian Garden area. The straight white line leaving from this general area and eventually dead-ending is **Plateau Point Trail.** Directly below the overlook and to the north, **Tonto Trail** wends its way across the blue-green Tonto Platform. Across the river, find the verdant area at the mouth of Bright Angel Canyon. The **North Kaibab Trail** passes through this area yards before ending at the river, just below Phantom Ranch. After turning to face east, find the saddle just south of O'Neill Butte; the **South Kaibab Trail** crosses this saddle.

2 Mather Point ★

Visitors who see the canyon only once often do it from here. People entering the park from the south, too, generally catch their first glimpse of the canyon from Mather Point, which

Desert View Drive

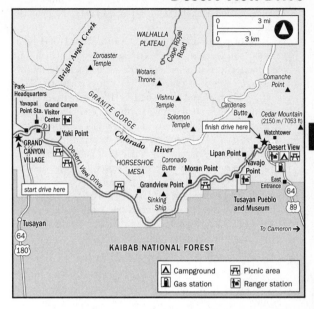

offers an expansive, 180-degree view. You can arrive at Mather Point on either the orange or blue shuttle buses or park in one of the four lots surrounding the Grand Canyon Visitor Center. Follow the paved pathway to the tall rock feature above the engraved pavement celebrating the native people traditionally affiliated with the Grand Canyon. Another minute of walking brings you to the canyon rim. Check the schedule in *The Guide* to see if there is a ranger program in **Mather Amphitheater** on the canyon rim. The rim trail to the east toward **Pipe Creek Vista** provides quiet spots for canyon viewing. The rim trail to the west takes you to popular **Mather Point** with a wheelchair accessible ramp all the way out to the end of the point for stunning views. You can continue along the rim trail toward **Yavapai Point.**

3 Grandview Point ★★

At 7,406 feet, this is one of the South Rim's highest spots. In the late 19th century, it was also one of its busiest. In 1890, Pete Berry, one of the canyon's early prospectors, filed a mining claim on a rich copper vein on **Horseshoe Mesa** (visible to the north of the overlook). To remove ore from the mine,

Berry blazed a trail to it from Grandview Point. He erected cabins and a dining hall on the mesa, then, as visitors began coming, added a hotel a short distance away from Grandview Point.

Built of ponderosa pine logs, **Grand View Hotel** flourished in the prerailroad days. To reach the hotel, which for a brief period was considered the canyon's best lodging, tourists took a grueling all-day stagecoach ride from Flagstaff.

In 1901, however, the Santa Fe Railroad linked Grand Canyon Village and Williams, putting an end, almost immediately, to the Flagstaff-to-Grandview stagecoach run. Once at Grand Canyon Village, few tourists ventured 11 miles east to Grandview Point, and the hotel went out of business in 1908. The mine fared no better. Plagued by high overhead costs, it shut down shortly after the price of copper crashed in 1907. Only a trace of the Grand View Hotel's foundation remains, but the historic **Grandview Trail** is still used by thousands of hikers annually (see chapter 4 for details), and debris from the old mine camp still litters Horseshoe Mesa.

4 Moran Point ★

This point is named for landscape painter Thomas Moran, whose sketches and oil paintings introduced America to the beauty of the canyon in the years before photography. After accompanying John Wesley Powell on a surveying expedition in 1873, Moran illustrated Powell's book, *The Exploration of the Colorado River and its Canyons.* The federal government bought one of Moran's paintings, *The Chasm of the Colorado,* and sent it to Congress. It and other works helped lure the first tourists to the canyon in the 19th century.

Moran Point is the best place from which to view the tilting block of rock known as the **Sinking Ship.** Standing at the end of the point, look southwest at the rocks level with the rim. You'll see the Sinking Ship beyond the horizontal layers of **Coronado Butte** (in the foreground). It's part of the **Grandview monocline,** a zone where rocks are bent in a single fold around a fault line. Looking down the drainage below Coronado Butte, you'll see the ancient (1.25 billion years old) **Hakatai Shale layer**'s red splotches that give Red Canyon its name.

The first white people to see the canyon probably saw it from somewhere on the rim between here and Desert View. In 1540, Spanish explorer Francisco Vásquez de Coronado was scouring the Southwest for the mythical Seven Cities of Cíbola, with its equally mythical fortune in gold. After hearing of a great river and settlements north of the Hopi pueblo of Tusayan, he sent a small force, led by Garcia Lopez de Cárdenas, to explore the area.

Hopi guides led Cárdenas and his men, who began the journey in armor, to the South Rim somewhere near here. Upon seeing the Colorado River, the Spaniards initially estimated it to be 6 feet wide. (It's closer to 200 in this area.) When Cárdenas asked how to reach it, the Hopi, who had been making pilgrimages to the bottom of the canyon for generations, professed not to know. For 3 days, Cárdenas's men tried unsuccessfully to descend to the river. In the process, they learned what many canyon hikers would later discover: What appeared to be easy from above was actually extremely difficult. They gave up, and no one of European descent returned to the canyon for 200 years.

3

5 ## Tusayan Ruin & Museum ★

By studying tree rings in the wood at these dwellings, archaeologists determined that parts of this 14-room stone-walled structure were built in 1185 by the Ancestral Puebloans. Among the pueblos that have been excavated near the Grand Canyon, Tusayan Ruin and Museum was the most recently occupied. By 1185, most of the Ancestral Puebloans had already left the canyon. For unknown reasons, however, this pueblo's dwellers stayed, despite a prolonged drought (known from tree rings), and despite the nearest year-round water source being about 7 miles away.

A self-guided tour takes you through this small, collapsed pueblo, which includes the stone foundations of two kivas, living areas, and storage rooms, all connected in a U-shaped structure.

This dwelling, like many Ancestral Puebloan abodes in present-day Northern Arizona, has a clear view of the **San Francisco Peaks,** including **Humphreys Peak,** which, at 12,633 feet, is Arizona's highest point. This mountain range formed when volcanic matter boiled up through weak spots in the earth's crust between 1.8 million and 400,000 years ago. The descendants of the Puebloans, the modern Hopi, believe that these peaks are home to ancestral spirits known as Kachinas.

Built in 1932, the **Tusayan Museum,** open daily 9am to 5pm (admission is free), celebrates the traditions of the area's indigenous peoples. Displays in this dimly lit historic building include traditional jewelry, attire, and tools, as well as historic photos. It's worth coming here just to see the 3,000- to 4,000-year-old split-twig figurines, made by members of a hunter-gatherer clan sometimes referred to as the Desert Culture. Excavators found these mysterious figurines of deer and sheep under cairns (piles of stones) in the canyon's caves. Allow about 30 minutes to tour the ruins and museum. A guided ranger tour called "Glimpses of the Past" is offered here at 11am and 3:30pm in summer.

Note: Vault toilets are available at the Tusayan Museum.

6 Lipan Point ★★

With views far down the canyon to the west, this is a marvelous place to catch the sunset. From here, you can see the **Colorado River** winding its way through soft, red shale before disappearing behind the black walls of the **Inner Gorge.** In the area between two of the river's sweeping curves, **Unkar Creek** has deposited a large alluvial fan. From A.D. 800 to 1150, the Ancestral Puebloans grew beans and corn in this rich soil. Archaeologists have found many granaries and dwellings in the area. At least some of the Puebloans migrated to the rim during summer to farm and to hunt the abundant game there.

7 Navajo Point

Like Lipan Point, Navajo Point offers fine views of the **Grand Canyon Supergroup,** a formation of igneous and sedimentary Precambrian rocks that, in many other parts of the canyon, has altogether eroded. Long, thin streaks of maroon, gray, and black that tilt at an angle of about 20 degrees layer this formation. They're visible above the river, directly across the canyon. As you look at these rocks, note how the level, brown **Tapeats Sandstone layer** (525 million years old), which in other locations sits directly atop the black Vishnu Formation, now rests atop the Supergroup—hundreds of feet above the schist. Where the Supergroup had not yet eroded away, the Tapeats Sandstone was often deposited atop it, protecting what remained.

8 Desert View ★

Here you'll find the **Watchtower,** a 70-foot-high stone building designed by Mary Colter, whose architecture style was fittingly organic. She modeled it after towers found at ancient pueblos such as Mesa Verde and Hovenweep. Like Colter's other buildings, this one seems to emerge from the earth, the rough stones at its base blending seamlessly with the rim rock.

The Watchtower is connected to a circular observation room fashioned after a Hopi kiva—a ceremonial room that often adjoined pueblo towers. To climb the Watchtower (which is free), you'll first have to pass through this room, now used as a gift shop selling Navajo rugs and Native American art, crafts, and jewelry. The shop is open daily 8am to sunset (shorter hours in winter), and the observation deck can be accessed until 30 minutes before sunset. The walls inside the Watchtower are decorated with traditional Native American art. Some of the finest work here is by Hopi artist Fred Kabotie, whose depiction of the Snake Legend, the story of the first person to have floated down the Colorado River, graces the Hopi Room. At the top is an enclosed observation deck, which, at 7,522 feet, is the South Rim's highest point. A roadway and parking lot have eased accessibility to Desert View.

The rim at Desert View offers spectacular views of the northeast end of the canyon. To the northeast, you'll see the cliffs known as the **Palisades of the Desert,** which form the southeastern wall of Grand Canyon proper. Follow those cliffs north to a significant rock outcropping, and you'll see **Comanche Point.** Beyond Comanche Point, you can barely see the gorge carved by the Little Colorado River.

In 1956, where the gorge intersects the Grand Canyon, two planes collided and crashed, killing 128 people. Most of the debris was removed from the area where the rivers unite, but a few plane parts, including a wheel, remain. (None are visible from here.)

The flat, mesalike hill to the east is **Cedar Mountain.** This is one of the few places where the story told by the rocks *doesn't* end with the Kaibab Limestone layer. Cedar Mountain and Red Butte (a hill just south of Tusayan along Hwy. 64) were both deposited during the Mesozoic Era (245–265 million years ago). They linger, isolated, atop the Kaibab Limestone, remnants of the more than 4,000 feet of Mesozoic deposits that once accumulated in this area. (Sedimentary rock like this is usually deposited when land is near or below sea level, as the land in this area used to be. It erodes when elevated, the way the Grand Canyon is now.) Though nearly all of these layers have eroded off the Grand Canyon, they can be seen nearby in the Painted Desert, the Vermilion Cliffs, and at Zion National Park.

This is the last overlook on Desert View Drive, and it has a **visitor center,** a general store, a snack shop, restrooms, and a gas station (gas is available here 24 hr. a day with a credit card). Rangers often give sunset talks here in summer. Past Desert View, Highway 64 continues east, roughly paralleling the gorge cut by the Little Colorado River. The canyon heads northward toward Lees Ferry, gradually becoming shallower and narrower. You can reach the banks of the Colorado River at Lees Ferry by vehicle. To get there, take Highway 89A and look for the signs to the short spur road leading to the river.

DRIVING TOUR 3: NORTH RIM: CAPE ROYAL DRIVE

START:	**Grand Canyon Lodge.**
FINISH:	**Point Imperial, at the park's northeastern end.**
TIME:	**About 4 hours—more if you do any hiking.**
HIGHLIGHTS:	**Sparse crowds and lovely views of the eastern canyon. If you start early, you can enjoy a picnic lunch at Vista Encantada.**
DRAWBACKS:	**Has only one viewpoint (Cape Royal) from which to see the central canyon. The Colorado River is not visible from as many points on this drive as on the South Rim drives.**

1 Cape Royal Trail ★★★

Lined by cliff rose and piñon pine, this gentle, paved .3-mile (each way) trail looks out onto stunning views. It first approaches a natural bridge, **Angels Window,** carved into a rock peninsula along the rim. Through the square opening under the bridge, part of the lower canyon, including a slice of the Colorado River, can be seen from the trail. This opening in the Kaibab Limestone layer formed when water seeped down through cracks, then across planes between rock beds, eventually eroding the rock from underneath.

The trail's left fork travels about 150 yards, ending at the tip of the peninsula above Angels Window, which, with sheer drops on three sides, is a thrilling place to stand.

The trail's right fork goes to Cape Royal's tip. From here, **Wotans Throne,** a broad mesa visible in the distance from many South Rim overlooks, looms only 1½ miles to the south. Also to the south, and nearly as close, is **Vishnu Temple.** Closer still is **Freya Castle,** a pinnacle shaped like a breaking wave. Across the canyon, the tiny nub on the rim is the 70-foot-high **Watchtower** at Desert View.

Cape Royal offers a spectacular view of the canyon at dawn and dusk; it's a popular wedding and picnic spot. *Note:* From Grand Canyon Lodge, drive 23 miles on the Walhalla Plateau directly to Cape Royal Trail. Make stops only on your way back to the lodge. That way, you can do the short hikes near Cape Royal while your legs are fresh, and stop at picnic areas, closer to the lodge, on your way back.

Cape Royal Drive & North Rim Trails

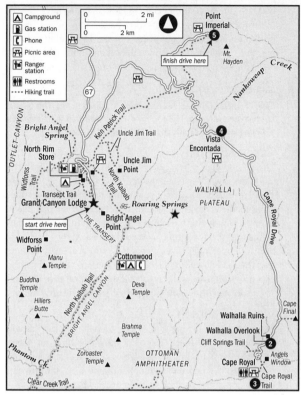

Optional Stop

The **Cliff Springs Trail** (3 miles north of Cape Royal, at a small pullout). This half-mile walk ends at a small spring in a side canyon, and is terrific for bird-watching. (See "Trails on the North Rim," in chapter 4.)

2 Walhalla Overlook ★

Ancestral Puebloans no doubt enjoyed the views from here. You'll see **Unkar Creek,** which, from here, looks like a tan line, snaking down toward **Unkar Delta.** Enriched by deposits from the creek, the delta's soil and abundant water made for excellent farming. Many Ancestral Puebloans lived there, growing corn, beans, and squash on terraces that caught runoff and left deposits of rich soil.

When the canyon heated up, the natives also spent time on the North Rim, at dwellings such as the ones across the street from this overlook. A flat dirt path leads to **Walhalla Ruins,** which includes the foundations of two small pueblos. In this area, too, the Ancestral Puebloans farmed, taking advantage of the extra moisture and a growing season lengthened by the warm breezes blowing out of the canyon. In addition to farming, the Puebloans also gathered food and hunted the abundant game on the rim.

Optional Stop

Cape Final Trail (about 5 miles south of Roosevelt Point). This gentle, 1.5-mile-long (one-way) hike follows an old jeep trail to an overlook at Cape Final. (See "Trails on the North Rim," in chapter 4.)

3 Roosevelt Point

This is one of the best places from which to see the Little Colorado River's gorge converge into the Grand Canyon. They meet at nearly a right angle, unusual in that most tributaries merge at close to the same direction as the larger rivers. Some geologists have used this observation to buttress arguments that the ancestral Colorado River exited the canyon via the Little Colorado River gorge, but little evidence supports that theory. The cliffs south of this junction, which form the canyon's southeast wall, are the **Palisades of the Desert.** Those north of the confluence are called the **Desert Facade.**

4 Vista Encantada

By starting your driving tour of the Walhalla Plateau early in the day, you can reach Vista Encantada in time for a late picnic lunch. You'll find several tables near the rim. While you picnic, you can look down an upper drainage of **Nankoweap Creek** and at the rock pinnacle known as **Brady Peak.**

5 Point Imperial ★★

A 3-mile spur road leads from Cape Royal Road to Point Imperial, which, at 8,803 feet, is the North Rim's highest point— and the best place on either rim from which to view the park's northeastern end. To the northeast, 3,000 feet below the overlook, you'll see the brownish-green plain known as the **Marble Platform.** The Colorado River cleaves this platform between Lees Ferry and where the Grand Canyon yawns open just east of here. Because the Marble Platform has the same rock layers as the Grand Canyon, geologists consider **Marble Canyon** to be the Grand Canyon's uppermost section.

Bordering the Marble Platform on the north are the **Vermilion Cliffs,** which run southwest to northeast. Located along the Utah-Arizona border, these cliffs are the next steps up in the **Grand Staircase,** a geological formation in which progressively younger rock formations rise like steps from Marble Canyon to southern Utah's Bryce Canyon. Where this formation turns southward (near Lees Ferry) is the unrelated edge of a fold called **Echo Cliffs.**

Looking southeast, you can see where the Little Colorado River's gorge intersects the Grand Canyon. Past that juncture, the **Painted Desert**'s landforms stain the horizon a rich red. This desert, made up of badlands and other erosional features carved from the Chinle Formation's soft clays, surrounds the Little Colorado River and one of its tributaries, the **Puerco River.** Like the Vermilion Cliffs, the Painted Desert is made up of "younger" rocks than are found in the Grand Canyon.

RANGER PROGRAMS & ORGANIZED TOURS

The park offers a host of seasonal ranger programs. A typical schedule includes daily guided hikes and walks, kids' programs, and discussions of geology, native plant and animal species, and natural and cultural history. Evening programs are offered nightly, year-round on the South Rim. All programs are free and open to everyone; just show up at the meeting places, which are scattered around the park (overlooks, trail heads, archaeological sites, and so on). For an up-to-date schedule, consult the park's newspaper, *The Guide,* or stop in at the Grand Canyon Visitor Center on the South Rim, or at the North Rim Visitor Center.

Bus Tours

Of the many private companies that offer bus tours, **Xanterra** presents the largest number of options. Among the tour choices are Desert View Tour (East Rim) and Hermits Rest Tour ($45 and $26, respectively, for adults; free for those 15 and under), sunset tours ($21), sunrise tours ($21) to one of several rim stops, and all-day outings that combine Desert View Drive with any other tour ($58). Unlike the free shuttles, these buses run on natural gas and Xanterra's drivers narrate the tours. Though they mean well and offer some valuable information, these guides were not hired for their command of natural science and history but rather for their educational entertainment. For advance reservations, call © **888/297-2757,** or visit www.grandcanyonlodges.com. Once at the canyon, visit the transportation desks at Yavapai, Maswik, or Bright Angel lodges, or call © **928/638-2631,** ext. 6015, to make reservations.

Open Road Tours (© **855/563-8830;** www.openroadtours usa.com) offers 1-day guided tours to the Grand Canyon's East Rim and Cameron Trading Post departing from Flagstaff at 9:30am and returning by 5:30pm. The cost is $95 for adults, $55 for children 11 and under.

ATTRACTIONS

Please refer to the map "Grand Canyon Village" on p. 107 in chapter 6 to find exact locations of the historic buildings on the South Rim.

South Rim

Most of the South Rim's historic buildings are concentrated in Grand Canyon Village, a National Historic District. Outside of the village, **Hermits Rest** on Hermit Road and the **Watchtower** on Desert View Drive are also of historical significance. For information about these two sites, refer to the Hermit Road (p. 35) and Desert View (p. 40) driving tours. Strange and beautiful, these historic buildings—like the canyon itself—take time to appreciate.

Mary Colter, a Minneapolis schoolteacher and trained architect who in 1902 began decorating the shops that sold Native American art on the Santa Fe Railroad line, designed more than a half-dozen of the canyon's historic buildings. Her landmarks include: Hopi House (1905), the Lookout (1914), Hermits Rest (1914), Phantom Ranch (1922), the Watchtower (1932), and Bright Angel Lodge (1935). Colter's work drew heavily on the architectural styles of Native Americans and Spanish settlers in the Southwest, long before these styles became fashionable among Anglos. The most noteworthy historic buildings in Grand Canyon Village are detailed below.

Bright Angel Lodge ★★ In the 1930s, Santa Fe Railroad representatives asked Mary Colter to design moderately priced accommodations for the many new tourists who had begun driving to the canyon. Colter laid out a number of cabins, as well as this rustic log-and-stone lodge, which would eventually house a lounge, restaurant, and curio shop. Completed in 1935, the lodge, near Grand Canyon Village's west end, looks low from the outside, but has a spacious lobby with wooden walls, flagstone floors, and a high, exposed-log ceiling. A remarkable hearth is in what was once the lounge and is now the **Bright Angel History Room.** Known as "the geological fireplace," it features the rock layers found in the canyon, stacked in the same order in which they naturally occur. Rounded, smooth river stones lie at the bottom of this bell-shaped hearth, and Kaibab Limestone, the rim rock, is on top. This educational room also tells the story of the Harvey Girls—young women who came west, starting in 1883 through the 1950s, to staff the Fred Harvey restaurants and hotels along the rail lines.

Buckey O'Neill Cabin ★ This is Grand Canyon Village's second-oldest surviving structure (the oldest is Red Horse Station, which was moved to the rim in 1890). Buckey O'Neill, who in the 1890s worked a number of local jobs, including sheriff, judge, reporter, and prospector, visited this cabin.

After discovering what he believed to be a rich copper vein in Anita, 14 miles south of the canyon, he pushed for the construction of a railroad line connecting Williams with the Grand Canyon—via Anita, naturally. A Chicago mining company bought out O'Neill, but the project collapsed when the mine turned out to be less than rich. In 1901, the Santa Fe Railroad, perhaps realizing that tourism here would pay far greater dividends than copper, bought the line and laid the remaining track.

When Mary Colter designed cabins for Bright Angel Lodge, she fought to preserve O'Neill Cabin, eventually building her own structures around it. Today, this cabin, a few feet west of Bright Angel Lodge, is the park's most upscale guest suite. Guests staying here may, however, feel like zoo animals as tourists try to peer inside. For more information, see chapter 6.

El Tovar Hotel ★★★ A year after the Santa Fe Railroad linked the South Rim with Williams, Fred Harvey commissioned Charles Whittlesey, an architect who had worked with Mary Colter on Albuquerque's Alvarado Hotel, to build a large luxury hotel on the rim. Whittlesey fashioned El Tovar after the Northern European hunting lodges of that period. Built of Oregon pine, this 100-room hotel offered first-class accommodations, attracting well-heeled East Coast visitors looking for a Western adventure and luminaries such as George Bernard Shaw and Theodore Roosevelt. The hotel received a multimillion-dollar face-lift for its centennial in 2005. To find it, walk 200 yards east along the rim from Bright Angel Lodge. For more about El Tovar, see chapter 6.

Grand Canyon Depot Built in 1909, this was the Santa Fe station and is one of America's three remaining log train depots. It closed after the last train from the Grand Canyon departed in 1968, then reopened in 1990, roughly a year after the railway resumed service. About 100 yards south of El Tovar, this two-story depot is built of logs that are flat on three sides, making for smooth interior walls and a rounded, rustic-looking exterior. Once home to the station agent and his family, the depot's second floor now houses Park Service offices. Photos of old trains parked at the depot decorate the walls. The **Grand Canyon Railway** makes its way every day from Williams to the Grand Canyon Depot, arriving in the morning and returning in the afternoon.

Hopi House ★★   Aware that travelers were captivated by the idea of meeting Native Americans, representatives of the Fred Harvey Co., best known for its railroad restaurants (and famed "Harvey Girls") alongside the Southwest's principal rail lines in the early 1900s, brought a group of Hopi artisans to Grand Canyon Village. At the same time that it was erecting El Tovar Hotel on the rim, the company commissioned Mary Colter to design a structure 100 feet east of the hotel that could serve as both a dwelling for the Hopi and a place to market their wares.

Colter fashioned Hopi House after the pueblos in Oraibi, Arizona. Completed in 1905, this stone-and-mortar structure rises in tiers, each level connected by exterior wood ladders and interior stairways; each level's roof serves as the porch for the level above. Inside, low doorways and nooks in the walls recall the snug quarters of real pueblos. The concrete floors are made to look like dirt, the plaster walls to look like adobe. Log beams support thatched ceilings.

Through 1968, Hopi artisans lived on the top floor of this building, while creating and selling their pottery, rugs, and jewelry on the lower floors. Nightly, they chanted and danced on a platform behind the building. Today, Hopi House still sells Native and non–Native American arts and crafts downstairs, and higher quality Native American art and jewelry on the second floor, which looks like an art gallery. Native American dancers perform just outside Hopi House afternoons in summer. Once used for religious purposes, the kiva on the second floor remains off-limits to non–Native Americans. Hopi House is open daily from 8am to 8pm (winter hours reduced).

Kolb Studio ★   In 1902, two brothers, Emery and Ellsworth Kolb, began photographing tourists descending the Bright Angel Trail on mules. After snapping the photos, they ran to Indian Gardens, where they had water to develop their plates, then raced back to the rim in time to sell the photos. Flush with profits from the business, in 1904, they started to build this home and studio beside Bright Angel Trail's head, along the rim at Grand Canyon Village's westernmost edge. Several years later, the brothers launched a more ambitious project: a motion picture of a raft trip through Grand Canyon. Completed in 1912, the film earned them international fame and drew throngs of people to the studio's viewing room.

After clashing regularly throughout the years, the two brothers eventually flipped a coin to determine who would have the privilege of remaining at their beloved Grand Canyon. Emery won two out of three tosses. So Ellsworth moved to Los Angeles, and Emery continued to live and work at Kolb Studio, introducing the brothers' film to audiences, continuing to photograph mule riders going down the Bright Angel Trail, and selling curios each day until his death at age 95 in 1976, after which the Park Service took over the building.

Today, Kolb Studio houses a nonprofit **gift shop** (in the former viewing room), which features books, gifts, and free exhibits year-round. There is no sales tax, and all proceeds are reinvested into the park's operating budget for educational purposes. Kolb Studio is open daily from 8am to 8pm (winter hours reduced).

Lookout Studio ★   Seeing the crowds drawn to Kolb Studio, the Fred Harvey Company launched a similar business, only closer to the railroad terminus. Mary Colter was hired to design the building, which she eventually named "the Lookout." Unlike some of her buildings, which were fashioned after occupied pueblos or well-preserved ruins, this one, on the canyon rim about 100 yards east of Kolb Studio, resembles a collapsed ruin. Its original chimney and low-slung roof looked like a pile of rocks and seemed barely higher than the canyon rim. To add to the effect, Colter planted indigenous plants on the roof. After its completion in 1914, tourists came here to buy souvenirs or to photograph the canyon from the deck, where a high-power telescope was placed. Today, Lookout Studio still serves much the same purpose. Lookout Studio is open daily from 8am to 8pm (winter hours reduced).

Verkamp's Visitor Center   A true visionary, John G. Verkamp may have been the first to sell curios at the Grand Canyon. In 1898, before the railroad even reached Grand Canyon Village, Verkamp was hawking souvenirs out of a tent on the grounds of Bright Angel Lodge. Although his first attempt at the business failed, Verkamp returned in 1905, after the trains began running, and opened a curio shop in a wood-shingled, Craftsman-style building 200 feet east of Hopi House. This time he succeeded. In 2006, the National Park Service purchased the family's interest and now operates a bookstore and **visitor center** here with displays of Grand Canyon history. **Ranger programs,** including history talks, often begin here. There's also a **walking history tour** on the floor of Verkamp's highlighting key moments in area history. Verkamp's is open daily from 8am to 8pm (winter hours reduced).

North Rim

Grand Canyon Lodge & Cabins ★   This lodge sits quietly on the North Rim, gracefully blending into its surroundings. Built in 1928 by Union Pacific Railroad workers, the original structure burned down in 1932 and was rebuilt in 1937. Inside, an expansive 50-foot-high lobby opens into an octagonal **sunroom** with three enormous windows affording dramatic views of the canyon. You can also enjoy the views in a chair on one of two long decks outside the sunroom. For a cool treat, descend the lodge's back steps and look directly below the sunroom. There, you'll find the romantic **Moon Room,** a popular spot for marriage proposals. Ranger programs are also offered every night in the lodge's **auditorium.** For more information, see chapter 6.

HIKES & OTHER OUTDOOR PURSUITS IN THE GRAND CANYON

There's no better way to enjoy the canyon than by walking right down into it and seeing all those rock layers and all that plant and animal life up close. You can day-hike partway into the canyon on a number of trails, or stay along any of the many rim trails. Hikers are urged not to try hiking to the bottom of the canyon and back in 1 day. The best time to hike into the canyon is mid-September to mid-May. During the summer months, hiking the rim trails is a better option, as hiking into the canyon can be uncomfortably hot.

4

AN OVERVIEW OF THE HIKING TRAILS

Though hiking below the rims is the most inspirational way to experience the canyon, it can also be dangerous, especially at midday during summer. Don't underestimate the physical toll that heat and vertical distances can take on even advanced hikers, and be sure to leave any canyon hikes in summer for the early morning. If it's too hot inside the canyon or you aren't up to climbing, consider walking on one of the South Rim's greenway or rim trails. The rim trails are especially nice in the North Rim's forests. However, flash floods can result in the closure of any of the trails.

SOUTH RIM   On the South Rim, **Bright Angel Trail** is the least difficult canyon trail for day hikers. It is well-maintained, proffers shade and drinking water, and is less steep than other canyon trails. Well-prepared hikers will be comfortable traveling 6 miles one-way to the end of **Plateau Point Trail** ★, which departs from **Tonto Trail** just north of where Tonto crosses Bright Angel Trail. If you go any farther on a day hike, there's a good chance that you'll run out of energy and daylight while climbing back to the rim. In summer's heat, day-trippers should not hike farther than **Indian Gardens** before turning back.

Other popular day hikes on the South Rim include the **South Kaibab Trail** to Cedar Ridge, **Hermit Trail** to Dripping Springs (via the **Dripping Springs Trail**) or Santa Maria Spring, and **Grandview Trail** to Horseshoe Mesa. The South Kaibab Trail, because of its steepness and lack of water and shade, is more strenuous than Bright Angel Trail, but it offers panoramic views. The Hermit and Grandview trails, which are not maintained and very steep in places, are even more rugged than the South Kaibab.

NORTH RIM   On the North Rim, the **North Kaibab Trail,** blessed with seasonal water and abundant shade, is the best option for day hikers descending into the canyon. Day hikers in good shape, as a rule, shouldn't go farther than Roaring Springs, which is 4.7 miles and 3,000 vertical feet below the trail head (check in advance with the visitor center to confirm water availability at Roaring Springs). Even strong walkers may have problems returning to the rim before sunset if they go past Roaring Springs on a day hike.

The trail descriptions later in this chapter cover many canyon paths, including turnaround points for day hikers. However, I've refrained from writing about some trails (including the **South Bass, North Bass, Nankoweap, Tanner, New Hance, Boucher, Thunder River, Bill Hall,** and **Deer Creek** trails) because of their remote locations or rugged conditions. You can ask questions about these trails and obtain free descriptions of them at the **Backcountry Information Center** (✆ **928/638-7875**), located across the train track near Maswik Lodge on the South Rim. The Backcountry Information Center on the South Rim is open year-round daily from 8am to noon and 1 to 5pm, and also offers information over the phone Monday through Friday from 1 to 5pm; the line is often busy, so be prepared to try more than once. Information is also available in the **Backcountry Reservations office** on the North Rim (about 11 miles south of the North Rim entrance gate or just more than a mile north of Grand Canyon Lodge, and marked by a sign; no phone number), which is open

An Overview of the Hiking Trails

HIKES & OUTDOOR PURSUITS

RECOMMENDED hiking DISTANCES

Here is a list of trails recommended for day hikers, and the farthest point that day hikers should go on them.

For Less Experienced Hikers:

Rim Trail (eastbound)	2.4 miles one-way
Rim Trail (westbound)	8 miles one-way
Trail of Time	1.3 miles one-way
Bright Angel Point Trail	.3 miles one-way
Transept Trail	1.5 miles one-way
Widforss Trail	5 miles one-way
Bright Angel Trail to Mile-and-a-Half House	1.5 miles one-way
North Kaibab Trail to Supai Tunnel	2 miles one-way

For Fit, Well-Prepared Hikers:

South Kaibab Trail to Cedar Ridge	1.5 miles one-way
North Kaibab Trail to Roaring Springs	4.7 miles one-way
Bright Angel Trail to Indian Garden	4.6 miles one-way
or to Plateau Point	6.1 miles one-way
Grandview Trail to Horseshoe Mesa	3 miles one-way
Hermit Trail to Santa Maria Spring	2.5 miles one-way
Hermit and Dripping Springs Trails to Dripping Springs	3.5 miles one-way

from mid-May to the end of November. For more detailed trail descriptions, look in guidebooks and individual trail guides sold through the **Grand Canyon Association** (© **800/858-2808;** www.grandcanyon.org).

Wherever you hike, carry plenty of water and know where the next water sources are. Eat and drink regularly so you don't create an electrolyte imbalance. If you hike into the canyon, allow yourself twice as much time for the trip out as for the descent. *Tip:* Always confirm with the visitor center or Backcountry Information Center the availability of water on the trails you intend to hike.

Backpacking for Beginners

By camping inside the canyon, you give yourself time to explore the park's lower elevations. However, the extreme temperature and elevation changes can make the Grand Canyon a nightmare for inexperienced or unprepared backpackers. The jarring descent strains your knees; the climb out tests your heart. Extreme heat often precludes hiking during the middle of the day, and water is scarce. Taking these hazards into account, a first-time backpacker should confine hikes to corridor trails.

PREPARING FOR YOUR BACKCOUNTRY TRIP
Packing Tips for Backpackers

What you carry (or don't) in your pack is just as important as your choice of trail. Warm temperatures and dry weather make the canyon an ideal place for traveling light. Lighten your load by carrying dry food such as instant beans and ramen noodles. In summer, go lighter still by leaving the stove at home and preparing cold meals. Some foods that are usually heated, such as ramen noodles or couscous, will soften in cold water—even inside a water bottle—over time. In early summer, carry a tent's rain fly or bivy sack instead of a tent. At this time of year, you're more likely to suffer problems related to heat—and heavy packs—than from the cold, so be sure you know how to rig your shelter, in case rain does fall.

Also, make sure you have enough water containers. I usually carry 4 to 5 quarts (or liters) in summer and sometimes, for long, waterless walks, bring even more. Start drinking water before you get thirsty, and refill your bottles whenever you have the chance. Eating carbohydrate-rich, salty food is just as important. If you guzzle too much water without eating, you risk developing an electrolyte imbalance that can result in unconsciousness or death. Loss of appetite is common during a hike. Eat every time you drink, even if you don't feel hungry. Also, carry powdered Gatorade or another electrolyte-replacement drink.

Obtaining Permits

Permits are required for all overnight camping in the backcountry that falls within the park's boundaries. This includes all overnight stays below the rims (except in Phantom Ranch's cabins and dorms) and on park land outside of designated campgrounds. Good for up to 11 people, each permit costs $10, plus an additional $5 per person per night (so the cost for four people, for example, would be $30).

Regular hikers can purchase a **Frequent Hiker Membership,** which costs $25 but waives the $10 permit fee for a year from the date of purchase.

The furthest in advance permit requests are accepted and considered by the Backcountry Information Center is the first of the month, 4 months prior to the proposed start month. For example, permits for all of May go on sale on January 1; permits for June go on sale February 1, and so on. To obtain a backcountry permit for the dates and use areas/campsites of your choice, ensure your request arrives at the Backcountry Information Center on the first day it will be accepted (but not before). Faxing is strongly recommended. Only written requests are accepted during the 4th month out. Written requests may be submitted by fax, letter, or hand delivered. All requests received by 5pm on the first day of the 4th month out will be placed in random order by computer. Verbal in-person requests are only considered for start dates 1 to 3 months out (not 4).

You can pick up the Permit Request Form and instructions in person at the **Backcountry Information Center** (𝄞 928/638-7875; www.nps.gov/grca) or download them from the website. Select "Backcountry Hiking" and then "Backcountry Permit" (the Permit Request Form is available as a PDF file). Once you fill out your Permit Request Form, take it in person to the Backcountry Information Center on the South Rim or North Rim; fax it to 𝄞 **928/638-2125** no earlier than the date the permits become available; or mail it postmarked no earlier than that date to: Grand Canyon National Park, P.O. Box 129, Grand Canyon, AZ 86023.

To increase your odds of receiving a permit, be as flexible as possible. It helps to request three alternative hikes, in order of preference, and more than one starting date. Keeping your group small also helps. No requests are taken by phone. Allow 1 to 3 weeks for processing after the Backcountry Information Center receives your form. Forms must be received at least 2 weeks prior to the dates requested. Faxing the form will get you a response much faster than mailing it. *Tip:* In the future, the Center may begin to accept permit requests online; check the National Parks website for updates.

The Backcountry Information Center takes calls weekdays between 1 and 5pm Mountain Standard Time at 𝄞 **928/638-7875.** You can also visit the office in person from 8am to noon and 1 to 5pm daily. Representatives can help if you have questions about a trail or about applying for a permit.

Permits are available from a few locations outside the park's developed areas—and outside the park. These locations include **Pipe Spring National Monument** (𝄞 928/643-7105) near Fredonia, Arizona; at ranger stations at **Jacob Lake, Meadview,** and **Lees Ferry;** and the **Bureau of Land Management office** in St. George, Utah (𝄞 **435/688-3246**). At the Pipe Spring, Meadview, and Lees Ferry locations, you may not always find a ranger capable of processing your request, and they only accept credit cards (no cash).

Preparing for Your Backcountry Trip

EXPLORING THE BACKCOUNTRY

For the purposes of this book, I've divided the park trails into three categories: rim, corridor, and wilderness. In the Grand Canyon, some of the rim trails and all of the corridor and wilderness trails are considered part of the backcountry.

RIM TRAILS As the name implies, rim trails are on the canyon's rim, rather than descending down into the canyon. Some rim trails stay in the park's developed areas; these are usually paved, with relatively gradual inclines. They can be very busy, but sometimes afford nice views. Other rim trails go farther away from developed areas and into the nearby piñon-juniper, ponderosa pine, and spruce-fir forests. These have a few steep or rugged stretches, but most are quite manageable. Many lead to scenic canyon overlooks and are often uncrowded.

CORRIDOR TRAILS When descending into the canyon for the first time, even experienced backpackers should consider one of the three corridor trails, **North Kaibab, South Kaibab,** or **Bright Angel,** discussed in detail below. Well-maintained and easy to follow, these are regularly patrolled by park rangers. Each has at least one emergency phone and pit toilet. Drinking water is available at several sources along both the Bright Angel and the North Kaibab trails (some of these sources are seasonal), but not on the South Kaibab. Check at the Backcountry Information Center or visitor center for current water availability before starting your hike. While hiking the corridor trails, you can spend your nights at **Bright Angel, Cottonwood,** or **Indian Garden campgrounds,** each of which has a ranger station, running water (seasonal at Cottonwood), and toilets.

WILDERNESS TRAILS By hiking on corridor trails, you can acclimate to the conditions in the canyon without having to negotiate the boulder-strewn and sometimes confusing wilderness trails, which also go into the canyon. Rangers are rare on wilderness trails, which are not maintained and can be difficult to discern, as they have washed away in some places, and, sometimes, descend steeply down cliffs. On the less traveled wilderness trails, help can be very far away if something goes wrong.

The corridor trails provide access to backcountry campgrounds, but most wilderness trails accommodate only at-large camping, meaning that it's up to each hiker to find a campsite. Unlike the campgrounds, the campsites along wilderness trails do not have purified water or ranger stations nearby, and only a few have pit

Exploring the Backcountry

HIKES & OUTDOOR PURSUITS

TRAIL difficulty LEVELS

Because of the huge elevation changes on the canyon trails, none can be called easy. In general, describing a trail as easy, moderate, or difficult oversimplifies the situation. For example, **Hermit Trail** is easy to follow and relatively gradual between the rim and just above Santa Maria Spring, but it's considerably more rugged after that. **Tonto Trail** is an easy walk in places, but has almost no water and very little shade. Here is a subjective ranking of the most popular trails that go from the rim into the canyon, in order from **least to most difficult:**

South Rim	North Rim
Bright Angel	North Kaibab
South Kaibab	Thunder River
Grandview	Bill Hall
Hermit	North Bass
Hermit/Dripping Spring/Boucher	Nankoweap

4

toilets. On the busiest wilderness trails, campers may be limited to designated sites.

TRAILS ON THE SOUTH RIM
Rim Trails

The **Rim Trail** on the South Rim extends from Hermits Rest to the South Kaibab Trailhead. It starts in Grand Canyon Village and goes both east and west along the rim, with the westbound section of the trail spanning 8 miles to Hermits Rest and the eastbound part extending 3.7 miles past Mather Point to Pipe Creek Vista and now another .8 miles to the South Kaibab Trailhead. Both sections can be very busy, especially near Grand Canyon Village, and both offer stunning canyon views while passing through less-than-pristine rim-top scenery. The eastbound section is paved (from Maricopa Point to Pipe Creek Vista) and easy to traverse; the westbound part is longer, more rugged, and has lonesome stretches. Much of the westbound section runs close to Hermit Road. The new educational **Trail of Time** extends 1.3 miles from Verkamp's Visitor Center to Yavapai Point in the eastbound section.

West on the South Rim Trail   Highlights: Beats riding the bus to the overlooks (though you can get on and off the bus at any of the viewpoints and walk as long as you like). **Drawbacks:** Seeing and hearing the buses, and the crowds at the overlooks.

Difficulty Level: One steep climb; tricky footing in isolated locations.

Don't let this trail's name confuse you. The Rim Trail on the South Rim meanders east and west along the canyon's South Rim, from South Kaibab Trailhead through Grand Canyon Village and all the way to Hermits Rest. (If you go looking for the canyon's west rim, you may end up in Lake Mead.) It parallels Hermit Road and passes through all the same scenic overlooks described in the Hermit Road driving tour (see chapter 3). Walking (instead of driving) this stretch is a great way to see the canyon while putting some elbow room between you and the crowds.

The trail is paved from South Kaibab Trailhead to Powell Point; unpaved between Powell Point and Monument Creek Vista; and paved between Monument Creek Vista and Hermits Rest. The 1.9-mile distance from the village to **Powell Point** is paved, with one 200-foot climb. Past Maricopa Point, the trail planes off and the pavement ends. For the next 4 miles, there's a well-defined dirt trail that meanders through piñon-juniper woodland along the rim (when not passing overlooks). The scenery is lovely, and the crowd thins as you move farther west. The nicest stretch lies between the **Abyss** and **Pima Point,** where the trail becomes the greenway and heads toward the canyon. This is one of the few places on the trail where you won't hear an occasional bus. Allow 2 to 3 hours to get from Powell Point to Hermits Rest, and about 1 hour to get from Grand Canyon Village to Powell Point.

As 16 miles might be too much hiking for 1 day, I recommend hiking out on this trail from Grand Canyon Village and taking the shuttle back (mid-Mar to mid-Oct). By doing so, you can avoid revisiting the same overlooks on the shuttle ride back—the shuttles stop at every turnout en route to Hermits Rest, but only stop at **Pima Point, Mohave Point,** and **Powell Point** on their way back to the village.

If you don't want to walk the whole 8 miles, here's a list of distances to help determine how far you've gone and whether you want to continue to the next lookout:

Trail head to Trailview I:	.7 miles
Trailview I to Maricopa Point:	.7 miles
Maricopa Point to Powell Point:	.5 miles
Powell Point to Hopi Point:	.3 miles
Hopi Point to Mohave Point:	.8 miles
Mohave Point to the Abyss:	1.1 miles
The Abyss to Pima Point:	2.9 miles
Pima Point to Hermits Rest:	1.1 miles

8 miles to Hermits Rest from Grand Canyon Village. **Access:** Rim-side sidewalk at Grand Canyon Village's west end. Water sources at Grand Canyon Village, Hermits Rest, Park Headquarters, and Yavapai Point. **Maps:** Trails Illustrated Topo Map, Grand Canyon Sky Terrain Trail Map.

East on the South Rim Trail   Highlights: Paved, easy to walk on, and close to the edge. **Drawbacks:** More crowded than the westbound section. **Difficulty Level:** The sidewalk is so wide, it's more like a road than a trail.

This smooth, paved trail connects Grand Canyon Village and **Mather Point.** Around the lodges, the path is a flat sidewalk teeming with people. Between Verkamp's Visitor Center and Yavapai Point is the new **Trail of Time,** a 1.3-mile walk from the village to Yavapai Geology Museum in which every meter (think of a long step) equals a million years of history. This interactive walk, representing 2 billion years of Grand Canyon history, allows you to see and touch rock samples from the canyon's various layers.

The crowds dissipate between the village's east edge and **Yavapai Point.** Near Yavapai Point, there are many smooth, flat rocks along the rim—great places from which to contemplate the canyon. Located 1.75 miles northeast of the village's historic district, Yavapai Point has a historic observation station (it was built in 1928) with large windows overlooking the canyon and geology-related exhibitions. From here, you can walk another .7 miles to Mather Point on a portion of the park's Greenway Trail, then past Pipe Creek Vista on to **South Kaibab Trailhead.** This 10-foot-wide, paved walkway is usually within a few feet of the rim, away from crowds and providing ever-changing canyon views. If you grow fatigued, you can catch shuttles at Mather Point, Yavapai Point, or Pipe Creek Vista. Allow about 1 hour to walk this trail.

2.4 miles to Mather Point. **Access:** Grand Canyon Village, along the rim behind El Tovar Hotel. Water sources at Grand Canyon Village, Park Headquarters, and Yavapai Point. **Maps:** Trails Illustrated Topo Map, Grand Canyon Sky Terrain Trail Map.

Corridor Trails

Bright Angel Trail ★★   Highlights: Long stretches near lush, cool creek beds. **Drawbacks:** During high season, you'll pass hundreds of hikers and some mules. **Difficulty Level:** Water sources, ample shade, and a wide, well-maintained surface make this the most accommodating trail into the canyon from the South Rim.

Both Native Americans and early settlers recognized this as a choice location for a trail into the canyon. First, there's an enormous fault line, along which so much erosion has taken place that even the usually sheer Redwall Limestone layer holds vegetation. Then there's the water—more of it than anywhere else on the

South Rim. The springs at Indian Garden supplied Grand Canyon Village as late as 1970.

For centuries, the Havasupai used this trail to descend from the rim, where they hunted in winter, to Indian Garden, where they farmed year-round. This went on until the 1920s when the Park Service expelled the remaining tribe members. Although most of the Havasupai now live on a reservation in the central canyon, a few of their **pictographs** (rock paintings made with mineral dyes) remain along the trail. Some are high on the rocks just past the first tunnel; others are on a sandstone overhang above **Two-Mile Corner,** the first switchback below **Mile-and-a-Half Rest House.**

When Pete Berry, Niles Cameron, and Ralph Cameron prospected for minerals here in the late 1800s, they improved the trail so that most people could hike it. As more visitors came to the canyon, Ralph Cameron realized that the trail might be more lucrative than gold. He bought out his partners, then used mining laws to take control of the land near and below Grand Canyon Village. Although the Santa Fe Railroad challenged his authority in the early 1900s, it wasn't until the 1920s that Cameron lost the trail. By then, he had charged countless mule riders a $1 fee to descend it.

If Cameron earned that much for every hiker on this trail today, he'd be doing just fine. More than 500,000 people hike the Grand Canyon's three corridor trails (South and North Kaibab, and Bright Angel) every year; Bright Angel is the most popular. It's busy, wide, dusty, and relatively gradual, with some occasional mule manure.

Walk down to **Mile-and-a-Half House** or **Three-Mile House,** which have shade, restrooms, an emergency phone, and seasonal drinking water. Or continue down to the picnic area near **Indian Garden** spring, where there's another restroom and lush vegetation and large cottonwood trees provide shade.

Watch the layers on this trail as you descend. As you move from the **Kaibab Formation** to the **Toroweap Formation,** the wall on your left gradually turns from cream-colored to pinkish-white. After the second tunnel, you'll start down through the steep buff-colored cliffs that form the **Coconino Sandstone.** As you do, compare the elevations of the cliffs on either side of the fault. The ones to the west have been offset and are 189 feet higher. At the bottom of the Coconino Sandstone, the **Hermit Shale,** deep red in color, is visibly eroding out from under the harder cliffs above it. This weakens the cliffs, which then break off along joints.

After dropping through the **Supai Group** and **Redwall layers,** the trail begins its long, direct descent to **Indian Garden;** as you near it, you'll begin to see plant species found near water, including willow, mesquite, catclaw acacia, even Arizona grape, a native species that produces tart but edible grapes. In spring, the redbud's

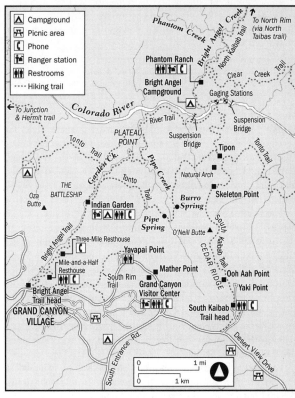

Legend:
- 🅰 Campground
- 🅰 Picnic area
- 🅲 Phone
- 👥 Ranger station
- 👥 Restrooms
- ···· Hiking trail

Phantom Creek

Bright Angel Creek

To North Rim (via North Taibas trail)

North Kaibab Trail

Phantom Ranch 👥👥🅲

Clear Creek Trail

Bright Angel Campground 🅰

Gaging Stations

← To Junction & Hermit trail

Colorado River

River Trail

Suspension Bridge

Suspension Bridge

Tonto Trail

PLATEAU POINT

Garden Ck.

Tonto Trail

Tipon ■

Pipe Creek

Tonto Trail

Natural Arch

THE BATTLESHIP

Oza Butte ▲

Indian Garden 👥🅰👥🅲

Burro Spring ●

Skeleton Point ■

Pipe Spring ●

O'Neill Butte ▲

South Kaibab Trail

CEDAR RIDGE

Bright Angel Trail

Three-Mile Resthouse 🅲

Yavapai Point 👥

Ooh Aah Point ■

Mile-and-a-Half Resthouse 👥🅲

South Rim Trail

Mather Point ■

Yaki Point ■

Bright Angel Trail head

GRAND CANYON VILLAGE

Grand Canyon Visitor Center 👥👥🅲

South Kaibab Trail head 👥👥🅲

South Entrance Rd.

Desert View Drive

0	1 mi
0	1 km

4

purple blooms are bright enough to be seen from the rim. Fit, well-prepared hikers may wish to hike 1.5 miles past Indian Garden on the **Tonto and Plateau Point trails.** Plateau Point Trail eventually crosses the Tonto Platform to an overlook of the Colorado River, 1,300 feet below.

Below Indian Garden, Bright Angel Trail follows **Garden Creek** down a narrow canyon in the **Tapeats Sandstone layer.** After leaving Garden Creek, the trail descends through the **Vishnu Formation** in a series of switchbacks known as **Devil's Corkscrew.** It then follows **Pipe Creek** to the **Colorado River** and the junction with **River Trail.** There, you'll find a small **rest house** with an emergency phone and toilet—but no pretreated drinking water. After staying near the river for 1.7 miles on River

Trail, you'll reach the **Silver Suspension Bridge.** Cross it to get to **Bright Angel Campground.** See "Backcountry Campgrounds," later in this chapter.

Allow for 2 to 4 hours round-trip (down and back) to Mile-and-a-Half House, 4 to 6 hours round-trip to Three Mile House, 6 to 9 hours round-trip to Indian Garden, and 8 to 12 hours round-trip to Plateau Point.

Round-trip trail length is 19 miles; 4.6 miles to Indian Garden; 7.8 miles to Colorado River; 9.3 miles to Bright Angel Campground. **Access:** Trail head is just west of Kolb Studio, near Grand Canyon Village. Water sources at Mile-and-a-Half House (seasonal), Three-Mile Rest House (seasonal), Indian Garden, Colorado River, Bright Angel Campground. **Map:** Grand Canyon Sky Terrain Trail Map.

South Kaibab Trail ★★★ **Highlights:** Panoramic views for much of the distance from the rim to the river. **Drawbacks:** Mules are on the upper trail. Parking is not available at the trail head. **Difficulty Level:** This trail is very strenuous. You won't find water, abundant shade, or shelter. It's also more dangerous than Bright Angel Trail—and steeper.

The South Kaibab Trail was the National Park Service's way of bypassing Ralph Cameron, who controlled Bright Angel Trail in the early 1900s. Cameron used mining laws to lay claim to the land around Bright Angel Trail and charged everyone $1 to descend it. Later, as a senator, he pushed to deny Park Service funding. In 1924, exasperated by Cameron's maneuverings, the Park Service began to build the South Kaibab Trail, which, like Bright Angel Trail, linked Grand Canyon Village with the Colorado River and Phantom Ranch. Unlike Bright Angel Trail, which follows natural routes into the canyon, this one was built using dynamite and hard labor.

The South Kaibab Trail begins with a series of switchbacks through the upper rock layers. After nearly a mile of hugging a cliff, the trail opens abruptly onto a dramatic panorama at an overlook known as **Ooh Aah Point** (allow 1–2 hr. to get here and back). As you descend through the **Kaibab Formation,** you'll see a few Douglas firs, remnants of the last ice age (and part of a shade-protected microclimate). After the ice age ended 10,000 years ago, the firs retreated off the South Rim, clinging only to a few due-north slopes where they received almost no direct sunlight. As the trail descends past the **Coconino Sandstone,** watch for evidence of cross-bedding—diagonal lines formed by windblown sand in an ancient desert.

Below the Coconino layer, the trail descends onto **Cedar Ridge** (allow about 2–4 hr. to get here and back), a platform that has restrooms and a hitching post for mules (but no water). This is an excellent place for day hikers to picnic and rest before hiking the

Trails on the South Rim

HIKES & OUTDOOR PURSUITS

1.5 miles back out. Continuing northward down the ridge, you'll reach a saddle underneath **O'Neill Butte,** with views 1,000 feet down to the **Tonto Platform** on either side. The trail then rounds the butte's east flank, eventually reaching another saddle. It descends in steep switchbacks through the **Redwall Formation,** then slices downhill across the Tonto Platform toward the **Inner Gorge.** From the Tonto Platform, make sure to glance back at the natural rock bridge in the cliffs. At the tip-off, where the trail begins its drop into the Inner Gorge, an emergency telephone and toilet are available.

As you begin your descent through the **Tapeats Sandstone layer,** you'll see the Colorado River between the dark, sheer walls of the Inner Gorge. The pink in the otherwise black walls is Zoroaster Granite, formed 1.2 billion years ago when molten rock was squeezed into the Vishnu Schist's fissures. From here, it's a 1-hour walk to the **Kaibab Suspension Bridge** and **Bright Angel Campground.**

Note: This is a good second hike to take after you've tried Bright Angel Trail and already know your abilities. You can't drive to the South Kaibab trail head; the park's free shuttle service begins ferrying hikers from the Backcountry Information Center to the trail head at least 1 hour before sunrise every morning. Allow at least 3 to 4 hours to get down, and at least 6 to 8 hours to return to the rim. Do not attempt a round-trip in 1 day.

6.7 miles to Colorado River; 6.8 miles to Bright Angel Campground. **Access:** Trail head near Yaki Point (Hwy. 64, E. Rim Dr., 5 miles east of Grand Canyon Village). Water sources at top of trail head, Colorado River, and Bright Angel Campground. **Map:** Grand Canyon Sky Terrain Trail Map.

Wilderness Trails

Hermit Trail ★★ Highlights: Late-afternoon sun feels good on cold days. **Drawbacks:** Less panoramic than other trails from the South Rim to the river. **Difficulty Level:** A moderate hike; steep in places; washouts and rock fall complicate route-finding. Cobblestone portions near the top are broken and rugged.

In 1912, Santa Fe Railroad managers sought to establish a route into the canyon that Ralph Cameron, the "owner" of Bright Angel Trail, couldn't control. The result was Hermit Trail, built 8 miles west of Grand Canyon Village. Paved with sandstone slabs and low walls on the outside, Hermit Trail was generally regarded as the best the canyon had to offer in the 1910s. The vine-covered shelter at Santa Maria Spring was built at about the same time, as was Mary Colter's new building, Hermits Rest.

Today, Hermit Trail remains wide at the top, with long, gradual switchbacks descending to the bottom of the **Coconino Sandstone** and onto the expanse of **Waldron Basin.** However, the old sandstone slabs have broken or slid in places, making the trail far more rugged than it was in the early 20th century. Because the upper trail is on west-facing cliffs, it's cool in the morning and hot in the afternoon. Below the Coconino Sandstone, the trail, passing a few low-lying piñon and juniper trees, intersects both **Waldron** and **Dripping Springs trails.** Go right both times. Near the head of the brick-red **Hermit Gorge,** the trail makes a few switchbacks down into the **Supai Group,** eventually reaching a water source, **Santa Maria Spring.** At 2.5 miles down, this spring is a good turnaround point for day hikers. To be safe, treat the water before drinking.

Past the spring, the trail heads toward the tip of **Pima Point,** remaining fairly level—except when negotiating areas covered by rockfall or when making short descents, via switchbacks, into the Supai Group rocks. Finally, reaching a break in the **Redwall layer,** it careens downhill in a series of tight switchbacks known as the **Cathedral Stairs.** Below the Redwall, the trail slices downhill, then makes a series of long switchbacks onto the **Tonto Platform.**

At the junction with Tonto Trail, Hermit Trail continues west (left) toward Hermit Creek. Later you'll reach another junction. The trail forking to the right descends to **Hermit Creek** between the Hermit Creek campsites and the Colorado River. Hikers camping at Hermit Rapids should take this shortcut. Others, including those using the Hermit Creek sites, should continue straight, passing this turnoff. In this area, you'll find remnants of the old Hermit Camp. Guests here in the 1920s were shuttled around in a Model T that had been transported to the camp in pieces and reassembled on-site—a luxury you may yearn for by this point.

If you do walk the 1.5 miles down the creek to the beach at **Hermit Rapids,** you'll pass several nice pour-overs and small pools. Along the walls, look for sacred datura, identifiable by large, teardrop-shaped leaves and white, lilylike flowers. You may have company at the beach—river trips frequently stop here to scout the rapids below the confluence.

Note: Backpackers planning overnight trips on Hermit Trail can receive special permits to drive on Hermit Road from the Backcountry Information Center. Allow 2 to 4 hours round-trip (down and back) to Waldron Basin, 5 to 8 hours round-trip to Santa Maria Spring, and 6 to 9 hours round-trip to Dripping Springs.

2.5 miles to Santa Maria Spring; 7.8 miles to Hermit Creek; 9.3 miles to Colorado River. *Access:* Parking area west of Hermits Rest. Water sources at Santa Maria Spring, Hermit Creek, and Colorado River. *Maps:* Grand Canyon (7.5 min.) quadrangle or Grand Canyon Sky Terrain Trail Map.

Hermit Trail & Dripping Springs (South Rim)

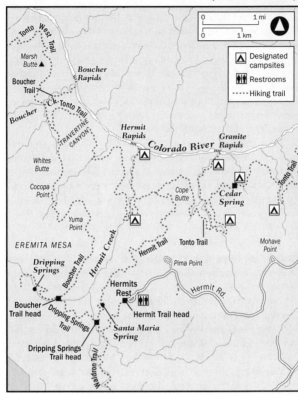

Map legend:
- 🏕 Designated campsites
- 🚻 Restrooms
- ···· Hiking trail

Map labels: Tonto West Trail, Marsh Butte, Boucher Trail, Boucher Rapids, Boucher Ck, Tonto Trail, Boucher, TRAVERTINE CANYON, Hermit Rapids, Colorado River, Granite Rapids, Whites Butte, Cocopa Point, Yuma Point, Cope Butte, Cedar Spring, Tonto Trail, EREMITA MESA, Dripping Springs, Hermit Creek, Boucher Trail, Hermit Trail, Tonto Trail, Mohave Point, Boucher Trail head, Hermits Rest, Pima Point, Hermit Rd, Dripping Springs Trail, Hermit Trail head, Santa Maria Spring, Dripping Springs Trail head, Waldron Trail

Dripping Springs Trail ★ Highlights: Uncrowded; ascends to springs in a deep alcove. **Drawbacks:** Does not afford expansive views; easy to get lost. **Difficulty Level:** Relatively easy, but with a few steep inclines and some genuinely scary exposures.

Dripping Springs Trail begins 1.2 miles down Hermit Trail. Though it doesn't offer expansive views of the inner canyon, hikers do enjoy the peace and solitude necessary to appreciate the desert's sounds, smells, and lighting. The most physically demanding portion of this hike is the 1,340-foot descent from the trail head of Hermit Trail to the junction with Dripping Springs Trail. On Dripping Springs Trail, it's a gradual westward climb to the springs themselves. (However, a few sections of trail near the head of

Hermit Gorge roll steeply and are narrow and exposed.) The trail eventually curves into an upper drainage of **Hermit Basin,** rounding the base of **Eremita Mesa.** The springs are partway up this drainage.

The 30-foot-thick rock overhang at **Dripping Springs** looks like a great place for a hermit to live. Perhaps this is why everyone assumed that Louis Boucher, the prospector who lived in this area in the early 1900s, *was* a hermit. It even looks a bit like the oversized fireplace at Hermits Rest, the building Mary Colter designed as her own tribute to a loner's way of life. Not much remains of Boucher's camp. But the springs still trickle out of the overhanging rock, through moss and maidenhair fern, and drip into a pool below. If you fill up, purify the water.

Note: Dripping Springs is also accessible via a short, steep trail from the rim directly above it. To purists, this is the real Dripping Springs Trail. Because the road to the original Dripping Springs Trail is now closed, the above route is preferable for most hikers.

3.5 miles from Hermit trail head to Dripping Springs. **Access:** Off Hermit Trail at the head of Hermit Gorge. Water sources at Dripping Springs (purify before drinking). **Map:** Grand Canyon (7.5 min.) quadrangle or Grand Canyon Sky Terrain Trail Map.

Grandview Trail ★★★   Highlights: Historic; provides views down into two side canyons. **Drawbacks:** Cobblestone ramps become slippery when wet or icy. In winter, crampons may be required. **Difficulty Level:** Suitable for most fit hikers; steep and exposed in a few locations near the top.

Hiking the Grandview Trail is a great way to take in human history along with canyon scenery. Strong day hikers can descend the 2,600 feet (over 3 miles) to **Horseshoe Mesa,** see the remnants of Pete Berry's turn-of-the-20th-century copper mine, and still make it back to the rim for dinner. Backpackers can use it to begin or close out loop hikes. However, because the cobblestone ramps below Grandview Point become slick in wet weather, avoid this trail during storms. Even if it's not raining, be sure to wear sturdy hiking boots.

The trail itself is part of the history. All but the top 430 feet of it was built in the 1890s. (The current upper section was completed around 1910 and was recently rebuilt.) In some places, the trailblazers used dynamite to blast away rock from sheer cliffs, forming ledges where none had been. In others, they pinned the trail against the walls by drilling holes into the rocks, pounding metal rods into the holes, then laying logs lengthwise above the rods. They then crammed rocks and dirt into openings and, as a finishing touch, paved the trail with cobblestones. Be sure to look at the trail from below to admire its structure.

For day hikers who are agile but not particularly strong, a smart place to turn around is at the saddle between upper Hance and Grapevine canyons. Known as **Coconino Saddle,** it's about .75 miles from the rim (the trail drops 1,600 ft. from the beginning to this point). Here, you'll find shade, flat resting spots, and views of both canyons. At the bottom of the **Coconino Sandstone,** the trail traverses east, then turns north, descending through the Hermit Shale and the Supai Group and onto Horseshoe Mesa. On the mesa, it intersects **Horseshoe Mesa Trail.**

Whether you go right, left, or straight at this junction, you'll eventually intersect the **Tonto Trail.** By going right, you'll descend 700 feet through the **Redwall Limestone** on the mesa's southeast side. Steep and rocky, this precarious route is the quickest path to water. Below the Redwall, a short spur trail leads to the perennial **Miner's Spring.** (Purify this water for safety.) You'll also find several mines here, including the **New Tunnel** (new in 1906), with a boiler and a compressor outside. In addition to being unstable, the mines have high levels of radon, so it's best to stay out of them.

By going left, you'll descend the mesa's west side to ephemeral **Cottonwood Creek,** past where the first miners lived. By going straight, you'll travel out onto the mesa's northwest "arm," where you'll see foundations of buildings from the mine camp, as well as old bottles, cans, and pieces of metal stoves. Also present, but less conspicuous, is evidence of past Native American activity: bits of chert (quartz rocks from which arrowheads were made) and old agave-roasting pits. A pit toilet is available for campers in this area, who must camp in designated sites.

Allow 1 to 2 hours round-trip (down and back) to Coconino Saddle, and 6 to 9 hours round-trip to Horseshoe Mesa.

3 miles from Grandview Trail trail head to Horseshoe Mesa; 6.8 miles to Tonto Trail (via the East Horseshoe Mesa Trail). *Access:* From Grandview Point (on Hwy. 64, 12 miles east of Grand Canyon Village). No water sources on Horseshoe Mesa. Water source at Miner's Spring, also called Page Spring (off the East Horseshoe Mesa Trail, well below Horseshoe Mesa's rim). *Maps:* Grandview Point (7.5 min.) and Cape Royal (7.5 min.) quadrangles or Grand Canyon Sky Terrain Trail Map.

Tonto Trail ★★ **Highlights:** Links many of the South Rim trails, creating some of the park's best loop hikes. **Drawbacks:** Long, shadeless, dry stretches make knowledge of water sources imperative. Can only be done as part of a multiday hike. **Difficulty Level:** Smooth and relatively level when not dipping into rocky, rugged drainages.

This 95-mile trail traverses much of the lower canyon atop the **Tonto Platform.** Rather than hike all of it, most people incorporate parts of it into shorter loop hikes, linking trails from the South Rim. Hiking here is often more strenuous than expected. Distances that look short on the map sometimes take a long time to cover, as the trail contours around numerous drainages that cut partway into the Tonto Platform. Because the platform has little to no shade, and because many of its water sources are seasonal, long hikes here in summer are ill-advised. Especially dangerous are the stretches between the Grandview and South Kaibab trails and between Slate Canyon and the South Bass Trail, both of which lack reliable water.

95 miles from Red Canyon (east) to Garnet Canyon (west). **Access:** Hance, Grandview, South Kaibab, Bright Angel, Hermit, Boucher, and South Bass trails all intersect Tonto Trail. Water sources at Hance, Cottonwood (usually), Grapevine, Pipe, Indian Garden, Monument, Hermit, and Boucher creeks, Indian Garden Spring, and the Colorado River in several locations. Ask at the Backcountry Information Center about water sources before hiking. **Map:** Grand Canyon Sky Terrain Trail Map or topographic map for section hiked.

TRAILS ON THE NORTH RIM
Rim Trails

The rim trails on the North Rim rank among the park's treasures. Start with **Transept Trail** or **Bright Angel Point Trail,** which are different sections of the same pathway. At the bottom of the stairs behind Grand Canyon Lodge, Bright Angel Point Trail goes to the left, while Transept Trail goes right. Bright Angel Point Trail is a short (.25-mile) paved path to a stunning overlook on a tiny peninsula between Transept and Bright Angel canyons. It's usually crowded, but well worth seeing. Transept Trail is longer, more thickly forested, and less crowded, but has fewer panoramic views.

Bright Angel Point Trail ★ Highlights: Stunning views of Transept and Bright Angel canyons. **Drawbacks:** Crowds at the overlook. **Difficulty Level:** Safe and easy, unless there's lightning.

This paved trail travels .25 mile along a narrow peninsula dividing Roaring Springs and Transept canyons. On the way, it passes a number of craggy outcroppings of the Kaibab Limestone layer, around which roots of wind-whipped juniper trees cling like arthritic hands. Though the trail stays at about the same level as the rim, junipers supplant ponderosa pines here because of the warm winds that blow out of the canyon; the lack of water in the permeable limestone is another reason. The trail ends at 8,148-foot-high **Bright Angel Point.** From this overlook, follow Bright Angel Canyon (with your eyes) to its intersection with the larger Colorado River gorge. On a quiet day, you can hear Roaring Springs, a tributary of Bright Angel Creek and the water source for both of the canyon's rims. You can hike this trail round-trip in a half-hour.

.25 mile each way. **_Access:_** By descending the back steps off the patios at Grand Canyon Lodge. Water source at Grand Canyon Lodge. **_Map:_** Grand Canyon Sky Terrain Trail Map.

Transept Trail ★   **Highlights:** Ponderosa pine forest and views of Transept Canyon. **Drawbacks:** May be busy, especially near Grand Canyon Lodge. Not a good choice for people with a fear of heights. **Difficulty Level:** Generally easy, though its undulations provide interval training.

Traveling 1.5 miles northeast along Transept Canyon's rim, this trail connects Grand Canyon Lodge and **North Rim Campground,** where bike rentals and the general store are also located. Passing through old-growth ponderosa pine and quaking aspen, it descends into, then climbs out of, three shallow side drainages, with ascents steep enough to leave people, especially those unaccustomed to the 8,000-foot altitude, short of breath. A small Native American ruin is on the way. It takes about 1½ hours round-trip to complete this hike.

1.5 miles each way. **_Access:_** Behind North Rim General Store (near the campground), or by descending the back steps off the patios at Grand Canyon Lodge. Water source at North Rim Store. **_Map:_** Grand Canyon Sky Terrain Trail Map.

Ken Patrick Trail ★   **Highlights:** A stretch skirts the rim; nice views of Nankoweap Creek drainages. **Drawbacks:** Mule-trampled near North Kaibab trail head parking lot, faint in other spots, and steeply rolling near Point Imperial. **Difficulty Level:** The longest, faintest, scratchiest—and all-around toughest—rim trail; no water accessibility.

This long, steeply rolling trail travels through ponderosa pine and spruce-fir forest between the head of **Roaring Springs Canyon** and **Point Imperial.** Along the way, it poses a number of challenges. Starting at the North Kaibab trail head, mules have pounded the trail's first mile into a dustlike flour (when not watered down into something resembling cake batter). Where the mules turn around after a mile, the trail becomes faint. It becomes even less distinct about 4 miles in, after passing the trail head for the old Bright Angel Trail.

After crossing **Cape Royal Road** (the only road that you'll encounter, about two-thirds of the way to Point Imperial), the trail descends into, then climbs out of, a very steep drainage overgrown with thorn-covered New Mexico locust. While challenging, the 3-mile stretch between the road and Point Imperial is also the trail's prettiest, following the canyon's rim above Nankoweap Creek's upper drainages. In these areas, you'll see plenty of scarlet bugler (identifiable by tubular red flowers with flared lower petals) and a number of Douglas firs interspersed with the ubiquitous ponderosa pines. Allow about 6 hours each way for this hike.

10 miles each way. **Access:** From the Point Imperial parking area's south side, or from the North Kaibab Trail's parking area (on the North Rim entrance road, 2 miles north of Grand Canyon Lodge). No water sources. **Maps:** Trails Illustrated Topo Map or Grand Canyon Sky Terrain Trail Map.

Uncle Jim Trail   Highlights: Views of Bright Angel and Roaring Springs canyons, much forest, and easy access which makes this a great option for a picnic. **Drawbacks:** Mule traffic. **Difficulty Level:** Has some hills, but is suitable for families.

A lasso-shaped loop accessible via the Ken Patrick Trail, the Uncle Jim Trail circles **Uncle Jim Point,** which divides Roaring Springs and Bright Angel canyons. This spot is named for a former game warden, Jim Owens, who slaughtered hundreds of mountain lions on the North Rim in the early 1900s. (His handiwork, part of a misguided predator-control program, likely contributed to an explosion in the deer population and an ensuing famine.) By taking the lasso's right branch, you'll soon reach an overlook near the tip of Uncle Jim Point. From here, you'll have views across Roaring Springs Canyon to Bright Angel Point. This overlook is a scenic, easily accessible spot for a picnic lunch. After passing it, the trail skirts the edge of Bright Angel Canyon before looping back. It takes about 3 hours round-trip to complete this hike.

5 miles round-trip (including Ken Patrick Trail). **Access:** 1 mile down Ken Patrick Trail from North Kaibab trail head parking area. No water sources. **Maps:** Trails Illustrated Topo Map or Grand Canyon Sky Terrain Trail Map.

Cape Final Trail   Highlights: An uncrowded, flat, boulder-free walk to a canyon overlook. **Drawbacks:** Parking area is easy to miss. **Difficulty Level:** Nice and easy.

Because this trail is relatively flat and boulder-free, it's a good choice for a first hike in the backcountry. It meanders through ponderosa pine forest on an old jeep trail, ending at **Cape Final,** where you'll have views of the northern canyon and **Juno Temple.** Budget roughly 2 hours round-trip for this hike.

2 miles each way. **Access:** An unmarked dirt parking area off the Cape Royal Rd., about 5 miles south of Roosevelt Point. No water sources. **Maps:** Trails Illustrated Topo Map or Grand Canyon Sky Terrain Trail Map.

Cliff Springs Trail ★   Highlights: Passes springs and an Ancestral Puebloan granary. **Drawbacks:** A few rocky stretches. **Difficulty Level:** Craggy spots can pose challenges.

Scenic and fairly short, this is a nice hike for families. Although the dirt trail seems at first to head into forest *away* from the canyon, it quickly descends into a narrow, rocky canyon that drains into the larger one—a reminder that the **Walhalla Plateau** is a peninsula in the Grand Canyon. Spruce and fir trees dominate the northern exposures in this side canyon, while ponderosa pines and piñon and juniper trees grow in the sunnier spots. Roughly a quarter-mile from the trail head, the trail passes a small **Ancestral Puebloan granary.** Then, after crossing a small drainage, the trail hugs the side canyon's north wall and passes under limestone overhangs and light green canopies of box elder trees (identifiable by their leaves in groups of three and their double-winged fruit). The springs drip from one of these limestone overhangs, where mosses carpet fissures in the rock. Don't drink the water, which may be contaminated. A waist-high boulder marks the end of the trail, which takes about 1 hour round-trip.

.5 mile each way. ***Access:*** A small pullout ½ mile north of Cape Royal on Cape Royal Rd. Water sources at Cliff Springs (purify before drinking). ***Maps:*** Trails Illustrated Topo Map or Grand Canyon Sky Terrain Trail Map.

Widforss Trail ★★ **Highlights:** A nice escape into ponderosa pine forest culminating with canyon views from Widforss Point. **Drawbacks:** Much of the trail is away from the rim, with the canyon out of sight. Frequented by mules. **Difficulty Level:** Distance and rolling terrain combine to make this a challenge.

This undeveloped, underused trail with expansive views is one of my favorite rim hikes in the park. It curves around the head of **Transept Canyon** before venturing south to **Widforss Point.** A brochure, sometimes available at the trail head, explains points of interest in the first 2 miles, during which the trail undulates through ponderosa pine and spruce-fir forest.

At the head of Transept Canyon, about halfway to Widforss Point, you'll pass several overlooks that make for good resting spots. You'll also see a balancing rock, formed when water seeping across planes eroded Kaibab Limestone beds from underneath.

Past the head of Transept Canyon, the trail heads south through old-growth ponderosa pine, and the canyon passes out of view. Under the red-orange-trunked trees, lupine blankets the forest floor with blue flowers. You'll also note a number of badly singed pines. The National Park Service allows prescribed burns in this and other areas, eliminating excess deadfall and undergrowth from the forest floor. Controlled fires like these are designed to bring the forest closer to its natural state. Before humans began suppressing blazes, natural fires swept through the ponderosa pine forest every 7 to 10 years. (For more on prescribed burns, see chapter 8.)

The trail, remaining hilly most of the way, reaches the rim again at Widforss Point. There, you'll have a nice view of five temples. The three to the southeast are **Zoroaster** (farthest south), **Brahma** (north of Zoroaster), and **Deva** (farthest north); to the southwest, **Buddha** sits like a sphinx with two long legs. Out of one of those legs rises **Manu.** A picnic table and several good campsites lie near the rim. Among the wildlife you may see on this hike are deer, bobcats, mountain lions, squirrels, coyotes, porcupines, snakes (gopher and king), and lizards. Allow about 5 hours round-trip.

5 miles each way. **Access:** A dirt road ⅓ mile south of Cape Royal Rd. Follow this road ¾ mile to the parking area, which is well-marked. No water sources. **Maps:** Trails Illustrated Topo Map, Grand Canyon Sky Terrain Trail Map, or free self-guiding trail map available at trail head.

Corridor Trails

North Kaibab Trail ★★ **Highlights:** Less crowded than Bright Angel Trail, it's great for a first backpack trip into the canyon. **Drawbacks:** At 14.4 miles and with a vertical drop of 5,850 feet, it's much longer, and drops farther, than the South Rim corridor trails. **Difficulty Level:** Descends gradually from rim to river. Ample water and shade. Tests endurance more than agility.

Forget the myth that corridor trails are easy. The North Kaibab Trail will test any hiker who attempts to go from rim to river (or vice versa) in a day. Compare its 14.4 miles to the South Rim corridor trails, Bright Angel and the South Kaibab, which are 9.2 and 6.7 miles, respectively. The drop, too, is a factor; the North Kaibab descends 5,850 feet, while the others fall about 4,800 feet from rim to river. Despite the length and the big vertical drop, the North Kaibab Trail is one of the best for backpackers first experiencing the canyon. The scenery is lovely, the trail's grades are manageable, and beautiful views look down two side canyons—Roaring Springs and Bright Angel. But unlike the South Rim corridor trails, you see less of the gorge cut by the Colorado River; this one's also less crowded.

The trail begins with a long series of switchbacks down the head of **Roaring Springs Canyon.** At an elevation higher than 8,000 feet, the first switchbacks are in thickly forested terrain that could just as easily be found in the Rocky Mountains. Aspen, Douglas fir, and Gambel oak shade the trail and hide many of the rocks in the **Kaibab and Toroweap layers.** The **Coconino Sandstone layer,** whose sheer cliffs hold too little soil for these trees, stands out against the greenery, its white rocks streaked black and tan by mineral deposits. The Coconino Overlook is clearly marked and stands about .75 mile from the trail head.

North Kaibab Trail (North Rim)

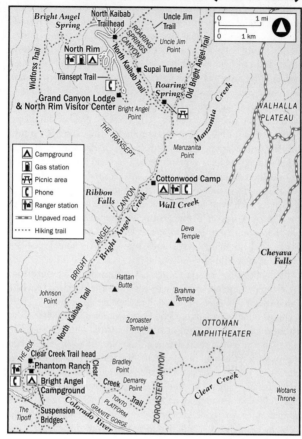

Bright Angel Spring
North Kaibab Trailhead
Uncle Jim Trail
ROARING SPRINGS CANYON
Uncle Jim Point
Old Bright Angel Trail
North Rim
North Kaibab Trail
Supai Tunnel
Widforss Trail
Transept Trail
Roaring Springs
Grand Canyon Lodge & North Rim Visitor Center
Bright Angel Point
WALHALLA PLATEAU
Manzanita Creek
THE TRANSEPT
Manzanita Point
Cottonwood Camp
Ribbon Falls
Wall Creek
BRIGHT ANGEL CANYON
Bright Angel Creek
Deva Temple
Cheyava Falls
Johnson Point
North Kaibab Trail
Hattan Butte
Brahma Temple
Zoroaster Temple
OTTOMAN AMPHITHEATER
THE BOX
Clear Creek Trail head
Phantom Ranch
Bright Angel Campground
Bradley Point
Demarey Point
Clear Creek
ZOROASTER CANYON
Clear Creek
Wotans Throne
The Tipoff
Suspension Bridges
Colorado River
TONTO PLATFORM
GRANITE GORGE
Trail

Legend:
- △ Campground
- Gas station
- ⛱ Picnic area
- ☎ Phone
- Ranger station
- ▭▭▭ Unpaved road
- ..... Hiking trail

The next major landmark is **Supai Tunnel.** At 2 miles from the trail head, and with shade, a restroom, and seasonal water, this is an ideal turnaround point for day hikers. Beyond the tunnel, the canyon warms up, and heat-tolerant plants such as squaw-bush, pale hoptree, piñon pine, and juniper appear. The trail descends in relatively gradual switchbacks through the **Supai Group,** then crosses a bridge over a creek bed. Past the bridge, the creek plummets. The trail travels along the south wall of **Roaring Springs Canyon,** on ledges above Redwall Limestone cliffs. A spire of Redwall Limestone known as the **Needle** marks where the trail begins its descent into the Redwall in a series of fairly steep switchbacks.

Roaring Springs, the water source for both rims, becomes audible just above the convergence of Bright Angel and Roaring Springs canyons. A .2-mile-long spur trail descends to the springs, where water pours from an opening in the **Muav Limestone layer** and cascades downhill, pooling at the bottom of the creek bed. Around those pools grow Arizona grape, scouring rushes, and box elder and cottonwood trees. You'll find shade, picnic tables, and usually drinking water here (verify water availability in advance with the visitor center). This is the farthest a day hiker should go.

Below the springs, 5.4 miles from the starting point, is a **pump house** (with a water faucet) and a heliport. From here, the trail begins a long, gradual descent to the Colorado River, traveling on or near the floor of Bright Angel Canyon for most of the way. The rocks along this stretch can be difficult to identify. In addition to the layers seen everywhere in the canyon, you'll find members of the **Grand Canyon Supergroup,** including the reddish-brown Dox Sandstone, purplish Shinumo Quartzite, orange-red Hakatai Shale, and numerous dikes and sills—places where lava filled cracks in the earth.

Two miles past Roaring Springs is **Cottonwood Campground.** By camping here on their way to and from the river, backpackers can extend their trips while hiking reasonable distances.

About a mile past Cottonwood Campground, a spur trail leads to **Ribbon Falls,** the centerpiece of a large natural amphitheater. The waterfall is usually a short detour off the North Kaibab Trail (when the water level is high, a sign points the way to Ribbon Falls and you'll walk across a bridge). Don't forego the chance to hike to the base of these falls, which roll off a high sandstone ledge and arc gracefully down, skimming an apron of travertine on the way. This apron formed when calcium carbonate precipitated out of the water as rock. You may see small, dark gray birds known as dippers (the name alone describes them) fishing in the pools around these falls.

About 2.5 miles past the falls, the trail enters a long stretch of narrows known as the **Box** and remains there, winding alongside Bright Angel Creek, until just above Phantom Ranch. To keep hikers dry in these narrows, the Civilian Conservation Corps (CCC) in the 1930s built three bridges over the creek and blasted ledges in the Vishnu Formation's cliffs. An immense flash flood swept away most of the originals—steel and all—in 1966. Today, this is the only maintained trail from the North Rim into the canyon.

Under no circumstances should you attempt to hike this trail from the rim to the river and back in 1 day.

2 miles to Supai Tunnel; 4.7 miles to Roaring Springs; 6.8 miles to Cottonwood Campground; 14.4 miles to the Colorado River. **Access:** On North Rim entrance road, 2 miles north of Grand Canyon Lodge; free parking available. Water sources at Roaring Springs (seasonal), Bright Angel Creek, Cottonwood Campground (seasonal), Phantom Ranch, Bright Angel Campground. **Maps:** Bright Angel Point (7.5 min.) and Phantom Ranch (7.5 min.) quadrangles.

Wilderness Trail

Clear Creek Trail ★   Highlights: A scenic, relatively flat spur off the North Kaibab Trail (from the bottom of the canyon), with views of Zoroaster Temple, Clear Creek, and the Colorado River. **Drawbacks:** Dangerously hot and dry in summer. **Difficulty Level:** Like the Tonto, smooth and relatively level when not dipping into craggy drainages.

After leaving the North Kaibab Trail, Clear Creek Trail climbs in steep switchbacks east of Bright Angel Creek, eventually reaching an overlook of the Colorado River, sandwiched between the dark walls of the Granite Gorge. The trail then travels east above the river, gradually ascending to the **Tonto Platform.**

Before it reaches that level, however, watch for the interface between the black, 2-billion-year-old **Vishnu Formation** and the flat brown facade of the **Tapeats Sandstone.** You can touch the point of contact between these layers; this is as close as you'll get to the Great Unconformity, the 1.2-billion-year gap in the geological record caused by erosion.

After reaching the Tonto Platform, the trail continues east (and then southeast), veering around the tops of numerous drainages, all beneath the imposing presence of **Zoroaster Temple** to the north. This long, shadeless stretch, where blackbrush and agave are among the tallest plants, makes Clear Creek Trail a risky place for summer hiking. Eventually, the trail crests a small rise, revealing a view of the confluence of the Colorado River Gorge and the drainage cut by Clear Creek. Turning northeast, the trail crosses Zoroaster Canyon and then traverses above Clear Creek before finally descending to the creek bed itself.

There are a number of nice campsites in the area just west of Clear Creek. From these campsites, you can head out on a number of excellent day hikes. Follow the creek 4 miles north to **Cheyava Falls,** a seasonal waterfall that, at 800 feet, is the canyon's tallest. Or, walk (and down-climb) 6 miles south to the Colorado River. The narrows en route to the Colorado are subject to flash floods and should be avoided during wet weather and spring runoff.

4

HIKES & OUTDOOR PURSUITS

Trails on the North Rim

Note: Remember that the North Rim is only open from mid-May to mid-October.

8.7 miles from Phantom Ranch to Clear Creek drainage. ***Access:*** .3 mile north of Phantom Ranch on the North Kaibab Trail. Water source at Clear Creek. ***Maps:*** Phantom Ranch (7.5 min.) quadrangle or Grand Canyon Sky Terrain Trail Map.

BACKCOUNTRY CAMPGROUNDS

The park's three backcountry campgrounds—**Bright Angel, Cottonwood,** and **Indian Garden**—are deep inside the canyon and accessible only via hiking trails. To stay at these campgrounds, you must be willing to hike long distances into the canyon carrying the necessary clothes, shelter, food, and water—and then hike back out with everything (including your trash). You will also need a permit from the park's Backcountry Information Center. If you lack either the necessary incentive or the necessary permit (or both), camp at one of the car campgrounds in the park's developed areas. There, you can sleep under the stars, a few feet away from your loaded vehicle. For more information, see chapter 5, "Camping with a Car in the Grand Canyon."

Bright Angel Campground ★★★   The **River Trail** (which begins at the foot of Bright Angel Trail), the **South Kaibab Trail,** and the **North Kaibab Trail** all converge below Bright Angel Campground, which lies on the Colorado River's north shore. The River Trail crosses the Colorado River on the Silver Suspension Bridge just west of the campground; the South Kaibab Trail crosses on the Kaibab Suspension Bridge just east of the campground. The North Kaibab Trail's lowest section parallels the campground on the opposite side of Bright Angel Creek. The campground lies 14.1 miles from the North Kaibab trail head; 9.3 miles from the Bright Angel trail head; and 6.8 miles from the South Kaibab trail head.

This long, narrow campground occupies a purgatory between the cool waters of Bright Angel Creek and the black cliffs of the Vishnu Formation, which, in summer, are hot as grills. A half-mile away, the Colorado River rumbles past, eddying against a beach that is a popular stopping point for raft trips. A walkway divides the campground, which is open year-round. Roughly half of the 32 campsites are on the cliff side; the other sites, which are nicer, are on the creek side. Most are shaded by cottonwood trees, a few of which Civilian Conservation Corps workers planted in the 1930s (though most of the CCC-planted trees washed away in a 1966 flash flood).

Phantom Ranch is a half-mile to the north. Though all three of the campgrounds inside the canyon boast lovely surroundings, the proximity of Bright Angel Campground to the Colorado River makes it especially stunning. The campground includes toilets, water, and a ranger station.

Cottonwood Campground ★★   As you hike up the North Kaibab Trail from the Colorado River, Bright Angel Canyon's walls part like the Red Sea below this campground. Between them rests a valley floor soft and damp enough to support a few cottonwood trees, most of which grow near the ranger station. Most of the 11 campsites are surrounded by shrub oak, whose low-slung branches barely shade the sites and picnic tables. Bright Angel Creek flows past the campground's west side. On a hot summer day, it's the only cool place around.

Halfway between the North Rim and the Colorado River, Cottonwood Campground is a great place to camp while en route to (or from) the waterway. As part of a 4-day hike from the North Rim, schedule a night here, a night at Bright Angel Campground, and another night at Cottonwood. But don't underestimate how hard it is to get here: The walk from the North Kaibab trail head to Cottonwood Campground covers 6.8 miles and drops 3,170 feet—nearly a half-mile longer than the entire length of the South Kaibab Trail, with nearly three-quarters of the vertical drop.

Cottonwood is the last camp in the canyon before you ascend to the North Rim. It lies 16.6 miles from the South Rim's Bright Angel trail head. It remains open year-round, though the ranger station is closed from November to April. There are toilets here; water is available seasonally.

Indian Garden Campground ★★   You can use this campground, 4.6 miles from the Bright Angel trail head and 3,100 feet below the rim, to break up hikes from the South Rim to the Colorado River. Its 15 sites are surrounded by lush riparian vegetation fed by Indian Garden Spring, just a short walk down the canyon. Toilets, water, and a ranger station are here. For a great 4-day hike from the South Rim, schedule 2 nights here and 1 night at Bright Angel Campground. Once you arrive at Indian Garden, you can hike to Plateau Point and enjoy marvelous vistas, or hike on the Tonto Trail.

OTHER SPORTS & ACTIVITIES
Air Tours

A handful of companies, all based at Grand Canyon National Park Airport in Tusayan, offer scenic airplane or helicopter rides over the canyon. With hundreds of thousands of people taking air tours over the canyon every year, the flights, which generate a great deal of noise in parts of the park and have raised safety concerns following a few crashes over the years, have become a politically charged issue. The use of quieter technology is being considered.

For many vacationers, however, the question is not whether to fly, but whether to take an airplane or a helicopter. The airplane flights, by and large, last longer and cost less. Most airplane tours remain airborne for 40 to 50 minutes and cost about $145 per person; most helicopter tours fly for 25 to 50 minutes, and range from $175 to $260. The planes also cover more ground, crossing the canyon near Hermits Rest and returning along the East Rim, near Desert View. The shorter helicopter tours, meanwhile, usually fly out and back in the same corridor near Hermits Rest (though some do go for the full loop). The helicopters cruise lower—just above the rim. And while they're not immune to an occasional bump, they tend to be smoother. (*Tip:* Whether you take an airplane or a helicopter, go early in the day for a smoother flight.)

The following companies offer air tours originating from Tusayan: **Papillon Grand Canyon Helicopters** (© **800/528-2418;** www.papillon.com); **Maverick Helicopters** (© **800/962-3869;** www.maverickhelicopter.com); **Grand Canyon Airlines** (© **866/235-9422;** www.grandcanyonairlines.com); and **Scenic Airlines** (© **800/634-6801;** www.scenic.com). Some of these companies also offer longer, more expensive tours that combine flights with short river cruises and lunch.

Condor Viewing

In recent years, many Grand Canyon visitors have spotted North America's largest land bird. Members of the vulture family, **California condors** cruise more than 100 miles a day, at speeds approaching 50 mph. When mature, condors are grayish-black except on their heads, which are orange and featherless. Under each wing, a triangular white patch—a characteristic field mark—will be visible.

In December 1996, six of these birds, whose wings can span 9½ feet, were released on the Vermilion Cliffs along Highway 89A, 26 miles from Lees Ferry. Since then, 10 or so condors have been released each year. The releases were part of a larger project aimed at reintroducing the birds to the wild after they nearly went extinct in the 1980s. Of the 198 California condors in the wild, 67 now live in the canyon country of northern Arizona and southern Utah.

Because condors primarily rely on eyesight to find their food, they sometimes follow turkey vultures and other scavengers. Other than size, the easiest way to tell the two species apart is the way they soar. Vultures hold their wings in a "V"; condors generally keep theirs in a flat plane.

Unless the condors change their habits, they will probably continue to make appearances above the South Rim and in Southern Utah in the years to come. In the summer of 2003, biologists confirmed that at least three pairs of California condors nesting in Arizona laid eggs. Two nests were unsuccessful, but one pair produced a young condor. It was the first time in hundreds of years that a condor had hatched and survived in Arizona. Unfortunately, the young condor died 2 years later; the cause of death was most likely malnutrition. Fourteen additional condors hatched and fledged in recent years, eight of which survive today.

North of the canyon, you might spot a condor by driving 14 miles east of Jacob Lake on Highway 89A to House Rock Valley Road (the first road to your left after you leave the national forest). Turn left (north) on BLM road 1065 and go 2 miles to a shade ramada, kiosk, and restroom; scientists leave food for the youngest birds atop the cliffs to the east. If condors are in the area, you'll probably meet workers who are tracking them. They carry a spotting scope and binoculars, and if asked, will likely help you see the birds.

Wherever you spot them, do not approach, feed, or otherwise disturb the condors. If you see one who appears to be hurt or sick, notify the **Peregrine Fund Condor Project** (✆ **928/355-2270;** www.peregrinefund.org). Be prepared to identify the time and location of the sighting and, if possible, the bird's wing-tag number. If you want to read more about these fascinating creatures, grab a copy of *Condors in Canyon Country* (Grand Canyon Association, 2007) by Sophie A. H. Osborn.

Cycling

Inside the park on the South Rim, cyclists are allowed on all paved and unpaved roads where motorized vehicles are allowed as well as on the **Greenway Trail.** The new paved Greenway Trail now connects the Grand Canyon Visitor Center with Pipe Creek Vista (1.3 miles) and the trail head of the South Kaibab Trail (another .8 miles). New sections of the Greenway Trail will be open in late spring 2012 connecting the Grand Canyon Visitor Center with the campground and on to the gateway community of Tusayan. Most of the Tusayan Trail will be unpaved. Cyclists are not permitted on hiking trails below the rim or pedestrian paths, including the rim trail between Mather Point and Monument Creek Vista. Hermit Road is open to cyclists year-round and makes for a terrific ride, but you'll need to yield to tour buses, shuttles, private vehicles, and people on foot.

On the North Rim, the entrance road is wide enough to accommodate experienced cyclists, and bicycles are permitted on all blacktop roads, as well as the Arizona and Bridle Path trails.

Outside the park, experienced cyclists enjoy the spectacular views on **Highway 67** (from Jacob Lake to the North Rim entrance) and the ride on **Highway 89** (from Fredonia, Arizona, to Jacob Lake), which travels through several climates.

Bicycles are now available for rent on the South Rim (except for in winter) at a temporary facility next to the Grand Canyon Visitor Center. A permanent bike rental and snack shop building should be open here by summer 2012. On the North Rim, there is a bike rental shop at the Sinclair Gas Station by the entrance to the North Rim Campground. To rent bicycles there or near the park, see "Bike Rentals," below. When planning a ride, keep in mind the high altitude.

MOUNTAIN BIKING

To mountain bike near the Grand Canyon, you'll need to cross out of Grand Canyon National Park into the **Kaibab National Forest,** which borders the park on both rims.

On the North Rim, avid cyclists flock to the **Rainbow Rim Trail,** an 18-mile stretch of single track (no motor vehicles allowed) that provides access to five remote canyon overlooks. Old logging roads, jeep trails, and footpaths crisscross other North Rim areas, providing a variety of cycling options. Visit the **Kaibab Plateau Visitor Center** in Jacob Lake (℗ **928/643-7298;** www.fs.usda.gov/kaibab/recreation) for directions, maps, road conditions, and trail descriptions.

On the South Rim, you'll find excellent mountain biking on the trails around the Grandview Fire Tower. To reach the tower, take Highway 64 east from Grand Canyon Village. About 1½ miles east of the Grandview Point turnoff, turn right (south). Leaving the park, follow this dirt road 1½ miles to Grandview Fire Tower and the trail head. Beginning here, you can ride more than 20 miles of intermediate-level single-track (with a few short, technically demanding stretches), much of it along the Coconino Rim.

Another trail system, with loops of 3.7, 10.2, and 11.2 miles, is near **Tusayan.** These loops follow old jeep trails through rolling hills in the ponderosa pine forest and have a few steep, rocky areas, though most of the terrain is only moderately difficult. To reach them, find the marked parking area ⅓ mile north of Tusayan on Highway 64's west side. A single trail goes north from there, eventually crossing under the highway through a concrete tunnel and providing access to the loops. (***Note:*** This is also a great place to run when staying in Tusayan.) For information on these trails and

Other Sports & Activities

HIKES & OUTDOOR PURSUITS

maps of the Tusayan Ranger District (© **928/638-2443**), visit the Forest Service office (weekdays 8am–4:30pm) a half-mile south of the park entrance on Highway 64.

BIKE RENTALS

Bicycles can now be rented on the South Rim from **Bright Angel Bicycle Rentals and Tours** (© **928/814-8704**; www.bike grandcanyon.com). In addition to bike rentals, they offer guided tours and also provide shuttle service along Hermit Road for those who prefer a shorter bike ride. Adult bikes cost $10 per hour, $25 for a half-day (4 hr.), and $35 for a full day; cost for children under 18 is $7, $15, and $25, respectively. Located next to the Grand Canyon Visitor Center, the rental shop is open from 8am to 6pm in high season. The company offering bike rentals on the South Rim could change in 2012.

For the South Rim, higher-end bicycles can be rented in Flagstaff at **Absolute Bikes** (© **928/779-5969**), 202 E. Route 66. Prices vary from $20 to $70 for a full day, $20 to $60 for a half-day.

On the North Rim, **Forever Resorts** (© **928/638-2611,** ext. 758) rents mountain bikes at the Sinclair Gas and Outfitter Station located at the entrance to the North Rim Campground. Adult mountain bikes cost $40 per day or $8.50 per hour; kid-size mountain bikes cost $25 per day or $4 per hour. Helmets are required and provided.

Outside the park, **Escape Adventures** (© **800/596-2953** or 435/259-7423; www.escapeadventures.com) in Moab, Utah, offers mountain and road bike rentals on a half- or full-day basis. Mountain bikes range from $35 for a half-day to $75 for a full day. Road bikes cost $55 for the first day, $45 for each additional day. For $225, you'll get a road bike for 7 days. Escape Adventures also offers multiday mountain bike tours of the North Rim; call or see the website for seasonal rates.

Downhill & Cross-Country Skiing

Arizona Snowbowl (© **928/779-1951**; www.arizonasnowbowl. com), located 7 miles north of Flagstaff on Highway 180, offers the best **downhill** skiing in the area. There are 32 trails serviced by four lifts, with runs for skiers and snowboarders of all abilities. The resort plans to introduce snowmaking equipment, which will help snow consistency. On weekends and holidays in summer, the **Scenic Skyride** takes customers to the top, where rangers give talks about the flora, fauna, geology, and history of the San Francisco peaks.

The crisp air, deep snow, and absolute silence make the North Rim a delightful place for cross-country skiing. The closest skiing to the park starts south of Jacob Lake, at the gate that closes **Highway 67.** You can park your car here, then ski south on the snow-covered highway. Snowmobiles are banned from the highway and the land east of it. To ski into the park (44 miles and several days' travel from the gate) and spend a night on the North Rim, you'll need to obtain a backcountry permit from the **Backcountry Information Center** (✆ 928/638-7875).

Cross-country skiing is unreliable on the South Rim. When there is sufficient snow, the Kaibab National Forest grooms trails near the Grandview Fire Tower. For information about which trails are open in winter, call the **Kaibab National Forest Tusayan Ranger District Office** at ✆ 928/638-2443.

Fishing

It's illegal to fish in the Colorado River without an **Arizona Fishing Permit.** (Those under 14 don't need a permit if they are with an adult who has one.)

One-day nonresident permits are available for $17 (5 days for $32) at the **Canyon Village Marketplace** (✆ 928/638-2262) in Grand Canyon Village; at **Marble Canyon Lodge** (✆ 800/726-1789 or 928/355-2225), a quarter-mile west of the Navajo Bridge on Highway 89; at **Lees Ferry Anglers Fly Shop** (✆ 800/962-9755 or 928/355-2261); and at **Cliff Dwellers Lodge** (✆ 800/433-2543 or 928/355-2228), 9 miles west of Navajo Bridge on Highway 89A. Fishing licenses are not available on the North Rim.

Once you get your fishing permit, the next challenge is getting to the best fishing spots. To fish inside park boundaries, you either have to hike to the Colorado River or be on a river trip and fish during breaks from rafting (for information about river trips, see "River Rafting," later in this chapter).

The best time to fish in the canyon is in fall and winter. The best trout fishing inside the park is at the canyon's eastern end, upstream of Phantom Ranch. The river is clear and cold (48°F/9°C) year-round directly below the dam, making this a great trout hatchery (and a chilling place for the native species, which evolved to live in muddy water and with extreme temperature variations). Downstream, the river gradually warms and gathers sediment from its tributaries, causing the trout population to dwindle and enabling the bottom-feeders to survive. The five most abundant fish species in the park are carp, speckled dace, flannel-mouth sucker, rainbow trout, and blue-head sucker.

Some of the Southwest's best trout fishing is just upstream of the park's easternmost boundary, between Glen Canyon Dam and Lees Ferry. Most of the hot spots in this 16-mile-long river stretch can be reached only by boat, but anyone can walk up a mile of shoreline from the Lees Ferry parking area. Lees Ferry fishing regulations allow the use of only artificial lures/flies and barbless hooks, and include the following limits: The daily bag limit is four fish, the possession limit is eight fish, the possession of live fish is unlawful, and the possession of fish longer than 12 inches is unlawful.

If you don't have your rod and waders with you, you can rent them, and boats too, from **Lees Ferry Anglers Guides and Fly Shop** (© 800/962-9755 or 928/355-2261; www.leesferry.com), which is now at Cliff Dwellers Lodge in Marble Canyon. This shop, the area's best, offers a complete guide service and carries a full line of fishing gear and tackle.

Horseback Riding

For horseback riding near the South Rim, go to **Apache Stables** (© 928/638-2891; www.apachestables.com), which operates from April through October; it's 1 mile north of Tusayan (off Hwy. 64), just outside the park's south entrance. Most of the horses here are "dog-friendly," as our guide put it. Because they're gentle and know the trails near the stables, you need only kick your steed periodically to make sure it keeps going. The rest of the time, you can relax and enjoy your horse's swaying motion and the ponderosa pine forest.

The friendly horses make this a great, albeit expensive, family activity. Children as young as 8 (and 48 in. tall) are allowed on the 1-hour trail rides, which, like the 2-hour ones, loop through the Kaibab National Forest near the stables. Other options are an evening trail ride and a wagon ride, both going to a campfire where participants roast marshmallows and other food they bring.

Prices are $89 for the 2-hour ride, $49 for the 1-hour ride, $59 for the campfire trail ride, and $26 for the campfire wagon ride. Participants should wear long pants and closed-toe footwear, and bring plenty of water. Backpacks are not allowed, but fanny packs are okay. Some age and weight restrictions may apply.

Mule Trips

Wearing floppy hats and clutching rain slickers, the day's mule riders gather at 7am (8am in winter) every day at a corral west of Bright Angel Lodge (on the South Rim) to prepare for their rides. You can almost hear the jangling nerves as they contemplate the prospect of descending narrow trails above steep cliffs on animals hardly famous for their willingness to comply. Although the mules walk close to the edges and have been known to back off the trails, accidents are rare, especially among riders who follow the

HIKES & OUTDOOR PURSUITS

Other Sports & Activities

wrangler's instructions. In fact, mule trips have been going into the canyon for more than a century without a single fatality from a fall.

The rides, while usually safe, can nonetheless be grueling. In fact, the National Park Service has limited the destination and number of mule rides, no longer allowing the 1-day trip to Plateau Point. Instead, there is now a rim ride offered to the Abyss, along with a limited number of mule rides still allowed down to Phantom Ranch. Most people's legs aren't used to bending around a mule, and the saddles aren't soft. In addition to the pounding, the canyon can be scorching, and chances for breaks are few. Because the rides are strenuous for both riders and mules, the wranglers strictly adhere to the following requirements: You must weigh less than 200 pounds (everyone is weighed), be at least 4 feet 7 inches tall, not be pregnant, and understand English. Acrophobes are discouraged from participating.

The least expensive ride—the half-day trip to the **Abyss Overlook**—stays on the rim. It travels from the Livery Barn in Grand Canyon Village through piñon pine forest to the Abyss Overlook. Riders have about 30 minutes here to take in the magnificent 3,000-foot vertical drop and stunning panorama. The total trip time is 3 hours. The cost is $121 and includes a bota bag for water and snacks.

The other rides are part of 1- or 2-night packages that include lodging and meals at **Phantom Ranch.** Going down, they follow Bright Angel Trail to the river, then travel east on the River Trail before finally crossing the river via the Kaibab Suspension Bridge. Coming back they use the South Kaibab Trail. The 10.5-mile descent takes 5½ hours; the 8-mile-long climb out is an hour shorter. The Phantom Ranch overnight costs $498 for one person, $880 for two, and $398 for each additional person (prices include tax). The Phantom Ranch 2-night trip, offered only from November to March, costs $702 for one person, $1,170 for two people, and $495 for each additional person. A duffel service is also available costing $64 per duffle bag.

Mule rides on the North Rim are through a small, family-run outfit called **Canyon Trail Rides.** Four types of rides, open to ages 7 and up, are offered; the easiest goes 1 mile along the rim on the Ken Patrick Trail before turning back. This 1-hour ride costs $40 per person, while the two half-day rides each cost $75 per person. One stays on the rim, following the Ken Patrick and Uncle Jim trails to a canyon viewpoint; the other descends 2 miles into the canyon on the North Kaibab Trail, turning back at Supai Tunnel. No one more than 200 pounds is allowed on the canyon rides; for the rim rides, the limit is 220. All riders must speak English.

Long pants are recommended, and you shouldn't bring anything more than a camera to carry. Water is provided.

River Rafting

There are a series of different Colorado River trips through Grand Canyon National Park. You can choose between single-day and multiday excursions, whitewater and smooth water, motorized and nonmotorized rafts, and commercial and noncommercial tours.

At the less expensive end are half-day, full-day, or overnight whitewater and smooth water trips, some of which start from Glen Canyon Dam or Lees Ferry (on the canyon's northeastern end), and others which launch from Quartermaster or Diamond Creek (on the canyon's western end). Noncommercial trips that launch from Diamond Creek and end at Lake Mead last 2 to 5 days. Permits for these whitewater trips are distributed on a first-come, first-served basis starting 1 year in advance. Motorized and nonmotorized whitewater rafting trips that launch from Lees Ferry and end at Diamond Creek vary in length.

Reserve 3- to 18-day professionally guided river trips 1 to 2 years in advance; 12- to 25-day noncommercial, self-guided trips are available to the public through a weighted lottery. Though motorized trips usually take at least 7 days to reach Diamond Creek, half-trip options exist for those who would prefer to hike in or out at Phantom Ranch. A full list of approved river concessionaires is available at www.nps.gov/grca under the "Plan Your Visit" section.

DAY TRIPS

Colorado River Discovery (✆ 888/522-6644; www.raftthe canyon.com) offers half-day guided smooth-water float trips from the base of Glen Canyon Dam to Lees Ferry (where most companies *begin* their trips). The excursions last about 5 hours and cost $85 for adults, $75 for children 12 and under. This trip is offered March 1 through November 30.

Grand Canyon Airlines (✆ 866/235-9422; www.grand canyonairlines.com) has teamed up with Colorado River Discovery to offer full-day guided smooth-water float trips from the base of Glen Canyon Dam to Lees Ferry. Round-trip bus transportation is provided to and from the Glen Canyon National Recreation Area transferring through Grand Canyon National Park and the Navajo Indian Reservation. Cost for this tour is $194 ($174 for ages 11 and under), including lunch. Tours are offered year-round, and include a flight over the canyon for an additional charge.

One-day guided motorized raft trips through the Grand Canyon's westernmost section are available through **Hualapai River Runners** (✆ 888/255-9550; www.hualapaitourism.com). This is the only 1-day whitewater rafting trip on the Colorado River. Riders begin at Diamond Creek's rapids and finish at Grand Canyon West (where a visit to the Skywalk can be added for $54). Time spent on the river is about 5½ hours and includes multiple cluster rapids. At the end of the day (weather permitting), participants are helicoptered off the river. Meeting time is 7:30am at Hualapai Lodge, on the Hualapai Indian Reservation in Peach Springs, and return time is between 6 and 7pm that same day. Lunch is included, and participants should bring a change of clothes, since they will get wet. These guided trips cost $355 per person and run from mid-March through October. The Hualapai Indian Reservation is about a 2-hour drive from Grand Canyon Village.

OVERNIGHT TRIPS

MOTORIZED Guided motorized trips are fastest, often covering the 277 miles from Lees Ferry (above the canyon) to South Cove (in Lake Mead) in 6 to 8 days, compared to as many as 18 days for nonmotorized trips. The motorized trips use wide pontoon boats (known colloquially as "bologna boats") that almost never capsize, making them slightly safer. Also, it's easier to move about on these solid-framed boats than on oar or paddleboats, a plus for people who lack mobility. Because of the speed, however, there's less time for hiking or resting in camp. If motorized trips are for you, consider using **Moki Mac River Expeditions** (© 800/284-7280; www.mokimac.com) or **Wilderness River Adventures** (© 800/992-8022; www.riveradventures.com).

NONMOTORIZED For mobile people who want to bask in the canyon's beauty, I strongly recommend guided nonmotorized trips, even if it means seeing half the canyon instead of it all. A motorless raft glides at close to the water's pace, giving passengers time to observe subtle, enticing patterns—swirls of water in eddies; the play of shadow and light as the sun moves across rock layers; each side canyon's opening, unfolding, and gradual closing. Without motors running, the river's sound provides a dreamlike backdrop to the journey.

There are two types of nonmotorized boats: paddleboats and oar boats. **Oar boats** are wooden dories or rubber rafts, each of which holds four or five passengers and a guide who does most or all of the rowing. If a guide is highly skilled, passengers on an oar-powered trip have an excellent chance of floating the entire river without having to swim in the 45°F (7°C) rapids. (The latest statistics on river-related deaths show commercial river trips to be as dangerous as playing golf. Far more people get hurt in camp than on the river.) If an oar-powered company appeals to you, I recommend **O.A.R.S.** ★★★ (© 800/346-6277 or 209/736-4677; see listing

Other Sports & Activities

HIKES & OUTDOOR PURSUITS

below), which has some of the most experienced guides on the river.

In a **paddleboat,** six passengers paddle, assisted by a guide who instructs and helps steer. This experience is ideal for fit people who want to be involved at all times. However, because of the participants' inexperience, paddleboats are probably more likely to capsize than oar boats or motorized rigs. And paddling can become burdensome during the long, slow-water stretches, especially when a headwind blows. **Canyon Explorations/Expeditions** (𝄢 **800/654-0723** or 928/774-4559; www.canyonexplorations.com) and **Outdoors Unlimited** (𝄢 **800/637-7238** or 928/526-4511; www.outdoorsunlimited.com) both have excellent reputations for paddle trips.

Another factor to consider before scheduling your trip is the season. In April, the cacti bloom in the lower canyon, splashing bright colors across the hillsides, and the river is relatively uncrowded. However, cold weather can occasionally make these trips a test of the spirit. In May, the weather is usually splendid, but the river is at its most crowded. June and July can be oppressively hot. In August, monsoons break the heat and may generate additional waterfalls along the river. From September 15 to the end of October, no motorized rigs cruise the river, so the canyon is quiet, though cold weather can be a problem.

RIVER RAFTING COMPANIES

Sixteen companies are authorized to provide rafting trips in the Grand Canyon. For a comprehensive list, visit the "River Trips" section of **www.nps.gov/grca** by first clicking "Plan Your Visit" and then "Things to Do."

Canyon Explorations   A more touchy-feely company referred to by some as "Cosmic Explorations," Canyon Explorations offers oar-powered and paddle trips with lengths varying from 6 to 16 days, including one trip with a string quartet, and two trips that set aside extra time for hiking.

P.O. Box 310, Flagstaff, AZ 86002. 𝄢 **800/654-0723** or 928/774-4559. www.canyonexplorations.com.

Moki Mac   A less-expensive choice, Moki Mac runs 8-day motorized trips from mid-April to early September, and oar-powered trips that last from 6 to 14 days from early May to mid-October.

P.O. Box 71242, Salt Lake City, UT 84171. 𝄢 **800/284-7280.** www.mokimac.com.

O.A.R.S.   This outfitter offers oar-powered and some paddle trips varying from 4 to 18 days.

P.O. Box 67, Angels Camp, CA 95222. ✆ **800/346-6277** or 209/736-4677. www.oars.com.

Outdoors Unlimited Oar-powered trips led by Outdoors Unlimited range from 5 to 15 days.

6900 Townsend Winona Rd., Flagstaff, AZ 86004. ✆ **800/637-7238** or 928/526-4511. www.outdoorsunlimited.com.

Wilderness River Adventures One of the Grand Canyon's larger outfitters, Wilderness River Adventures offers motorized and oar-powered Colorado River trips varying from 3 to 16 days.

P.O. Box 717, Page, AZ 86040. ✆ **800/992-8022.** www.riveradventures.com.

CAMPING WITH A CAR IN THE GRAND CANYON AREA

T his chapter focuses on camping with a vehicle—that is, camping in or near an RV or automobile. Most car campgrounds have individual parking pullouts, sites for tents, picnic tables, fire rings or grills, toilets, and drinking water. Campgrounds inside Grand Canyon National Park now have recycling bins, as well. A few so-called "primitive" campgrounds lack running water. Located in remote areas, these often consist of little more than open space and a pit toilet. In addition to car campgrounds, the Grand Canyon area is home to a handful of RV parks, where recreational vehicles can tap into water and electricity during overnight stays.

5

Numerous car campgrounds and RV parks are available in and near the national park's developed areas (as well as one primitive car campground near the western canyon). Within the park, camping is permitted at designated campsites only. Make reservations well in advance—spaces fill up fast. In addition to the campgrounds listed in this chapter, many other car campgrounds and RV parks are available farther from the canyon, in Flagstaff, Williams, and Kanab.

For more information about camping in the Grand Canyon area, see "Backcountry Campgrounds," in chapter 4.

CAMPING INSIDE THE PARK
Near the South Rim

Desert View Campground ★   At dusk, coyotes' yips drift over this mostly tent campground, which sits in piñon-juniper woodland at the park's eastern edge. Elevated, cool, and breezy, its peaceful surroundings offer no clue that bustling Desert View Overlook lies within walking distance. The floor of the woodland makes for smooth tent sites, the most secluded being on the outside of the loop drive. The only drawback: The nearest showers are 26 miles away at Camper Services in Grand Canyon Village. The restrooms here have flush toilets and sinks, but no hot water. During high season, this first-come, first-served campground sometimes fills up by noon. To secure a site, arrive in the morning and self-register. Some sites have fire pits and picnic tables. Backcountry permits are not required here.

26 miles east of Grand Canyon Village on Hwy. 64. No phone, no advance reservations. www.nps.gov/grca. 50 sites. No hookups. Maximum vehicle or trailer length: 30 ft. $12 per site. 7-day limit. AE, DISC, MC, V. May to mid-Oct.

Mather Campground ★   Despite having 319 campsites within a relatively small area, this remains an excellent campground near Grand Canyon Village. Piñon and juniper trees shade the sites, which are spaced far enough apart to afford relative privacy. The Aspen and Maple loops are especially roomy. Also, it's good to be near, but not too near, the coin-operated showers in the Camper Services building next to the campground. The general store and post office at Market Plaza lie within easy walking distance. Free shuttle buses connect Mather Campground with the Visitor Center, as well as scenic overlooks and trail heads. Wood and charcoal fires are permitted in provided campsite grills only.

Because Mather is the only campground in Grand Canyon Village, it tends to fill up before the others. From December 1 to March 1, the campground is open on a first-come, first-served basis. No reservations are taken for these months, but sites are easy to get. For the rest of the year, you can make reservations up to 6 months in advance by calling the toll-free number listed below. For same-day reservations, check at the campground entrance. Even when the campground is booked, sites sometimes become available when campers leave early or cancel. There's no waiting list, however, and no set time for the new spaces to be given away. By coming in the morning, you can avoid waiting in line at the campground entrance.

Near Grand Canyon Village on South Rim. ✆ **877/444-6777** for advance reservations, or 928/638-7851 for campground-specific information. www.recreation.

Grand Canyon Area Campgrounds

Cameron Trading
Post RV Park **12**
De Motte Campground **4**
Desert View Campground **7**
Diamond Creek Campground **1**
Flintstone Bedrock City **11**
Grand Canyon Camper Village **9**
Jacob Lake Campground **3**
Kaibab Camper Village **2**
Kaibab Lake Campground **13**
Mather Campground **8**
North Rim Campground **5**
Ten X Campground **10**
Trailer Village **6**

Campgrounds in the Grand Canyon Area

CAMPGROUND	RIM	TOTAL SITES	RV HOOKUPS	DUMP STATION	TOILETS	DRINKING WATER	SHOWERS
Cameron Trading Post RV Park	South	36	36	yes	no	yes	no
Desert View Campground	South	50	no	no	yes	yes	no
Diamond Creek Campground	South	open tent camping	no	no	yes	no	no
Flintstone Bedrock City	South	unlimited tent sites	27	yes	yes	yes	yes
Grand Canyon Camper Village	South	300	250	yes	yes	yes	yes
Jacob Lake Campground	North	53	no	no	yes	yes	no
Kaibab Camper Village	North	112	52	yes	yes	yes	yes
Kaibab Lake Campground	South	82	no	no	yes	yes	no
Mather Campground	South	323	no	yes	yes	yes	yes
North Rim Campground	North	86	no	yes	yes	yes	nearby
Ten X Campground	South	72	no	no	yes	yes	no
Trailer Village	South	84	84	nearby	yes	yes	nearby

gov. 319 sites, 4 group sites. No hookups. Maximum vehicle or trailer length: 30 ft. $18 per site Apr 1–Nov 30; $15 per site Dec 1–Mar 31; $12 tent only (no car). AE, DISC, MC, V. Year-round.

Trailer Village The neighbors are close, the showers far (about ½ mile away), and the vegetation sparse. In such basic surroundings, you might want to draw the curtains and stay in your RV. The beauty of a hookup is that it lets you do just that. Each site includes a picnic table, barbecue grill, and electrical hookup with cable TV. If, however, you want to venture outside during your stay, scout the property before taking a site. A few sites at the north end of the numbered drives have grass, trees for shade, room for a tent, and one neighbor-free side. If you'd like to leave your RV altogether, you can catch a shuttle bus at a stop near the campground.

Camping Inside the Park

CAMPING WITH A CAR

FIRE PITS/ GRILLS	LAUNDRY	PUBLIC PHONES	ADVANCE RESERVATIONS	FEES	DATES OPEN
no	no	yes	yes	$25 per site	year-round
yes	no	nearby	no	$12 per site	May to mid-Oct
yes	no	no	no	$35 per person	year-round (weather permitting)
no	yes	yes	yes	$14 two-person tent, $16 electric hookup, $18 water/ electric, $2 each additional person	year-round
yes	yes	yes	yes	$40+ water/electric, $35 electric, $25 tent sites	year-round
yes	no	no	no	$17 per site	May to mid-Oct
yes	yes	yes	May 15–Oct 15	$35 hookups, $17 dry sites, $17 tent sites, $85 cabin-style room	
yes	no	no	no	$18 per site	May 1–Sept 30
yes	yes	yes	Mar–Nov	$18 Apr–Nov, $15 rest of year	year-round
yes	yes	yes	yes	$18–$25 per site, $6 tent only (no car)	May 15–Oct 15
yes	no	no	no	$10 per site	May–Sept
yes	yes	nearby	yes	$35, plus $3 each additional person	year-round

Like the lodges inside Grand Canyon National Park, Trailer Village is overseen by Xanterra—and therefore subject to the same rules as the lodges (except pets are allowed here). That means reservations can be made in advance. If you don't have reservations, check at the campground entrance even if the sign says no openings exist. A few spots open up in the late morning when campers depart early. (Because reservations are guaranteed by credit card, few additional spots open at night.) Trailer Village is adjacent to Mather Campground.

Near Grand Canyon Village on South Rim. ✆ **888/297-2757** for advance reservations or 928/638-2631 for same-day reservations, campground questions. www.grandcanyonlodges.com. 84 sites with full hookups. $35 per site for 2 people, plus $3 for each additional adult (17 and over). AE, DISC, MC, V. Laundry facilities; dump station nearby (closed in the winter). Year-round.

Near the North Rim

North Rim Campground ★★★ Shaded by ponderosa pines and situated alongside Transept Canyon (a side canyon), this is a delightful place to pass a few days. The pines, which shade a soft, smooth forest floor, are spaced just far enough apart to allow for group sports and other activities. The 1.5-mile-long Transept Trail links the campground to Grand Canyon Lodge. A service station, the North Rim General Store, a laundromat, and showers ($2 for approx. 6 min.) are all within walking distance. The most spectacular sites are the rim sites, which overlook the canyon. These cost an extra $7 but are worth it—they're some of the prettiest anywhere. Campfire programs are offered at 7pm nightly in the amphitheater.

With only 87 sites, the North Rim Campground fills up for most of the summer. You can book a spot up to 6 months in advance. Even if you show up without a reservation and find the SORRY, CAMPGROUND FULL sign on the entry booth, ask about cancellations. The best time to do so is between 10am and 11am when sites made available by the preceding night's cancellations go up for sale.

The campground sometimes stays open on a limited basis after October 15, until snow closes Highway 67, but you'll need to self-register, and few services are available in the park.

On Grand Canyon North Rim (44 miles south of Jacob Lake on Hwy. 67). *©* **877/444-6777** or 518/885-3639 for advance reservations. www.recreation. gov. 83 sites (12 tent-only sites), 3 group sites. No hookups. $18–$25 per site; $50 per group site (up to 25 persons); $6 tent only for rim-to-rim hikers (no car). AE, DISC, MC, V. May 15–Oct 15 and on limited basis until snow closes highway.

CAMPING OUTSIDE THE PARK
Near the South Rim

Flintstone Bedrock City ☺ Cartoon lovers will be curious about this kitschy Flintstones-themed campground, restaurant, and store, whose multihued, faux-stone buildings cling like putty to the windswept land at the intersection of highways 64 and 180. In addition to peddling the ubiquitous Grand Canyon T-shirts and dead-scorpion paperweights, the gift shop sells all manner of Flintstones paraphernalia, including bibs, sweatshirts, T-shirts, key chains, and magnets. **Fred's Diner** serves up dishes such as the "Chickasaurus Sandwich" and the "Bronto Burger" for less than $5.

One advantage to having a prehistoric theme is that no one can tell whether your campground is run-down, and indeed there are signs this place is struggling to hang on. The buildings here seem about as old as caves, so nothing looks out of character. One problem, however, is obvious: the proximity of some tent sites to Highway 64. Amenities here include a play area with a Flintstone train ride, volleyball court, "dinosaur" slide, coin-op laundry, gift shop, Internet kiosk, TV, and game room.

In Vallé (at junction of Hwy. 180 and 64). ℂ **928/635-2600.** Unlimited tent sites, 27 hookups. $5 entrance to "Bedrock City Park" plus $14 for a 2-person tent; $16 electric hookup; $18 water/electric hookup; $2 each additional person. AE, DISC, MC, V. Year-round.

Grand Canyon Camper Village The advantage of this RV park and campground is its location. Just a mile south of the park entrance in Tusayan, it lies within easy walking distance of stores and restaurants on one side, and of Kaibab National Forest on the other. Disadvantages include relatively narrow (average width: 27 ft.) campsites, the noise from the nearby airport, and the throngs of people at the campground. At least the restrooms are clean, the coin-operated showers hot, and the laundry facility up and running. There's also a playground and camp store, as well as free Wi-Fi.

In Tusayan (1½ miles south of the park on Hwy. 64). ℂ **928/638-2887.** www.grandcanyoncampervillage.com. 50 tent sites, 250 hookups. $25 tent sites; $35 electric; $40 and up water/electric. MC, V. Year-round.

Kaibab Lake Campground ★★ The campsites at this Forest Service campground are on a forested hillside above Kaibab Lake's reddish waters. There's no swimming in the lake (as it's a reservoir for Williams), but the fishing for trout and catfish isn't bad. There are restrooms here but no showers. The Grand Canyon is 60 miles away.

4 miles north of Williams on Hwy. 64. ℂ **928/699-1239.** 80 sites, 2 campsites accessible for people with disabilities; no hookups. $18 per site. No credit cards. May 1–Sept 30.

Ten X Campground ★★ Wooded group campsites make this Forest Service campground the most peaceful open-air accommodations within 20 miles of the South Rim. With plenty of distance between you and your neighbors, this is a great place to linger over a fire and roast marshmallows; all sites have fire pits and grills, and the campground host sells wood. Later, you'll find the soft, needle-covered floor perfect for sleeping. Showers are at Mather's Campground in Grand Canyon Park Village, which is nearby. Some sites can be reserved a minimum of 3 days in advance, while others are on a first-come, first-served basis. If you're driving up from Flagstaff or Williams, consider snagging a site before going to the canyon for the day.

2 miles south of Tusayan on Hwy. 64. ✆ **928/638-2443.** www.recreation.gov. 72 sites, no hookups or showers. $10 per site. AE, DISC, MC, V. May–Sept.

Near the North Rim

DeMotte Campground ★★   Forty first-come sites are available at DeMotte, the closest campground to the North Rim outside the Park (5 miles north of the entrance station). This Forest Service campground sits at 8,760 feet (10 ft. higher than Telluride, Colorado), in spruce-fir forest, so it's sure to be cold, especially at night. So cold, in fact, that it closes in mid-October because the water in the pipes freezes. The road through the campground curves sharply and some of the spaces are small, so this place may not work for large RVs. Because this campground is relatively small and located just outside the park entrance, it tends to fill up early. Try to get a site on your way into the park instead of on your way out. The campsite host will come around to collect your fee. Drinking water, toilets, and cooking grills are available at the campground.

5 miles north of the park boundary on Hwy. 67. ✆ **928/643-8100.** 40 sites, no hookups. $17 per site, second vehicle $8. No credit cards. No reservations. Mid-May to mid-Oct.

Jacob Lake Campground ★★   Nestled into rolling hills covered with ponderosa pine forest, this is a beauty of a Forest Service campground. It reopened in 2009 after being closed for a year of renovations. Towering pines shade sites only a short drive from Jacob Lake Lodge, which lies 45 miles (75km) north of the North Rim. This campground, which seldom fills up, offers free evening naturalist programs. Reservations are not accepted—a ranger will come around in the morning to collect your fee.

U.S. 89A, just north of Jacob Lake. ✆ **877/444-6777.** www.recreation.gov. 53 sites, no hookups. $17 per vehicle, second vehicle $8. No credit cards. No reservations. May to mid-Oct.

Kaibab Camper Village ★★   Compared to the South Rim RV parks, where sagebrush is often the largest plant in sight, this North Rim RV and tent park looks like it came out of a fairy tale. Throughout the campground, ponderosa pines pierce the sky like Jack's mythical beanstalk. This is easily the prettiest RV park setting in the Grand Canyon area. Generators are forbidden so that everyone can enjoy the quiet. There are two public showers ($2.25 for 5 min.) and laundry facilities; all that's missing is flush toilets. Though the toilets are hooked up to a larger septic system, they resemble portable toilets in every other way, including the fact that they're dark as caves at night. There's a convenience store selling firewood and basic camping supplies at the entrance.

¾ mile west of Hwy. 67, just south of Jacob Lake. ℂ **928/643-7804** (when open); 800/525-0924 (Mon–Fri 8am–5pm) or 928/526-0924 (when closed). www.kaibabcampervillage.com. 50 tent sites, 62 RV sites (52 hookups, 10 dry sites). $35 for hookups (up to 4 people); $17 for dry sites (up to 4 people); $17 for tent sites (up to 2 people), plus $4 for each additional person. Cabin-style room available for $85. MC, V. Mid-May to mid-Oct (weather permitting).

Near the Park's Eastern Entrance

Cameron Trading Post RV Park This is no-frills RV camping: Hookups are in a field, with no showers and only a few cottonwood trees for shade. A few sites at the campground's north end overlook the Little Colorado River gorge—especially scenic when the river is flowing. Though there's nothing in the way of recreation at the campground, the Cameron Trading Post, with its restaurant and Native American art, is across the street.

U.S. 89 across from Cameron Trading Post. ℂ **800/338-7385.** www.cameron tradingpost.com/lodge.html. No tent sites, 36 full hookups. $25 per site. AE, DISC, MC, V. Year-round.

Near the Western Canyon

Diamond Creek Campground ★ This campground at the confluence of Diamond Creek and the Colorado River is the only place where you can drive (with a tribal permit) to the river inside the Grand Canyon and camp alongside it. The gravel road, descending from 4,600 feet in Peach Springs to 1,325 feet at the campground, sometimes gets washed out, but high-clearance vehicles can negotiate it when it's not raining or wet. If you plan to stay here, begin the drive down at least a couple of hours before sunset, as the road is too difficult to navigate at night. Surrounded by cliffs of granite and schist, the campground sits at a lovely spot. Pick up your tribal permit before 4pm at Hualapai Lodge (at the top of the hill) before driving down to Diamond Creek. Hiking and fishing are both possible; you'll need permits from the lodge. There's also a small grocery store next to the lodge where you can pick up some supplies.

Despite its beauty, there are a few real drawbacks to the campground. You probably won't be alone; the beach serves as a popular launch point and pullout for raft trips. Also, there are only two portable toilets, and you'll need to bring your own drinking water and pack out your garbage. If you don't commandeer one of the two metal ramadas (simple roof shelters), pitch your own so you don't broil in the midday sun. Since this campground is just above the canyon's lowest point, it's one of the region's hottest places. Portable stoves are permitted. Note that the campground often experiences strong winds in March and April.

Hualapai Indian Reservation (18 miles from Peach Springs, 19 miles from Hwy. 66 on Diamond Creek Rd.). ℰ **888/868-9378.** Open tent camping. $33 per person for camping; $25 for sightseeing only. AE, DISC, MC, V. Year-round (weather permitting). Pay and register before entering at the Hualapai River Trips Office, daily 8am–4pm at Hualapai Lodge in Peach Springs.

Camping in Kaibab National Forest

Park visitors can camp for free in **Kaibab National Forest ★★**. The Forest Service's rules are simple: Camp in designated areas away from paved roads and water, and at least a mile from designated campgrounds. (No camping is allowed near Hull Cabin or Red Butte.) Pack out your garbage, including used toilet paper, and remove any signs that you've been there. Bury human waste in holes 4 inches deep, 6 inches across, and at least 100 yards from water or creek beds. Where fires are allowed, use established fire rings, fire pans, or mound fires. Completely douse campfires before leaving. If the forest seems dry, check with a local Forest Service office about campfire restrictions.

The dispersed camping in the National Forest on the North Rim is among the best anywhere. A number of Forest Service roads lead to canyon overlooks close to where you can spend the night, such as **Crazy Jug Point** and **Parissawampitts Point,** which offer lovely views of the central Grand Canyon but require long, bumpy drives.

For maps and information on dispersed camping on the North Rim, visit the **Kaibab Plateau Visitor Center** (ℰ **928/643-7298**) in Jacob Lake, open daily 8am to 5pm from mid-May to mid-October.

PICNIC & CAMPING SUPPLIES

To maximize your dollars, stock up on camping items at a grocery store in a larger city, if possible. In general, prices are lowest in Flagstaff and rise steadily as you near the canyon, peaking at the Canyon Village Marketplace inside the park.

South Rim

The Canyon Village Marketplace ★ In Grand Canyon Village's business district, this general store is the park's largest and most comprehensive retailer. Customers come here for groceries, canyon souvenirs, liquor, electronic and automotive goods (though supply is somewhat limited), outdoor clothes, camping provisions, and hiking and backpacking gear. Some camping equipment can be rented overnight, including tents, sleeping bags, backpacks, stoves, daypacks, trekking poles, and hiking boots. The knowledgeable staff members gladly offer information about park trails and camping. There's also a tasty deli here, as well as an ATM at the Chase bank next door.

In Grand Canyon Village. ☏ **928/638-2262.** June–Sept daily 7am–9pm; Oct–May daily 8am–7pm.

Desert View Store   The Desert View Store has souvenirs, beer and wine, a limited selection of groceries, and camping supplies.

At Desert View (off Hwy. 64). ☏ **928/638-2393.** Daily 9am–5pm (summer 8am–6pm).

North Rim

North Rim Country Store   The North Rim Country Store lies outside the park, just across from DeMotte Campground and near Kaibab Lodge. It has a gas station and convenience store selling basic groceries, camping supplies, beer, wine, ice, firewood, and hunting supplies. There's also an ATM, a restroom, and telephones here (which you might need since cellphone coverage in this area is nonexistent).

Hwy. 67, 26 miles south of Jacob Lake. ☏ **928/638-2383.** www.northrimcountry store.com. May 15–Nov 1 daily 7am–7pm.

North Rim General Store   The North Rim General Store is small but well-supplied with groceries, gifts, sundries, beer and wine, and a limited supply of camping equipment, including flashlights, stoves, cooking ware, sleeping bags, mats, ponchos, and insect repellant. However, it cannot outfit backpackers. Free Wi-Fi is available here, which can be accessed inside or from one of the outdoor tables (even when the general store is closed).

Adjacent to North Rim Campground. ☏ **928/638-2611.** Daily 7am–8pm (may vary).

5

CAMPING WITH A CAR | Picnic & Camping Supplies

WHERE TO STAY & EAT IN GRAND CANYON NATIONAL PARK

This chapter lists lodging and dining options inside Grand Canyon National Park. Many additional hotels and restaurants exist in the nearby Arizona communities of Tusayan, Williams, and Flagstaff, as well as in Kanab, Utah. Rooms in Flagstaff, Williams, and Kanab—all three of which are more than 50 miles from the park—generally cost less than comparable ones inside the park. That said, hotels inside the park offer remarkable value given their quality and proximity to the canyon. The park's two concessionaires operate more than 900 rooms across seven lodges, including Phantom Ranch. Tusayan, 1 mile from the park's south entrance, tends to be more expensive than the park. When planning a visit to the Grand Canyon, I recommend reserving a place inside the park for at least 1 night. This lets you savor the canyon's twilight hours without having to drive far in the dark.

If you're hoping to spend the night at or near the rim, be sure to call well in advance of your stay. During busy seasons, especially summer, the lodges in the park and in Tusayan frequently fill up, forcing would-be lodgers to backtrack away from the park.

If you tire of relatively new rooms with Southwestern motifs, a few historic hotels and lodges remain. In the park, stay at the breathtaking **Grand Canyon Lodge** (your only option on the North Rim, which books full up

reserving **A ROOM INSIDE THE PARK**

Lodging inside the park on the South Rim is handled by **Xanterra** (℡ **888/297-2757** or 303/297-2757; www.grandcanyon lodges.com), and on the North Rim by **Forever Resorts** (℡ **877/386-4383** or 480/998-1981; www.grandcanyonforever.com). Book well ahead. The most desirable rooms, like those at Grand Canyon Lodge, El Tovar, or Bright Angel's rim cabins, can fill up a year in advance. All lodges usually sell out from mid-March to mid-October (in summer, you can often find a room more easily for late Aug or early Sept). It is possible to reserve a room up to 13 months in advance (which you would need to do for Phantom Ranch) and the rate is guaranteed for the first night, even if the price increases later. If you're flexible with dates and travel in fall or winter, you can usually find rooms 1 or 2 months in advance. Because Xanterra and Forever Resorts both allow cancellations without penalty up to 48 hours in advance, you can sometimes grab a room at the last minute, even at the busiest times. A few rooms become available each day, so try walking into the lodge of your choice to ask about vacancies there or nearby. Checkout is 11am, so the staff will know by that time whether a room will be available.

Rates listed in this chapter are for double-occupancy rooms during high season, which lasts March through October and includes holidays. Prices may fall substantially in the off season at off-rim lodges (prices remain the same year-round at El Tovar, and Bright Angel, Kachina, and Thunderbird lodges). A 7.74% tax will be added. Xanterra and Forever Resorts accept American Express, Diner's Club, Discover, MasterCard, and Visa. Kids under 16 stay free with their parents. Pets are not allowed in accommodations inside the park (service animals are permitted), and no smoking is permitted at any of the lodges.

The hotels do not have specific street addresses. When you enter the park, you receive a map pinpointing their locations. Most of the rooms in the park have relatively new furnishings, as well as telephones and televisions. Only El Tovar, Yavapai East (at Yavapai Lodge), and Maswik North have air-conditioning; Thunderbird and Kachina lodges have evaporative cooling systems. The only conspicuous difference in decor is at upscale El Tovar.

to a year in advance), the exquisite **El Tovar Hotel** (the park's most upscale lodging), or **Bright Angel Lodge** (a favorite among families, hikers, and history buffs). The park's concessionaires retain these three accommodations' historic character—other park lodgings tend to be more motel-style. If you stay on the North Rim, which is open only during the warmer months, expect greater serenity but fewer services than you'll find on the South Rim.

See "Gateway Towns," chapter 7, for more information about where to stay and eat, and what to do, outside of the national park.

SOUTH RIM LODGING
Expensive

El Tovar Hotel ★★★ 📷   The grande dame of the South Rim hotels serves as a dark, cool counterpoint to Mary E. Jane Colter's warm, pueblo-style buildings. Completed in 1905 to accommodate the influx of adventurous, well-heeled East Coasters traveling on the Santa Fe Railroad, the hunting-style lodge stands just steps from the rim and casts a long shadow over Grand Canyon Village. A pointed cupola sits like a witch's cap atop its three stories of Oregon pine and native stone, and spires rise above an upstairs deck. Inside, tourists wander through historic corridors that lead past the dimly lit lobby to the elegant dining room. El Tovar looks much as it did at its inception, when it offered all manner of luxury, including a music room, art classes, and a rooftop garden.

While these amenities have gone the way of the Flagstaff-to–Grand Canyon stagecoach, the hotel remains the canyon's most upscale, and the only one to offer room service. During the last renovation, rooms were given a significant face-lift: For example, bathrooms got pedestal sinks, hand-laid tiles, and beveled mirrors. The deluxe rooms now offer more space, and some have balconies. Twelve individually themed suites, including the **Zane Grey Suite** (which has a porch) and the **Charles Whittlesey Suite** (named after the hotel's architect, this one has blueprints of the building's original design), start at $335. The most stunning accommodations by far are the three **view-suites,** each of which boasts a sitting room and a private deck overlooking the canyon. These suites, which cost $426, often fill up a year or more in advance. Stay at El Tovar if you can, but remember that you don't have to be a guest to enjoy spending time here.

www.grandcanyonlodges.com. ☏ **928/638-2631** (main switchboard) or 888/297-2757 (reservations only). Fax 303/297-3175. 78 units. Standard rooms $178–$209; deluxe rooms $273; suites $335–$426. AE, DC, DISC, MC, V. **Amenities:** Restaurant (international) in a stunning dining room; lounge w/veranda overlooking the rim; concierge; room service. *In room:* A/C, flatscreen TV, fridge, hair dryer.

Moderate

Maswik Lodge ★ 🏷   Built in the 1960s, Maswik Lodge sits in a wooded area that's a 5-minute walk from the rim. If you're not up

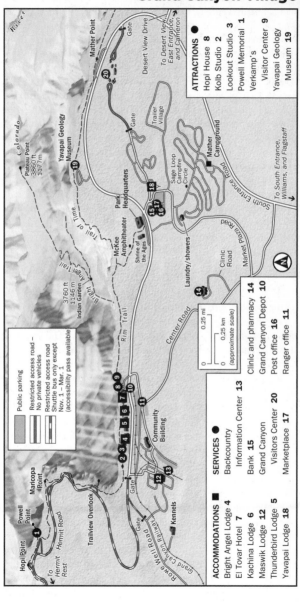

ATTRACTIONS ●

Hopi House **8**
Kolb Studio **2**
Lookout Studio **3**
Powell Memorial **1**
Verkamp's
  Visitor Center **9**
Yavapai Geology
  Museum **19**

SERVICES ●

Backcountry
  Information Center **13**
Bank **15**
Grand Canyon
  Visitors Center **20**
Marketplace **17**

Clinic and pharmacy **14**
Grand Canyon Depot **10**
Post office **16**
Ranger office **11**

ACCOMMODATIONS ■

Bright Angel Lodge **4**
El Tovar Hotel **7**
Kachina Lodge **6**
Maswik Lodge **12**
Thunderbird Lodge **5**
Yavapai Lodge **18**

Public parking

Restricted access road –
No private vehicles

Restricted access road
Shuttle bus only except
Nov. 1 – Mar. 1
(accessibility pass available)

0   0.25 mi
0   0.25 km
(approximate scale)

to walking, catch a free shuttle in front of the lodge, which also offers a transportation desk, cafeteria, gift shop, and sports bar with billiards and air hockey. The guest rooms fill 16 two-story wood-and-stone buildings known as Maswik North and South. Most **Maswik North** rooms feature vaulted ceilings, large bathrooms with vanities, private balconies, and forest views, making them among the park's loveliest accommodations. Because of their spaciousness and price, they're an excellent family value—and it's easy to get a roll-away bed if needed. Rooms in **Maswik South** are older, a bit smaller, and have less pristine views. They are the least desirable rooms in the park, but are also less expensive than most other options.

Maswik is an especially smart choice for those traveling with children (lodgings here can easily fit a roll-away bed), and all rooms include two queen-size beds or one king. During summer, Maswik also rents out 40 guest rooms in 10 rustic, thin-walled cabins. If you're staying anywhere at Maswik, bring a flashlight, as the area is dark at night.

www.grandcanyonlodges.com. *C* **928/638-2631** (main switchboard) or 888/297-2757 (reservations only). Fax 303/297-3175. 278 units. Maswik South $92; Maswik North $173; cabin rooms $92. AE, DC, DISC, MC, V. **Amenities:** Cafeteria; sports lounge; Internet kiosk. *In room:* TV. In Maswik North only: A/C, fridge, hair dryer.

Thunderbird and Kachina Lodges ★ The '60s-era dormitory architecture is impossible to miss in these lodges' flat roofs, decorative concrete panels, and metal staircases. The exteriors notwithstanding, the hotel has since been renovated, and has both a friendlier look and an excellent location next to the rim. Inside, rooms are basic but comfortable, with wide windows and upgraded bathrooms. Most upstairs units on the more expensive canyon side offer at least a partial canyon view. Check-in for Thunderbird takes place at Bright Angel Lodge; for Kachina, it's at El Tovar.

www.grandcanyonlodges.com. *C* **928/638-2631** (main switchboard) or 888/297-2757 (reservations only). Fax 303/297-3175. 55 units at Thunderbird, 49 at Kachina. Street-side $173; canyon-side $184. AE, DC, DISC, MC, V. *In room:* TV, fridge, hair dryer.

Yavapai Lodge The largest lodge at the canyon, Yavapai lies a mile from the historic district but is close to the Canyon Village Marketplace, the post office, and Chase bank. Built between 1970 and 1972, the lodge houses a large cafeteria and gift shop. Its 358 rooms, renovated in 2010–11, are spread among 10 single-story buildings known as **Yavapai West** and six two-story wood buildings collectively called **Yavapai East.** Yavapai West rooms are reminiscent of a Route 66–style motel, offering guests the convenience of parking right in front of their door. Yavapai East's units are larger, with king-size beds, modern furnishings, and air-conditioning. As many of them offer forest views, they're worth the extra money. The paths connecting the buildings are dark at night, so bring a flashlight.

www.grandcanyonlodges.com. ⓒ **928/638-2631** (main switchboard) or 888/ 297-2757 (reservations only). Fax 303/297-3175. 358 units. $114 Yavapai West; $163 Yavapai East. Winter rates $90–$110. AE, DC, DISC, MC, V. **Amenities:** Cafeteria; Internet kiosk. *In room:* Flatscreen TV, hair dryer. In Yavapai East only: A/C, fridge.

Inexpensive

Bright Angel Lodge ★★ 🔥 Guests of Bright Angel Lodge, which was renovated in 2007, stay in tightly clustered buildings along the rim west of the main lodge. In the 1930s, the Fred Harvey Co. sought to develop new, affordable lodging for the many visitors who had begun driving to the canyon. The company contracted Mary Colter to design the lodge and cabins. She built the cabins around several historic buildings, including the park's old post office and the Bucky O'Neill Cabin, the rim's oldest continually standing structure. Since those days, Bright Angel Lodge has become the South Rim's hub—and most crowded area. Visit the Bright Angel History Room for artistic and literary highlights of the legacies of Fred Harvey, Mary Jane Colter, and the Santa Fe Railway at the Grand Canyon.

Low-end accommodations start with clean, spare rooms in two long buildings adjacent to the main lodge. The lodge rooms are the park's least expensive, and each has a double bed and desk but no television; some also share bathrooms. Rooms in the historic cabins are slightly more expensive but still an excellent value. Most of these popular cabins house two guest rooms; the majority of them have open-frame ceilings and windows with bright-colored frames. The units nearer the rim are quieter than the ones along Village Loop Road, where traffic can get heavy. At the high end of the price range are the 12 rim-side cabins, which offer views of the canyon and probably the neatest overnight experience available at the canyon. Four include fireplaces; the historic **Bucky O'Neill Cabin,** one of the park's oldest structures, has a fireplace, a wet bar, and canyon views. The rim-side cabins tend to fill up far in advance, so plan ahead.

www.grandcanyonlodges.com. ⓒ **928/638-2631** (main switchboard) or 888/ 297-2757 (reservations only). Fax 303/297-3175. 34 units, 14 with bathroom, 10 with sink only, 10 with sink and toilet; 55 cabin units. $71 double with sink only; $81 double with sink and toilet only; $92 double with bathroom; $113 historic cabin; $145–$178 historic rim-side cabin; $340 rim-side Bucky O'Neill Suite. AE, DC, DISC, MC, V. **Amenities:** Restaurant; snack bar; lounge; Internet kiosk. *In room:* Ceiling fan in rim-side and historic cabins, TV in most rooms, fridge in rim cabins.

LODGING INSIDE THE CANYON

Phantom Ranch ★★ This has got to be one of the world's most remote accommodations. Accessible only by floating down the Colorado River or by hiking (or riding a mule) to the bottom of the Grand Canyon, Phantom Ranch is the only park lodging below the rims, and it often sells out on the first day of availability—13 months in advance. To reserve a spot, call as early as possible. If you arrive at the canyon without a reservation, contact the **Bright Angel Transportation Desk** (𝄃 **928-638-2631,** ext. 6015) to put yourself on the waiting list for either of the following 2 days (you must then be present the next morning if your name is called). Hikers will have an easier time getting lodging here in winter, when fewer mule rides head down.

The reason for the booked slate? Clean sheets never felt better than at the bottom of the Grand Canyon, cold beer never tasted as good (not even close), and a hot shower never felt so, well, miraculous. The ranch's nine air-conditioned cabins are a simple pleasure. Mary Colter designed four of them—the ones with the most stone in the walls—using rocks from nearby Bright Angel Creek. Connected by dirt footpaths, these cabins sit, natural and elegant, alongside picnic tables, under cottonwood trees' shade. Inside each cabin, there's concrete flooring, a desk, and 4 to 10 bunk beds, as well as a toilet and a sink. A shower house for guests sits nearby.

While most of Phantom Ranch was completed in the 1920s and 1930s, four 10-person male and female dorms, each with its own bathing facilities, were added in the early 1980s. Used exclusively by hikers, these are ideal for individuals and small groups looking for a place to bed down; larger groups are better served by reserving cabins, which provide privacy and a lower per-person price than the dorms.

During the day, some guests hike to Ribbon Falls or along the River Trail, while others relax, read, or write postcards that, if sent from here, will bear a unique postmark: "Mailed by mule from the bottom of the Grand Canyon." In the late afternoon, guests and hikers from nearby Bright Angel Campground gravitate to the canteen, which sells snacks and serves meals. Note, though, that guests must book meals in advance. (For more about dining here, see "Where to Eat Inside the Canyon," later in this chapter.)

At the bottom of the canyon, ½ mile north of the Colorado River on the North Kaibab Trail. www.grandcanyonlodges.com. 𝄃 **928/638-2631** (main switchboard) or 888/297-2757 (reservations only). 7 4-person cabins, 2 cabins for up to 10 people, 4 10-person dorms. $43 dorm bed; $90 cabin (for 2); $11 each additional person. Most cabins are reserved as part of mule-trip overnight packages (see "Mule Trips," in chapter 4). Duffel service (baggage service via mule) $65 (each way). AE, DISC, MC, V. **Amenities:** Restaurant. *In room:* A/C, no phone.

LODGING ON THE NORTH RIM

Grand Canyon Lodge ★★★   I love this lodge, a timeless stone and log structure that stands majestically at the edge of the North Rim over one of earth's most breathtaking panoramas. The lodge's architect, Gilbert Stanley Underwood, was best known for designing edifices such as train stations and post offices. After opening in 1928 and burning in 1932, the lodge reopened in 1937 and seems to have grown into the landscape. Its green-shingled roof merges with the needles on nearby trees, its log posts match their trunks, and its Kaibab limestone walls blend with the rim rock. Beyond the grand lobby, with its 50-foot-ceiling and exquisite Native American rugs, the octagonal **Sun Room** features leather sofas and chairs pointed toward three enormous picture windows overlooking the canyon. Two long decks with faux-wood chairs flank this room, providing a platform from which to view the canyon from outside. Just below lies another romantic lookout, the **Moon Room,** which is a favorite for marriage proposals. The lodge also houses a deli, saloon, and breathtaking dining room offering panoramic views of the world wonder before it (see "Where to Eat on the North Rim," later in this chapter).

One hundred forty cabins made of the same materials as the lodge have sprouted like saplings around it (unlike El Tovar, none of the units connect to the main lodge). There are four types of cabins: **Western Cabins** and **Rim Cabins,** with rustic wood furnishings, gas fireplaces, fridges, bathtubs, and small vanity rooms, are the most luxurious. Rim Cabins generally fill up on their first day of availability, which is 13 months in advance. The two other types of accommodations here—**Pioneer Cabins** and **Frontier Cabins**— feel more rustic inside. Tightly clustered along Transept Canyon's rim, they feature exposed-log walls and ceilings, electric heaters, and showers instead of bathtubs. Pioneer Cabins were all renovated in 2009 with new handmade furnishings, and each cabin has two guest rooms—one with a queen bed, the other with twin bunks and a futon. For $157 to $167, a family of five can stay in comfort in a Pioneer Cabin. Frontier Cabins each have one guest room with a double bed and a twin bed. Getting the right shower temperature requires delicate balancing. A few inexpensive motel rooms are also available here. Though comfortable and quiet, their ambience doesn't compare with the cabins' historic feel.

Tip: If you plan to dine at the lodge, be sure to reserve well in advance of your arrival. Note there's limited cellphone coverage here; Wi-Fi access, however, is available at the General Store, a short drive away. The lodge auditorium offers nightly ranger programs.

At North Rim, 214 miles north of South Rim on Hwy. 67. www.grandcanyon forever.com. ℂ **877/386-4383** (reservations) or 928/638-2611 (main switchboard) or 877/386-4383. Fax 928/638-2554. 218 units. $121 Frontier Cabin; $116 motel unit; $157–$167 Pioneer Cabin; $177 Western Cabin; $187 Rim Cabin. AE, DC, DISC, MC, V. **Amenities:** Restaurant; deli; coffee shop and bar. *In room (except for Frontier Cabins):* Fridge, hair dryer.

WHERE TO EAT ON THE SOUTH RIM

Arizona Room ★★ STEAKHOUSE   This is the locals' first choice for dinner and a less time-consuming option than El Tovar. The informal restaurant dishes up the South Rim's most consistently tasty meals. Entrees include hand-cut New York strip steaks, mustard rosemary prime rib, honey-lime grilled chicken, and blackened wild salmon. My favorite is the baby back ribs with prickly pear or spicy chipotle barbecue sauce. To accompany your meal, choose from a variety of midpriced California wines or flavored margaritas. Arriving before the Arizona Room's 4:30pm dinner opening isn't a bad idea, since the wait can be an hour long at sunset (the large windows facing the canyon are a huge draw). The restaurant is open for lunch, too, offering a barbecue-centric menu. Consider the roasted pistachio chicken salad sandwich and a cup of smoked corn chowder.

At Bright Angel Lodge. ℂ **928/638-2631.** Reservations not accepted. Lunch $10–$13; dinner $17–$28. AE, DC, DISC, MC, V. Daily 11:30am–3pm and 4:30–10pm. Closed for lunch Nov–Feb, and for dinner Jan–Feb.

Bright Angel Restaurant ☺ AMERICAN   This busy restaurant serves decent coffee-shop food. Basic breakfast and lunch fare such as build-your-own omelets, French toast, burgers, and large salads usually pass muster. At dinnertime, the restaurant supplements the lunch menu by adding no-fuss entrees such as grilled tri-tip steak, sour cream chicken, roast pork loin, and three-cheese lasagna. A kids' menu and activity book are also available. This is a good place for families, who can dine without worrying much about the children's behavior.

Also in Bright Angel Lodge is **Canyon Coffee House,** which opens at 5:30am and serves coffee drinks, as well as light breakfast items. Come evening, the coffeehouse becomes a cocktail lounge.

At Bright Angel Lodge. ℂ **928/638-2631.** Reservations not accepted. Breakfast $6–$13; lunch $8–$11; dinner $11–$26. AE, DC, DISC, MC, V. Daily 6:30am–10pm.

Canyon Village Deli DELI Many Park Service employees duck into this delicatessen (inside the General Store) for lunch. Here, you can sit in a corner booth, read the paper, and watch tourists pass. Food options include cold and hot sandwiches, salads, fried chicken, mashed potatoes, pizza, fruit, pastries, and ice cream.

In the South Rim's Canyon Village Marketplace (at Market Plaza). © **928/638-2262**. Menu items $4–$8. AE, DISC, MC, V. Daily 8am–7pm (can vary seasonally).

Desert View Snack Bar CAFETERIA The premade sandwiches, burgers, and hot dogs here will sustain you until you make it back to Grand Canyon Village. Breakfast offerings, including eggs and French toast, draw campers from nearby Desert View Campground.

At Desert View, 25 miles east of Grand Canyon Village on Hwy. 64. © **928/638-2360**. Reservations not accepted. Menu items $3–$9. AE, DC, DISC, MC, V. Daily 8am–7pm (can vary seasonally).

El Tovar Restaurant ★★★ INTERNATIONAL One hundred years after opening its doors, this restaurant remains a memorable dining experience. Best of all is the stunning dining room, which features banks of windows at the north and south ends and Oregon pine walls graced with murals depicting Native American dances.

At dinner, a Southwestern influence spices the Continental cuisine. Consider starting with the mozzarella roulades with prosciutto, tomatoes, olives, and a basil pesto. Delicious main courses include the salmon tostada (best prepared medium rare) served with corn salsa and a tequila vinaigrette; the enormous New York strip accompanied by buttermilk-cornmeal onion rings; and roasted half duck with a cherry merlot sauce. The rich French onion soup is an excellent lunch choice. At breakfast, sample the coffee—it's the park's best—and order the eggs Benedict with smoked salmon. All entrees are served in large portions, and children can order half-portions at discounted prices. The restaurant's pastry chef prepares irresistible desserts. Service is friendly and refined, and the waiters are well trained to help match the award-winning wines.

In El Tovar Hotel. © **928/638-2631**, ext. 6432. Reservations accepted for dinner only. Breakfast $5–$13; lunch $7–$17; dinner $23–$32. AE, DC, DISC, MC, V. Daily 6:30–10:45am, 11:15am–2pm, and 5–10pm.

Maswik and Yavapai Cafeterias CAFETERIAS For the price of a burger, fries, and a soft drink at the Tusayan McDonald's, you get a full meal at either Maswik or Yavapai cafeteria. Though the food costs about the same at both places, there are some key differences: Maswik was recently renovated and more closely resembles a food court, where meals come complete with side dishes. One Maswik station serves Mexican fare; another provides home-style entrees such as roast turkey, meatloaf, chicken, or fish; a third offers pastas; and a fourth serves burgers, hot dogs, and grilled chicken sandwiches. There's also a new pizza pub here open from 11am to 11pm.

At Yavapai, you can mix and match from different stations, picking up baked chicken from one, pizza from another, mashed potatoes from another—and, when you put it all together, a case of indigestion. The inexpensive salad bar is priced by weight. Both cafeterias offer Dreyer's soft serve ice cream, as well as box lunches to go for less than $11.

At Maswik and Yavapai lodges, respectively. © **928/638-2631.** Reservations not accepted. Breakfast $3–$8; lunch and dinner $4–$11. AE, DC, DISC, MC, V. Maswik daily 6am–10pm. Yavapai daily 6am–9pm (closed early Nov to mid-Feb, except on holidays).

WHERE TO EAT INSIDE THE CANYON

Phantom Ranch ★★ AMERICAN At the bottom of the Grand Canyon, whether you travel in by foot or by mule, pretty much anything tastes good. Would the food at Phantom Ranch taste as great on the rim as it does alongside Bright Angel Creek? That's hard to say.

Every evening, just three options are offered: a steak (drench it in steak sauce and you're in heaven) or vegetarian dinner at 5pm, and a hearty beef stew at 6:30pm. The vegetarian plate includes a black bean burger and the same side dishes as the steak dinner: vegetables, cornbread, baked potato, and salad. Dessert is chocolate cake.

The family-style, all-you-can-eat breakfasts are excellent, with heaping platters of eggs, bacon, and pancakes laid out on long tables in the canteen. The sack lunch ($13) includes a bagel, cream cheese, summer sausage, juice, an apple, peanuts, raisins, chips, and cookies. Alternatively, you could pack your own lunch and, if necessary, supplement it with snacks from the canteen.

Because the cooks here produce only a certain amount of food, hikers must reserve meals ahead of time through Xanterra (p. 105) or at the Bright Angel Transportation Desk. As a last resort, inquire upon arrival at Phantom Ranch to find out whether any meal reservations remain. Up until 4pm, you can do this at the canteen. After 4pm, ask at the side window behind the canteen. Between 8am (8:30am in winter) and 4pm and from 8 to 10pm, anyone is allowed in the canteen, which sells snacks, soda, beer, wine, first-aid items, souvenirs, and film. The lemonade is fantastic.

Inside the canyon ½ mile north of the Colorado River on the North Kaibab Trail. To reserve meals more than 1 day in advance, call ☎ **888/297-2757;** to reserve next-day meals, contact the Bright Angel Transportation Desk at ☎ **928/638-2631,** ext. 6015. Steak dinner $43; vegetarian meal $27; stew $27; sack lunch $13; breakfast $22. AE, DC, DISC, MC, V (DC not accepted for advance reservations).

WHERE TO EAT ON THE NORTH RIM

Deli in the Pines AMERICAN   This snack bar serves simple breakfast, lunch, and dinner options, including cereals, sandwiches, pizza whole or by the slice, pasta dishes, and hot dogs. Grab one of the tables or booths, or take it to go. If all you desire is good coffee, stop by the Roughrider Saloon (straight across from the deli), which doubles as a cafe from 5:30 to 10:30am.

In Grand Canyon Lodge (west wing). ☎ **928/638-2611.** Reservations not accepted. Breakfast $3–$7; lunch and dinner $4–$8 (whole pizzas up to $22). AE, DISC, MC, V. Daily 7am–9pm.

Grand Canyon Lodge Dining Room ★★ CONTINENTAL This is, without question, one of the world's most scenic restaurants. Long banks of west- and south-facing windows look out on Transept Canyon and help warm this dining room, gently lit by table candles by night. The high, open-framed ceiling absorbs guests' clamor. The menu incorporates sustainable agricultural products. At dinner, consider starting with the blue crab and artichoke dip served with house fried tortilla chips, or with the assortment of chargrilled vegetables accompanied by a sunflower dipping sauce. Fresh Utah ruby trout is served nightly as a main course with a different sauce (mine came with a light pear, apple, and raisin butter sauce), the 10-ounce prime rib is a perennial favorite, and the thinly sliced bison will make your mouth water. A sampling of the lunch menu includes beef stew, Angus hamburgers, veggie burgers, chicken or turkey sandwiches, and Navajo tacos; a lunch buffet with pasta and salad is also offered. Both the breakfast and lunch buffets cost less than $15.

Note: There are only nine window-adjacent tables, which cannot be reserved. Though you can opt to wait (likely for an hour or more), you will still not be guaranteed a window seat. However, you can see through the windows from any part of the dining room, and are always welcome to walk up to them for a closer view. The quality of service varies.

At Grand Canyon Lodge. ℂ **928/638-2611.** Reservations recommended for dinner, not accepted for breakfast or lunch. Breakfast and lunch $6–$15; sack lunch $10–$12; dinner $13–$35. AE, DC, DISC, MC, V. Daily 6:30–10am, 11:30am–2:30pm, and 4:45–9:45pm.

GATEWAY TOWNS

The Grand Canyon isn't Northern Arizona's only wonder. The surrounding area on the Colorado Plateau ranks among the world's most stunning places. It's a sparsely populated landscape of 12,000-foot-high volcanoes and 3,000-foot-deep red-rock canyons—linked by the planet's largest ponderosa pine forest. Lonely highways lace the countryside, inviting exploration. During your travels, you can track California condors or watch elk wander the forests. You can walk the same paths and stand in rooms used for centuries by America's indigenous peoples, then learn about the cultures of their modern descendants. You can chat with cowboys in Williams or venture to Flagstaff's cultural attractions, including the Lowell Observatory and the Museum of Northern Arizona. The many diversions won't detract from your trip to the canyon; they'll simply enhance your appreciation of the entire area.

FLAGSTAFF ★★

150 miles north of Phoenix; 32 miles east of Williams; 78 miles south of Grand Canyon Village

Home to **Northern Arizona University,** the **Museum of Northern Arizona,** and **Lowell Observatory** as well as dozens of trendy restaurants and bars, Flagstaff invites you to nurture your intellect, dine on gourmet food, and reduce your stress level. While it remains a medium-size mountain town, "Flag" (as it is sometimes called locally) is at the same time a vibrant student center and one of Arizona's important economic hubs. The 12,000-foot-high San Francisco Peaks, which are often snow-capped, rise just north of Flagstaff's historic downtown, with its friendly shops and galleries that attract a mix of students, locals, and tourists. Downtown has experienced a revival, and Flagstaff boasts a

Flagstaff

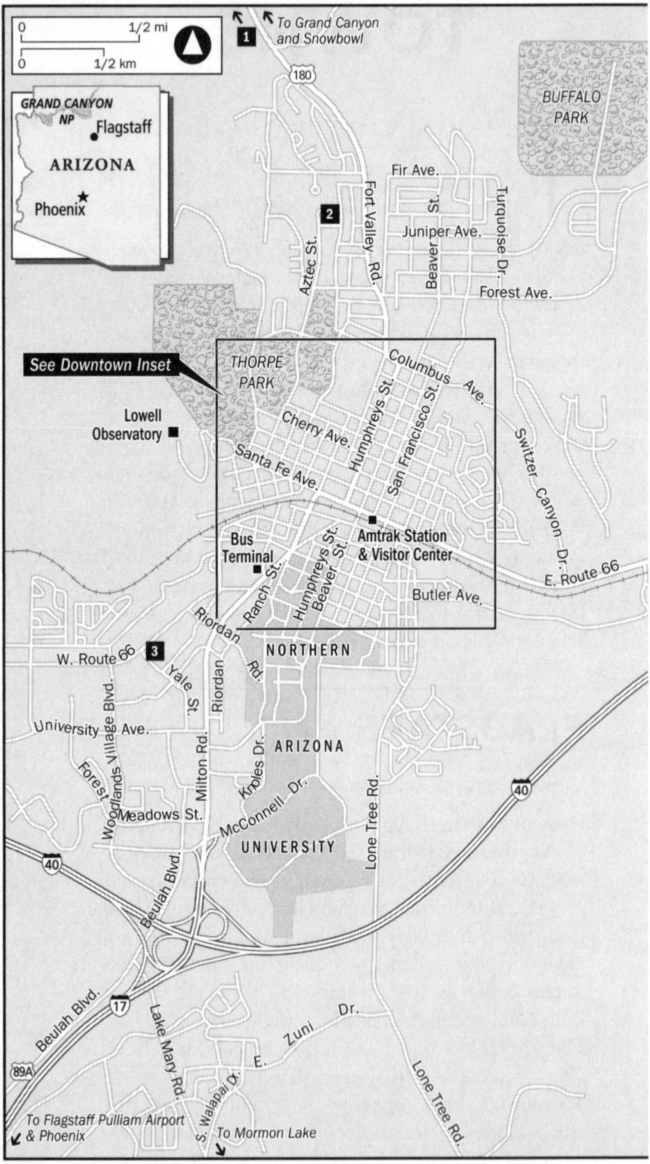
0 1/2 mi
0 1/2 km
GRAND CANYON NP
Flagstaff
ARIZONA
Phoenix
To Grand Canyon and Snowbowl
180
BUFFALO PARK
Fir Ave.
Juniper Ave.
Forest Ave.
Aztec St.
Fort Valley Rd.
Beaver St.
Turquoise Dr.
See Downtown Inset
THORPE PARK
Lowell Observatory
Columbus Ave.
Cherry Ave.
Humphreys St.
San Francisco St.
Santa Fe Ave.
Switzer Canyon Dr.
Amtrak Station & Visitor Center
Bus Terminal
Ranch St.
Humphreys St.
Beaver St.
E. Route 66
Butler Ave.
Riordan Rd.
NORTHERN ARIZONA UNIVERSITY
W. Route 66
Yale St.
Riordan
University Ave.
Woodlands Village Blvd.
Milton Rd.
Knoles Dr.
Forest
Meadows St.
McConnell Dr.
Lone Tree Rd.
40
Beulah Blvd.
17
89A
Lake Mary Rd.
E. Zuni Dr.
S. Walapai Dr.
Lone Tree Rd.
To Flagstaff Pulliam Airport & Phoenix
To Mormon Lake

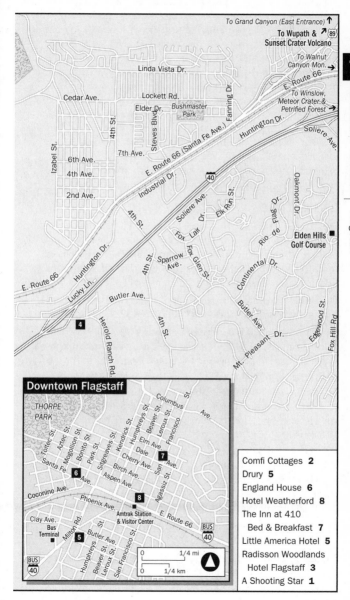

To Grand Canyon (East Entrance) ↑
To Wupath & ↗ 89
Sunset Crater Volcano

To Walnut
Canyon Mon. →

E. Route 66

To Winslow,
Meteor Crater &
Petrified Forest →

Linda Vista Dr.

Cedar Ave.

Lockett Rd.

Elder Dr.

Bushmaster
Park

Fanning Dr.

Huntington Dr.

Soliere Ave.

Steves Blvd.

4th St.

7th Ave.

E. Route 66 (Santa Fe Ave.)

Izabel St.

6th Ave.

4th Ave.

Industrial Dr.

I-40

Oakmont Dr.

2nd Ave.

4th St.

Soliere Ave.

Elk Run St.

Rio de Flag Dr.

Elden Hills
Golf Course

Fox Lair Dr.

E. Route 66

Huntington Dr.

Lucky Ln.

4th St.

Sparrow
Ave.

Fox Glen St.

Continental Dr.

Butler Ave.

Butler Ave.

Edgewood St.

Fox Hill Rd

4

Herold Ranch Rd.

4th St.

Mt. Pleasant Dr.

Downtown Flagstaff

THORPE
PARK

Columbus
Ave.

Toltec St.

Aztec St.

Mogollion St.

Bonito St.

Park St.

Humphreys St.

Beaver St.

Leroux St.

Francisco

Santa Fe
Ave.

Sitgreaves St.

Kendrick St.

Elm Ave.

Dale
Ave.

7

Cherry Ave.

San
Francisco St.

Coconino Ave.

Birch Ave.

Aspen Ave.

Agassiz St.

6

Phoenix Ave.

8

Clay Ave.

Milton Rd.

Amtrak Station
& Visitor Center

E. Route 66

BUS
40

Bus
Terminal

5

Butler Ave.

Humphreys St.

Beaver St.

Leroux St.

San Francisco St.

BUS
40

0   1/4 mi
0   1/4 km

Comfi Cottages **2**

Drury **5**

England House **6**

Hotel Weatherford **8**

The Inn at 410
  Bed & Breakfast **7**

Little America Hotel **5**

Radisson Woodlands
  Hotel Flagstaff **3**

A Shooting Star **1**

thriving music and nightlife scene, impressive cultural events, and numerous outdoor activities. **Downtown Heritage Square** has become the city's liveliest area, offering concerts, movies, and an evening art walk the first Friday of each month.

If you thought trains were a thing of the past, think again. Freight trains regularly clatter past downtown, shaking cappuccinos and drowning out street musicians before continuing their transcontinental routes. Each day roughly 100 trains pass through, and city leaders have successfully installed directional signals at railroad crossings in order to reduce the need for blowing train horns. **Route 66,** flanked by motels with colorful names such as the Pony Soldier, Geronimo, and El Pueblo, parallels the tracks. In addition, Flagstaff is an "international dark sky city" adhering to special lighting ordinances limiting the amount of light emanating from the area. This makes star gazing from here all the more fascinating.

Essentials

GETTING THERE By Car Flagstaff is off I-40, one of America's main east-west interstates. I-17 also starts here and heads south to Phoenix. U.S. 89A connects Flagstaff to Sedona by way of Oak Creek Canyon. U.S. 180 links Flagstaff with Grand Canyon Village, and U.S. 89 goes from Flagstaff to Page.

By Plane Flagstaff's Pulliam Airport, 3 miles south of town off I-17, is served by **US Airways** (© **800/428-4322**) from Phoenix.

By Train Flagstaff is also served by **Amtrak** (© **800/872-7245** for reservations, or 928/774-8679 for station information only) from Chicago and Los Angeles. The train station is at 1 E. Rte. 66.

VISITOR INFORMATION The **Flagstaff Visitor Center,** 1 E. Rte. 66 (© **800/842-7293** or 928/774-9541; www.flagstaff arizona.org), is open Monday through Saturday 8am to 5pm, Sunday 9am to 4pm. The Amtrak station and Hertz rental are also located here.

GETTING AROUND By Rental Car Car rentals are available from **Avis** (© **800/331-1212** or 928/774-8421), **Budget** (© **800/763-2999** or 928/213-0156), **Enterprise** (© **800/736-8222** or 928/774-9407), **Hertz** (© **800/654-3131** or 928/774-4452), and **Alamo/National** (© **800/227-7368** or 928/779-1975).

By Taxi If you need a taxi, call **Friendly Cab** (© **928/774-4444** or 928/214-9000).

By Bus **Mountain Line** (© **928/779-6624;** www.mountainline. az.gov) provides public bus transit around the city every day. The fare for an all-day pass is $2.50 for adults, $1.25 for seniors and those under age 18.

ORIENTATION Downtown Flagstaff is just north of I-40. Milton Road, which becomes I-17 to Phoenix at the road's southern end, passes Northern Arizona University on its way downtown, where it merges with Route 66. Part of Route 66, Santa Fe Avenue parallels the railroad tracks, linking the city's historic downtown with its east side. Downtown's main street is San Francisco Street, while Humphreys Street leads north out of town to U.S. 180 toward the San Francisco Peaks and the Grand Canyon's South Rim.

SUPERMARKETS & GENERAL STORES If you want to stock up on food before you hit the road, here are several places to stop: **Albertson's,** 1416 E. Rte. 66 (© **928/773-7955**), open daily 6am to midnight; **Basha's,** 2700 Woodlands Village Blvd. (© **928/774-3882**), open daily 5am to 11pm; **Basha's,** 1000 N. Humphreys St. (© **928/774-2101**), open daily 6am to 10pm; and **Fry's,** 201 N. Switzer Canyon Dr. (© **928/774-2719**), open daily 6am to midnight. Fry's also has a pharmacy.

What to See & Do

Lowell Observatory ★★★ ☺ Percival Lowell, an amateur astronomer, realized that Flagstaff's dry, thin air made the town a choice location for observing the heavens. A keen interest in Mars led this Boston aristocrat to build an observatory atop a hill here in 1894. From it, he studied the skies for the next 22 years. Though Lowell never discovered life on Mars, the research he did at his observatory has contributed greatly to our knowledge of astronomy. In the past century, the work done at Lowell Observatory led to Pluto's discovery, a map of the moon, and evidence of an expanding universe.

Today, in addition to conducting research, the observatory's 20 or so passionate research staff and astronomers educate and entertain the public. Day and night, staff members help visitors peer through telescopes at stars far across the galaxy. (Call or check the website for a schedule of programs, and plan to wear warm clothes, particularly if you come at night.) During the day, tours of the observatory and historic rotunda library are offered between 10am and 4pm. The solar system exhibit is one of the most interesting, and the Steele Visitor Center offers exciting interactive displays and photographic exhibits, suitable for adults and kids. There's also a "Pluto Walk" in which each inch represents a million miles of our solar system. *Note:* Because of the high elevation (7,200 ft.), breathing is more difficult here than at sea level.

1400 W. Mars Hill Rd., Flagstaff. © **928/774-3358.** www.lowell.edu. Admission $10 adults, $9 seniors and students, $4 ages 5–17, free for children 4 and under.

Visitor center June–Aug daily 9am–10pm; off-season and nighttime hours vary (call for specific program information).

Museum of Northern Arizona ★★

Founded in 1928 by a Flagstaff couple concerned about the widespread removal of artifacts from the area, this museum explores the Colorado Plateau's history, science, and cultures. Its **Geology Room** presents displays about the area's unique landforms, the **Ethnology Room** sheds light on the Hopi, Navajo, Pai, and Zuni people, and the **Special Exhibits Gallery** frequently shows art from the region. But the best attraction here—one of the best anywhere—is the display of Native American artifacts, culled from the museum's five-million-piece collection. Always beautiful and occasionally moving, they're arranged in a thoughtful context that illuminates the history and spirit of the Native American people. The Easton Collection Center opened here in summer 2009 and houses items from MNA's extensive anthropological and biological collections. There's a gallery and bookshop here, as well as a nature walk just outside the museum.

3101 N. Fort Valley Rd. (U.S. Hwy. 180), Flagstaff. ℰ **928/774-5213.** www. musnaz.org. Admission $7 adults, $6 seniors, $5 students with ID, $4 children ages 7–17, free for children 6 and under. Daily 9am–5pm.

Sunset Crater Volcano National Monument ★

Sunset Crater is one of the world's best preserved cinder cone volcanoes. It was formed near the end of the 11th century atop a weak spot in the earth's crust. An underground gas chamber exploded, spewing tons of cinders around the newly created vent in the earth. Within a few months of the explosion, cinders had piled up to form a 1,000-foot-tall pyramid-shaped crater. Lava poured intermittently from openings near the bottom of the crater for the next decade, snaking across the land before ossifying in choppy mounds that to this day appear viscous. In one final flourish of activity, small eruptions deposited ash colored by oxidation in red and yellow atop the otherwise black cone.

The activity produced a landscape of eerie shapes and striking, subtle colors. During an expedition in the late 1800s, explorer John Wesley Powell saw this colorful cone, perhaps in the low light in which it is most striking, and named it Sunset Crater. Today, the national monument has a picnic area, visitor center, and several walking trails. Try to get here early in the morning or late in the afternoon, when the colors are richest. The Sunset Crater trails stay open until dusk. In summer (usually at 10:30am and 2pm), rangers offer free coffee or hot chocolate over a chat about the monument.

If you're driving from Flagstaff and plan to also visit Wupatki National Monument (p. 123), come here first and then take the northward loop to Wupatki. You may wish to continue to Cameron and then to the east entrance of the canyon on Highway 89.

15 miles north of Flagstaff on Hwy. 89. © **928/526-0502.** www.nps.gov/sucr. Admission $5 adults, free for children 15 and under. Admission (good for 7 days) also covers entrance to Wupatki National Monument. Cash, credit cards, or National Park passes only at entrance gate. May 1–Oct 31 daily 8am–5pm; Nov 1–Apr 30 daily 9am–5pm.

Walnut Canyon National Monument ★★ 📷

The Sinagua (a subgroup of the Ancestral Puebloans, also called Anasazi) occupied this wooded canyon for roughly 125 years from about 1125 to 1250. They built hundreds of dwellings on ledges under natural rock overhangs on sunny east- and south-facing cliffs, and tucked granaries into the smallest openings. Atop the canyon rims, they dug out terraces and check dams to help keep their crops moist, and erected pit houses and pueblo-style dwellings.

Though most of the terraces and check dams have collapsed, 300 cliff dwellings remain. Twenty-five alcoves are on the **Island Trail,** a 1-mile loop that descends 185 feet (with more than 240 steps) below the visitor center. Many others are visible from the trail, on the canyon walls. This is a steep climb, and somewhat challenging in hot weather. Another relatively flat .7-mile trail travels along the canyon's rim, affording views of these rooms, as well as coming close to the rim-top ruins. This is a lovely canyon and, with just 125,000 visitors annually, one of the quietest national monuments. It's also a biological "hot spot" with extraordinary plant and animal diversity.

10 miles east of Flagstaff off I-40 (exit 204). © **928/526-3367.** www.nps.gov/waca. Admission $5 adults, free for children 15 and under. Cash only at entrance gate or visitor center. May 1–Oct 31 daily 8am–5pm; Nov 1–Apr 30 daily 9am–5pm.

Wupatki National Monument ★

As their population grew in the 1100s, many of the Sinagua, Cohonina, and Kayenta Anasazi people moved onto the land north of Sunset Crater. Today, hundreds of ruins from this period are scattered across Wupatki National Monument. Some of the most remarkable are near the visitor center, including a mysterious ball court with walls 6 feet high, and **pueblo ruins** made from the same Moenkopi Sandstone atop which they're built. A **blowhole,** which releases air from underground cracks, may have had special significance to the Native Americans who settled nearby.

Other ruins are scattered along the road that loops through the monument, usually in elevated spots with expansive views of both the Painted Desert and San Francisco Peaks. Most of the Sinagua left in the 1200s and are believed to have become the modern-day Hopi (and perhaps Zuni).

If you're driving from Flagstaff and plan to visit both Sunset Crater Volcano National Monument (p. 122) and Wupatki National Monument, it makes most sense to drive first to Sunset Crater, then take the northward loop to Wupatki.

35 miles north of Flagstaff on Hwy. 89. © **928/679-2365.** www.nps.gov/wupa. Admission $5 adults, free for children 15 and under. Admission (valid for 7 days) also good for Sunset Crater Volcano National Monument. Cash or credit card only at entrance gate. Visitor center daily 9am–5pm.

Where to Stay
MODERATE

An excellent and relatively new hotel in Flagstaff is **Drury,** at 300 South Milton Rd. (© **928/773-4900**), located next to Northern Arizona University. Other recommended accommodations are **Radisson Woodlands Hotel Flagstaff** (© **928/773-8888**), 1175 W. Rte. 66, and the B&B **England House** (© **877/214-7350** or 928/214-7350), 614 W. Santa Fe Ave., where rates range from $75 to $200 for double occupancy.

Comfi Cottages ★★ ☺ In the 1970s, Pat Wiebe, a nurse at the local hospital, began purchasing and renovating small homes in Flagstaff. Today, she rents out nine of these quaint cottages, all but one of which were built in the 1920s and 1930s. Wiebe has modernized the cottages somewhat, adding thermostat-controlled fireplaces, televisions, DVD/VCRs, and washer/dryers. She goes out of her way to make accommodations comfortable, and treats her guests like they're part of the family.

In every unit, you'll find fresh-cut flowers, antiques, cupboards stocked with breakfast foods, and rag dolls from her personal collection. Outside of each cottage is a picnic table and gas grill; most also have bicycles and sleds in the garage. These cottages, which sleep 2 to 10 people, can make you feel as if you've acquired a new home, in which kids are welcome. There's a lovely property at 710 W. Birch, with upstairs and downstairs units resembling contemporary town homes. Another property, at 919 N. Beaver, is a three-bedroom, two-bath house built in the 1930s by the same architect, Charles Whittlesey, who designed the Grand Canyon's El Tovar hotel. Like most of the others, these are just a short walk from Flagstaff's historic business district.

1612 N. Aztec St., Flagstaff, AZ 86001. www.comficottages.com. © **888/774-0731** or 928/774-0731. Fax 928/773-7286. 9 units in different locations in Flagstaff. $150–$320 double. Rates include breakfast. DISC, MC, V. Inquire about pets. **Amenities:** Free bicycle use. *In room:* A/C, TV, DVD/VCR, kitchen, Wi-Fi (free).

The Inn At 410 Bed & Breakfast ★★★ 🍴 Gordon Watkins runs the most charming, friendly B&B anywhere in the vicinity of the Grand Canyon. Peering into each of his nine guest rooms here is like flipping through pages in an issue of *House & Garden*. Each expertly decorated room is daringly different, yet tasteful. The romantic **Tea Room** sits adjacent to the first-floor living area, elegantly furnished with a king bed, fireplace, mahogany wood-work, porcelain tea sets, and a Jacuzzi bathroom. The stunning **Monet's Garden** suite is reminiscent of a French country garden, featuring a two-person Jacuzzi tub and private sitting area that opens to the garden. The refined **Conservatory** room celebrates classical music. Its elegant sitting room is accented by a fireplace and French sitting chairs; in the corner stands a violin and a music stand, with walls decorated with music-sheet wallpaper and prints of the masters. All the guest rooms here have gas fireplaces; three have jetted tubs.

The inn will gladly help you arrange outdoor activities, such as hiking and biking outings, and you're within easy walking distance to downtown shops and restaurants. The gourmet Southwestern breakfast includes juice, fresh fruit, a homemade pastry, and a non-meat entree. Afternoon refreshments are served in the elegant main sitting room. Ginger and Sissy are two lovely spaniels you'll often find lingering around the sitting area. Gordon is a terrific host.

410 N. Leroux St., Flagstaff, AZ 86001. www.inn410.com. © **800/774-2008** or 928/774-0088. Fax 928/774-6354. 9 units. $160–$210 double. MC, V. **Amenities:** Small gym; Wi-Fi (free). *In room:* A/C, cable TV w/DVD/VCR, fridge, hair dryer, MP3 docking station, no phone.

Little America Hotel ★ Strangely enough, one of the most highly regarded chain hotels in Flagstaff adjoins a truck stop. Even though it doesn't look like much from the outside, the interior is a different story. Little America's rooms are lavishly decorated in French colonial style and extremely spacious—they have sitting areas, dressing areas, dining tables, and oversize tubs. Guest rooms facing the forest cost $20 more and are quieter because there's less train noise. An even better surprise: Five hundred mostly wooded acres, owned by the hotel, provide access to Flagstaff's urban trail system and, farther out, the Arizona Trail. From Thanksgiving through January, a million holiday lights sparkle on the forest trees. Closer to the rooms, there's a large outdoor pool, sand volleyball courts, horseshoe pits, and a 2-mile walking and jogging trail through ponderosa pines. And if, by chance, you need 60 gallons of diesel, a trucker's hat, or coffee in an imposing Styrofoam cup, you won't have to go far.

2515 E. Butler (off I-40 exit 198), Flagstaff, AZ 86001. http://flagstaff.littleamerica. com. © **800/352-4386** or 928/779-7900. Fax 928/779-7983. 247 units, 8 spe-cialty suites. High season $149–$189 double; low season $99–$139 double. AE, DC,

DISC, MC, V. **Amenities:** Restaurant; lounge; complimentary shuttle to airport or train station; fitness center; Jacuzzi; outdoor pool (seasonal); room service. *In room:* A/C, TV w/pay movies and video games, fridge, hair dryer, Wi-Fi (free).

A Shooting Star ★★ 🎁 Innkeeper Tom Taylor's mesmerizing solar-paneled house serves as a B&B, observatory, and photography and music recording studio. Most guests come to this remote location under Arizona's clear dark skies to witness an amazing astronomy program (presented by Tom and included in the rate) that lets you view the moon, stars, and other planets through the lens of a powerful telescope. Tom is a brilliant astro-photographer, and his photos decorate the interior of the northern white pine log house along with astronomy books, telescopes, and musical instruments. Three guest rooms—aptly named Galileo, Einstein, and Cassini—sit just off the great room, where guests come together under 25-foot ceilings to discuss the wonder of the stars. The house fronts the San Francisco peaks and sits next to a national forest, offering a breathtaking panorama in all directions. Tom joins guests for the full gourmet breakfast, and he welcomes other musicians who wish to play music with him. It's also possible to reserve in advance dinner at the inn. *Note:* Flagstaff lies 20 minutes from here, and there are no services nearby.

27948 N. Shooting Star Lane (21 miles north of Flagstaff at milepost 236 on Hwy. 180), Flagstaff, AZ 86001. www.shootingstarinn.com. © **928/606-8070.** 3 units. $225 double. Rates include breakfast. AE, DISC, V. **Amenities:** Wi-Fi (free). *In room:* No phone.

INEXPENSIVE

A recommended, inexpensive to moderate chain motel in Flagstaff is **Springhill Suites,** 2455 S. Beulha Blvd. (© **928/774-8042**). Rates are from $109 for double occupancy.

Hotel Weatherford 🏷 Constructed in 1898, this historic three-story hotel in downtown Flagstaff transports you back to the turn of the 20th century. Come here for the history, location, and nightlife rather than for luxury or quiet accommodations. The **Zane Grey Room,** which serves drinks on the hotel's third floor at night, boasts a hand-carved Brunswick bar next to a fireplace and across from an original painting by the legendary 19th-century landscape artist Thomas Moran. Zane Grey wrote *The Call of the Canyon,* a copy of which is proudly displayed in this room. The guest rooms, only some of which have private bathrooms, are simple and eccentric. Three "queen suites" offer queen-size beds, sitting areas with antique furnishings, and claw-foot tubs. The rest of the rooms remain just as they were at the end of the 19th century: just a bed, chair, and dresser with no TV or phone. If you're planning to stay here, rest up plenty in advance—then join the party, starting with a meal at **Charly's,** the hotel's Southwestern pub-style restaurant.

23 N. Leroux, Flagstaff, AZ 86001. www.weatherfordhotel.com. ✆ **928/779-1919.** Fax 928/773-8951. 11 units, 3 with shared bathrooms. $49–$79 double with shared bath; $89 double with private bath; $139 queen room. AE, DC, DISC, MC, V. Parking behind the hotel. **Amenities:** Restaurant, Charly's (Southwestern/American, p. 129); 2 excellent bars. *In room (2 rooms only):* A/C, TV.

Where to Eat
EXPENSIVE
Brix ★★ AMERICAN/WINE BAR   Adjacent to the Inn at 410, this casually elegant restaurant and wine bar competes only with Cottage Place as Flagstaff's finest dining room. Closely spaced candlelit tables fill the inside, and there's a charming outdoor patio with heat lamps for those who prefer fresh air. The contemporary American menu draws inspiration from local farmers; its selections are mostly organic. The menu changes with the seasons and might include choices such as seared fresh fish, steak frites, farm-raised chicken, and homemade pasta with a vegetarian sauce. Delicious side dishes include artisanal macaroni and cheese and grilled eggplant and squash. Patrons are also welcome to come just for wine and cheese. Expect a balanced variety of international wines, with more than 30 selections served by the glass. A casual sister restaurant to Brix, **Criollo,** at 16 N. San Francisco St. (✆ **928/774-0541**), serves impressive Latin-inspired local food.

413 N. San Francisco St., Flagstaff. ✆ **928/213-1021.** www.brixflagstaff.com. Reservations recommended. Main courses $23–$34. AE, DISC, MC, V. Sun–Thurs 5–9pm; Fri–Sat 5–10pm.

Cottage Place ★★ 📷 COUNTRY FRENCH   The quiet serenity of Flagstaff's most elegant restaurant is ideal for special occasions, a wonderful spot to peacefully celebrate your vacation to the Southwest. Original artwork decorates three rose-colored rooms, where soft conversations are heard from candlelit tables. Chateaubriand (for two) is chef-owner Frank Branham's signature dish. It's carved tableside with béarnaise and smoked Gouda gratin potatoes. As for other entrees, I find it hard to choose between the rack of lamb, which is seared on an open-flame broiler and accompanied by a port wine demi-glaze and English mint sauce, and the Gorgonzola filet: beef tenderloin pan-seared and flavored with a Gorgonzola crust. All entrees are served with soup du jour or house salad. A six-course tasting menu is offered nightly, with or without matching wines, and there's also a reduced price "twilight menu" offered from 5 to 6pm, which comes with soup or salad and an entree.

126 W. Cottage Ave., Flagstaff. ℂ **928/774-8431.** www.cottageplace.com. Reservations recommended. Dinner $26–$36; chateaubriand for 2 $77. AE, MC, V. Wed–Sun 5–9:30pm.

Josephine ★ CONTINENTAL   This modern American bistro in the historic Milton Clark house serves the best lunches in town. The bungalow-style building was the first constructed in Flagstaff (1911) using indigenous malpais rock. A large stone hearth forms the centerpiece of the main dining room and bar, with smaller rooms adjacent. The chef uses quality ingredients and local products (organic when available) to create a fresh, creative menu. A couple light choices at midday are the salmon BLT and the "Po-Boy" crab cake sandwich. For dinner, favorites include shrimp macaroni and cheese, pork *osso buco,* and cocoa chili-encrusted beef tenderloin medallions. The menu suggests wines to be paired with each of the entrees. Service here is friendly and informal, and portions are somewhat smaller than you might find elsewhere. Enjoy seating on the garden patio in summer.

503 N. Humphreys St., Flagstaff. ℂ **928/779-3400.** Reservations accepted. Lunch $9.50–$13; dinner entrees $20–$30. AE, DISC, MC, V. Summer Mon–Sat 11am–2:30pm and 5–9pm, Sun 5–9pm, brunch Sat–Sun 8am–2:30pm; winter Mon–Fri 11am–2:30pm and 5–9pm, Sat 5–9pm. Closed Sat lunch and Sun in winter.

Tinderbox Kitchen ★★★ AMERICAN   Opened in May 2009, Tinderbox Kitchen quickly established itself as Flagstaff's hottest new table. Co-owners Kevin Heinonen and chef Scott Heinonen have created an inspirational menu centered on American comfort food, although it's been kicked up several notches above "comfort." The menu varies daily, and is packed with creative entrees such as succulent seared scallops served with creamed corn and wild rice hush puppies, jalapeño mac-'n'-cheese topped with a duck leg confit, juniper-cured venison, buffalo meatloaf, and a fresh fish selection prepared any number of ways. Dishes are carefully presented and extremely flavorful, although substitutions are "politely declined." The decor matches the contemporary simplicity of the cuisine, with a dozen interior tables complemented by a handful on the back patio. An international wine list with moderate price points accompanies the menu. Call in advance to inquire about possible chef's tasting menus.

34 S. San Francisco St., Flagstaff. ℂ **928/226-8400.** www.tinderboxkitchen. com. Reservations recommended. Lunch $8–$15; dinner $18–$28; 4-course meal $50. AE, DISC, MC, V. Mon 5–9pm; Tues–Sat 11am–2pm and 5–9pm. Closed Sun.

MODERATE

Beaver Street Brewery AMERICAN   This whistle-stop cafe became Flagstaff's first microbrewery, and I still find the food, beer, and service better here than at Flagstaff Brewery. Potbellied stoves and railroad artwork decorate the high-spirited dining room, with an open-view kitchen and a popular bar attached. As an appetizer, try a cheese fondue or pizza chips, which are sprinkled with Parmesan, Romano, mozzarella, and a dash of garlic. Pub-style platters include bratwurst sausages, shrimp tacos, barbecue dishes, sandwiches, and wood-fired pizzas: The Enchanted Forest is smothered with portobello mushrooms, fresh spinach, roasted bell peppers, and French brie on an artichoke-olive-pesto base topped with walnuts, ground black pepper, Parmesan, and basil. And it doesn't make a whole lot of sense to come here without trying one of the fresh brews—among the best are raspberry ale, the locally popular Indian pale ale (IPA), and Railhead red ale. You can watch sports and play pool at the Brews and Cues bar next door, which stays open until 2am weekends, 1am weekdays.

11 S. Beaver St., Flagstaff. © **928/779-0079.** Lunch and dinner items $9–$20. AE, DISC, MC, V. Sun–Thurs 11am–11pm; Fri–Sat 11am–midnight (limited menu after 10pm serving pizza and appetizers).

Charly's SOUTHWESTERN/AMERICAN Charly's is spacious and cool, both inside, where the 12-foot-high ceilings of the Hotel Weatherford (built in 1897) provide breathing room, and on the sidewalk, a favorite place for summertime dining. Try the *posole*—New Mexican hominy with pork, chili, and spices served in a flour tortilla bowl—or the Navajo tacos served with fry bread. Besides steaks, fish, and burgers, the restaurant also offers a number of vegetarian dishes that make for welcome light dining. After dinner, you can dance at the adjacent bar, which features live entertainment on weekends and pours 20 beers on tap. The hotel's bars are among the town's hottest nightspots, and are open well after Charly's kitchen closes.

In historic Hotel Weatherford, 23 N. Leroux St., Flagstaff. © **928/779-1919.** Reservations accepted. Breakfast $6–$10; lunch $10–$14; dinner $20–$27. AE, DC, DISC, MC, V. Daily 8am–10pm.

Cuvée 928 ★★ AMERICAN/WINE BAR Restaurant–wine bars have grown increasingly popular in Flagstaff, and this is the most spirited. Young professionals congregate here for appetizers, specialty cocktails, and delightful California and international wines (the 3–6pm happy hour is a local favorite). Patrons can even choose their wines right out of the impressive cellar. The food is so good the restaurant has continued to expand, with creative entrees written on a board above the bar. Among the original selections is a "crawfish croute," a corn buttermilk biscuit smothered in a rich New Orleans–inspired Creole sauce with crawfish tail meat and a side of grilled asparagus. The chef uses many organic and local products, and Flagstaff's only original hot sauce is served here. For lunch, there's a wonderful array of sandwiches (try the beef brisket), wraps, panini, salads, and other light bites. This is one of the few establishments offering a late-night menu on weekends. Cuvée 928 opens up on to Heritage Square, which is home to concerts, art walks, and movies on weekend nights.

6 E. Aspen Ave., Flagstaff. ✆ **928/214-9463.** www.cuvee928winebar.com. Lunch $8–$12; dinner $15–$26. AE, DISC, MC, V. Mon–Thurs 11am–9pm; Fri–Sat 11am–midnight. Closed Sun.

Karma ★ SUSHI/TAPAS   A sexy venue for dinner and drinks, Karma flaunts a hip vibe created by fashionable waitstaff and patrons. Don't think traditional Japanese: Creative sushi rolls using wild salmon, spicy tuna, delectable lobster, or a variety of other fresh fish define the menu; the Asian fusion selections also include a teriyaki grill with chicken or salmon, hot braised tofu, and pan-fried wheat noodles with shiitake mushrooms. The Black Cat Roll packs in spicy lobster, asparagus, mango, and avocado with black sesame. Sushi and sashimi combos for two or more are also available. You can come just for drinks, as well: The bartenders take pride in their exotic cocktails, cold sake, and imported Japanese beers—including wheat-free rice beers. Happy hour happens weekdays from 3 to 6pm.

6 E. Rte. 66, Flagstaff. ✆ **928/774-6100.** www.karmaflagstaff.com. Sushi $4–$13; entrees $8–$17. AE, DC, DISC, MC, V. Mon–Sat 11am–10pm; Sun 4:30–10pm.

INEXPENSIVE

Black Bean Burrito Bar & Salsa Co. ★ 🍴 MEXICAN   In a Mexican food–challenged region, extravagant burritos turn up in the most basic of environments. At the Black Bean, you'll eat out of plastic drive-in baskets while sitting at a counter that opens onto a pedestrian walkway. The burritos, which come with a choice of seven different salsas of varying kick, are delicious and enormous, with the heft of hand weights. Just don't expect an authentic Mexican meal: This place offers creative specialty wraps (which envelop steamed or stir-fried ingredients), including exotic flavors such as Thai peanut tofu and roasted jalapeño chicken, in addition to more standard bean, chicken, and steak burritos. If you're here in the morning, order a tasty breakfast burrito.

12 E. Rte. 66, Gateway Plaza, Ste. 104, Flagstaff. ✆ **928/779-9905.** Reservations not accepted. Menu items $2–$8. MC, V. Daily 8am–9pm.

Fratelli Pizza ★ 🍴 PIZZERIA   This is not a place to come for a relaxing, romantic, or even sit-down dinner. There are just a small number of tables to sit at, so most people order takeout. There's not much more to say about Fratelli, except that its pizza is Northern

Arizona's best. The authentic hand-tossed pies come with a selection of traditional, vegetarian, and specialty toppings. Antipasto, salads, and giant calzones also enliven the menu, as do a handful of beer and wine selections.

119 W. Phoenix Ave., Flagstaff. © **928/774-9200.** Reservations not accepted. Pizza $11-$21. AE, DISC, MC, V. Sun-Thurs 11am-9pm; Fri-Sat 11am-10pm.

Macy's European Coffee House Bakery ★ ☖ VEGETARIAN/BAKERY   Students, artists, intellectuals, and proud locals pack this bohemian cafe most every morning. Macy's may not be able to save the world, but its healthy organic food, vegetarian dishes, homemade pastries, and fresh roasted coffee and specialty blends encourage people to slow down and smell the latte. Breakfast items include steamed eggs, vegan waffles, granola, and biscuits and gravy. Soups, salads, and creative sandwiches dominate the lunch menu. Order at either of the two counters, and note that anything can be made wheat-free, dairy-free, nut-free, or for vegans. Free Wi-Fi is available, and Monday is chess night. Besides the busy indoor tables, outdoor seating is available in warm weather.

14 S. Beaver St., Flagstaff. © **928/774-2243.** Reservations not accepted. Entrees $3-$8. MC, V. Daily 6am-8pm.

TUSAYAN ★

1 mile south of Grand Canyon National Park; 60 miles north of Williams; 80 miles NE of Flagstaff; 340 miles north of Tucson

More a tourist outpost than a town, Tusayan's short stretch of modest hotels, restaurants, and shops extends no more than a half-mile on both sides of the highway. There are no houses, and most Tusayan residents live in company-provided apartments or trailers behind the town's businesses. Employers pay dearly to lure workers here (many increasingly from outside the U.S., particularly during high season), and to convince suppliers to lug their goods 60 miles off the interstate. So Tusayan is neither cheap nor particularly memorable, with gas, hotel rooms, and food that cost about 20% more than they would in other gateway towns. However, Tusayan's location next to the Grand Canyon's South Rim makes it the best option for folks who don't have a lodging reservation inside the park and wish to stay closer than Flagstaff or Williams.

Essentials

GETTING THERE   By Car   If you drive, make sure to fill your gas tank before setting out for Tusayan and the Grand Canyon; there's only one service station between Tusayan and Flagstaff, the nearest major city, which is almost 80 miles away. From Flagstaff, it's possible to take U.S. 180 and U.S. 64 directly to Tusayan.

By Plane Grand Canyon National Park Airport in Tusayan is served by two airlines flying out of Las Vegas: **Scenic Airlines** (℅ 800/634-6801 or 702/638-3300; www.scenic.com), which charges $229 each way, and **Vision Air** (℅ 702/261-3850; www.visionholidays.com), which charges $199 each way.

Outside of these options, you'll have to fly into Phoenix, Las Vegas, or Flagstaff and then arrange ground transportation to Tusayan and the national park.

GETTING AROUND **By Car** The nearest available rental cars are in Flagstaff. There's one gas station in Tusayan and another at Desert View inside the park's east entrance (though this station is seasonal). Be forewarned that gas at these stations costs about 50¢ more per gallon than in Flagstaff, downtown Williams (away from I-40), or Cameron, so make sure to top off in those places if you can.

By Taxi **Xanterra** offers 24-hour taxi service to and from the airport, trail heads, and other park destinations (℅ 928/638-2631).

SUPERMARKET **Tusayan General Store** is 1 mile south of the park entrance on Highway 180/64 (℅ 928/638-2854). There's also a post office and ATM here. It's open daily 7am to 10pm in summer, and 8am to 9pm during the slower times of the year. Or, try the larger **Canyon Village Marketplace** in the park's business district (p. 102).

What to See & Do

Grand Canyon IMAX Theater/National Geographic Visitor Center ★★ ☺ *Grand Canyon—the Hidden Secrets* is the most watched IMAX film ever, and it seems like it's been playing in Tusayan forever. Every inch of the six-story-high, 82-foot-wide screen is taken up by stunning footage of the canyon. Among the highlights of this 34-minute film: whitewater rafting that makes you feel as if you might drown, insects magnified to the size of buildings, and aerial footage from inside some of the canyon's rock narrows. Adjacent to the theater are a small food court and a National Geographic visitor center with information from the Arizona Office of Tourism. You can buy entrance passes to the Grand Canyon here. The Peregrine Fund (www.condorcliffs.org) now offers a "Condor Encounter Live Bird Show" just outside multiple times per day.

On Hwy. 64 in Tusayan (no address listed, but impossible to miss), 1½ miles south of the park's south entrance. ℅ **928/638-2468.** www.explorethecanyon.com. $13 adults, $9.50 ages 6–10, free for children 5 and under. Mar–Oct daily 8:30am–8:30pm; Nov–Feb daily 10:30am–6:30pm. Showings at half past the hour every hour.

Where to Stay
EXPENSIVE

Best Western Grand Canyon Squire Inn ★   There's a lot to
do at this hotel, which prides itself on being the Grand Canyon's
only full-service resort. Kids will love the family recreation center,
which includes a six-lane bowling alley, billiards, and video games.
Adults tend to gravitate to the fine-dining **Coronado Room** restaurant and **Saguaro Sports Bar,** Tusayan's popular watering
hole. Guest rooms feature rustic wood furnishings and Southwestern accents. Standard rooms, in two older buildings left from the
Squire Motor Inn (1972), are no larger than the rooms at the other
area motels. Costing about $20 more than standard rooms, deluxe
rooms are more spacious and have upgraded bathrooms with
Roman tubs.

P.O. Box 130 (1½ miles south of park on Hwy. 64), Grand Canyon, AZ 86023. www.
grandcanyonsquire.com. (℃) **800/622-6966** or 928/638-2681. Fax 928/638-
2782. 250 units. High season $159–$189 double; low season $109–$129 double.
AE, DC, DISC, MC, V. **Amenities:** 2 restaurants, including Coronado Room
(p. 135); 2 bars (lounge and sports bar); exercise room; Jacuzzi; outdoor pool
(seasonal). *In room:* A/C, TV, fridge upon request, hair dryer, Wi-Fi (free).

Canyon Plaza Resort ★   In summer, guests here sun themselves around the large outdoor swimming pool and hot tub. In
winter, they head for the hotel's stunning atrium, where tropical
plants and palm trees shade an indoor Jacuzzi spa with a waterfall.
As the area's hot tubs go, this one is the most enticing, with jets to
massage every aching joint. When guests finally finish soaking,
they find themselves occupying some of the town's nicest accommodations, including a handful of rooms with private decks and
refrigerators. A few rooms bordering the atrium have only tiny
windows to the outside (and larger ones facing the atrium). Ask for
a room with a large exterior window if darkness bothers you. Open
from 6:30am to 10pm daily, **JJK's,** the hotel's family-style restaurant, offers three buffets (popular with tour groups), as well as
menu selections.

P.O. Box 520 (on Hwy. 64, 1 mile south of park entrance, next to IMAX theater),
Grand Canyon, AZ 86023. www.grandcanyonplaza.com. (℃) **800/995-2521** (res-
ervations only) or 928/638-2673. Fax 928/638-9537. 176 units, 56 suites. Apr 1–
Oct 20 $180–$250 double; Oct 21–Mar 31 $100 double. AE, DC, DISC, MC, V.
Amenities: Restaurant; lounge; 2 Jacuzzis; outdoor pool (seasonal); sauna.
In room: A/C, TV, fridge (suites only), hair dryer, minibar (60 rooms), Wi-Fi (free).

Grand Hotel ★★   Modeled after an Old West lodge, the
Grand's lobby features an enormous fireplace, hand-woven car-
pets, and hand-oiled, hand-painted goatskin lanterns. Imitation

ponderosa pine logs rise from the stone-tile floors to the high ceiling. Inviting rooms include prints of the canyon and simple Southwest furnishings. The choicest ones are the third-story rooms with balconies facing away from the highway. **Canyon Star Restaurant**, specializing in mesquite-smoked barbecue and Southwestern cuisine, serves three meals daily and offers nightly entertainment in summer. Of Tusayan's bars, the most appealing by far is Canyon Star Saloon. Below its stamped-copper ceiling, patrons belly up to the bar; some of the stools are old saddles. The hotel will pack box lunches ($18) for guests who order them the night before, and has a coffee bar in the lobby.

P.O. Box 3319 (on Hwy. 64, 1½ miles south of park entrance), Grand Canyon, AZ 86023. www.grandcanyongrandhotel.com. (C) **888/634-7263** or 928/638-3333. Fax 928/638-3131. 121 units. High season $189 standard, $209 balcony; low season $99 standard, $119 balcony. AE, DISC, MC, V. **Amenities:** Restaurant, Canyon Star (p. 135); bar; concierge; exercise room; Jacuzzi; indoor pool. *In room:* A/C, TV, hair dryer, Wi-Fi (free).

MODERATE

A midpriced chain hotel in Tusayan is **Red Feather Lodge** ((C) **800/538-2345** or 928/638-2414), on Highway 64, 1 mile south of the park. Next door is a **Holiday Inn Express** ((C) **888/ 473-2269** or 928/638-3000). Rates typically range from $90 to $150 for double occupancy.

INEXPENSIVE

Grand Canyon Inn 🏷 Travelers can sometimes save $30 on a room simply by driving 23 miles south from Tusayan to this family-run motel in Vallé, at the dusty crossroads of highways 180 and 64. All rooms are decorated the same, with two queen beds and simple Southwestern decor. Rooms in the newer section cost $20 more than those in the '50s-era motel across Highway 64 from the main inn. There's an expensive gas station next door. If you're looking for a variety of activities outside the motel, keep driving to Williams or Flagstaff.

P.O. Box 755 (in Vallé, at junction of Hwy. 180 and Hwy. 64), Williams, AZ 86046. www.grand-canyon-inn.com. (C) **800/635-9203** or 928/635-9203. Fax 928/635-2345. 73 units. Aug 1–Oct 31 $59–$89 double; Nov 1–Apr 30 $59–$79 double; May 1–July 31 $69–$89 double. AE, DISC, MC, V. **Amenities:** Restaurant; bar; outdoor pool; Wi-Fi in lobby (free). *In room:* A/C, TV, no phone (in older motel rooms).

7-Mile Lodge 🏷 This is the cheapest motel in town. Instead of taking reservations, the owners of this lodge start selling spaces at around 9am and usually sell out by early afternoon. If you need a reasonably priced place to stay, think about stopping here on your way into the park. Don't be put off by the motel's cramped office—surprisingly, the rooms are decent and large enough to hold two queen-size beds. Thick walls and doors muffle the noise of planes from the nearby airport.

P.O. Box 56 (1½ miles south of Hwy. 64 park entrance), Grand Canyon, AZ 86023. ℂ **928/638-2291.** Reservations not accepted. 20 units. High season (spring to early fall, holidays) $89 double; low season (rest of year) $79 double. AE, DISC, MC, V. *In room:* A/C, TV, no phone.

Where to Eat

Canyon Star Restaurant ☺ REGIONAL   The entertainment at this festive restaurant seems designed to give tourists exactly what they hope to find in the American West. Most nights, a lonesome cowboy balladeer performs for diners. Specialty items include the barbecue buffalo brisket, slow-roasted baby back ribs, and the 12-ounce New York strip. Salmon and trout are usually served, and there's a commendable kids' menu ($9). For something on the lighter side, try the "very berry" balsamic vinaigrette salad with fresh berries. The adjacent **Canyon Star Saloon** is Tusayan's leading hangout with six regional beers on tap.

In Grand Hotel on Hwy. 64 (1½ miles from park's south entrance), Tusayan. ℂ **888/634-7263** or 928/638-3333. Breakfast $9–$14; lunch $8–$18; dinner $20–$30. AE, DISC, MC, V. Daily 6–10am, noon–4pm, and 5–10pm.

Coronado Dining Room ★ CONTINENTAL   Tasty food and attentive service make this Tusayan's most upscale restaurant. The lavender-colored tables and chairs, dim lighting, and beautiful prints of the canyon create a more formal atmosphere than at other Tusayan eateries (even though the dining room looks like the destination point for a time machine to the 1970s). The restaurant puts a heavy emphasis on steaks, including filet mignon, New York strip, rib-eye, and prime rib; a few chicken and seafood dishes are thrown in for good measure. The most delicious entree may be the sumptuous elk tournedos served with sweet red wine demi-glacé. Fresh, dark bread accompanies the meal. The adjoining, family-oriented **Canyon Room** offers breakfast and a buffet lunch.

In Best Western Grand Canyon Squire Inn (1½ miles south of park on Hwy. 64), Tusayan. ℂ **928/638-2681,** ext. 4418. Reservations recommended. Entrees $17–$30. AE, DC, DISC, MC, V. Daily 5–10pm.

We Cook Pizza and Pasta ☺ ITALIAN   In this restaurant's lengthy name, the owners neglected to mention how much they charge. Prices here are high, even by Grand Canyon standards, especially for a place without table service. A large 16-inch combo pizza for four to six people ("the Works," they call it) will set you back $30, and pasta dishes range from $10 to $17. After paying, you'll have to sit at one of the long picnic tables and wait for your number to be called. Since you can't reserve tables here, the only way to shorten your wait is by phone-ordering in advance. Despite all that, the pizza is pretty tasty. There are also a handful of pasta dishes, such as the Cajun chicken fettuccine, and an all-you-can-eat salad bar. The adjacent **Carvel** ice cream shop dares you to add more cholesterol to your meal. This restaurant has a very casual family feel.

On Hwy. 64 (1 mile south of park entrance), Tusayan. ✆ **928/638-2278.** Reservations not accepted. Pizza $10–$30; pasta and calzones $10–$17; sandwiches $8; salad bar $8. DISC, MC, V. Summer daily 11am–10pm; winter daily 11am–8pm.

WILLIAMS ★★

59 miles S. of Grand Canyon; 32 miles W. of Flagstaff; 220 miles E. of Las Vegas

All told, this is a friendly, safe, and very small town for families hoping to experience the Old West without battling the new traffic. With timber above it, ranches below it, and railroads running through it, this town of roughly 3,000 residents attracted one of the West's most raucous crowds after its 1892 incorporation. Cowboys, loggers, prospectors, trappers, and railroad workers all frequented the brothels, gambling houses, bars, and opium dens on the town's infamous **Saloon Row.** Though quieter now, Williams has done an especially good job of packaging its lively past. Much of Saloon Row and many other 19th-century buildings have been restored. The town's renovated train depot now serves as the start and finish point for the Historic Grand Canyon Railroad's daily runs. To entertain tourists, gunslinging cowboys stage raucous (corny, but fun) shootouts in the streets every summer night. In winter, there's an oval-shaped ice-skating rink next to the city's recreation center and within walking distance of the train. Don't look for much nighttime activity though: The only restaurant you'll find open after 10pm is **Denny's.** You'll also need your own car to get around, as there are no car rental agencies or taxis in Williams.

Essentials

GETTING THERE   By Car   Williams is on I-40 just west of the junction with Highway 64, which leads north to the Grand Canyon's South Rim. Watch out for elk and deer crossing Highway 64 as you head north from Williams.

By Train   Amtrak (✆ 800/872-7245) has a small station in Williams. A free shuttle bus brings departing passengers from the drop-off into town, to the station for the **Historic Grand Canyon Railway** (✆ 800/843-8724), which offers daily round-trip service linking Williams and Grand Canyon Village. For more on this historic railway, see "What to See & Do," below.

VISITOR INFORMATION For more information about the Williams area, contact the **City of Williams Visitor Information Center,** 200 W. Railroad Ave., Williams, AZ 86046-2556 (✆ **800/ 863-0546** or 928/635-1418; www.experiencewilliams.com, or www.williamschamber.com). It's open 8am to 5pm daily (until 6:30pm in summer), and a vending machine in the building sells park entrance permits (the machine accepts credit cards).

SUPERMARKET **Safeway,** which also has a bakery and deli, is at 637 W. Rte. 66 (✆ **928/635-0500**); it's open daily from 5am to 10pm (hours may vary in winter).

What to See & Do

Bearizona ★ ☺ This new drive-through attraction allows you to experience bison, mountain goats, wolves, bighorn sheep, and—as the main attraction—black bears, all roaming freely in a 160-acre wildlife park. Guests, traveling slowly in their cars, can observe herd and pack life as it exists in nature, and the amount of wildlife wandering close to the roads is impressive. In addition to this 3-mile wilderness drive, guests can park and stroll through the 20-acre Fort Bearizona which features smaller animals in protected areas, including adorable bear cubs, wolf pups, bobcats, foxes, porcupines, piglets, goats, and more. There's also a petting area for children to interact with the most docile creatures, as well as a snack bar and gift shop. If you've never confronted bears in the wild (and let's hope you haven't), this may be the safest opportunity you'll get.

1500 E. Route 66 (take I-40 exit 165), Williams. ✆ **928/635-2289.** www.be arizona.com. Admission $16 adult, $8 youth 4-12, free for children 3 and under. Summer daily 8am-8pm (6pm last entry); winter reduced hours. Closed Jan-Feb.

Grand Canyon Railway ★★★ ☺ This historic train ride is a beautiful way to visit the Grand Canyon. The trip starts at the historic **Williams Depot** next to the Grand Canyon Railway Hotel. Built in 1908, this concrete building is on the National Register of Historic Places. It survived only because the railroad realized in the 1970s that demolishing it would cost more than letting it be. It now houses a gift shop and cafe, and the two steam engines once used to pull the train have been retired and are now on display in front. Today's stainless steel diesel train pulls a maximum of 15 cars accommodating up to 1,000 people, and the 100-year-old railroad carries more than 180,000 passengers annually.

At 9:30am every morning, after local cowboys stage a Wild West gunfight outside the depot, conductors help passengers board the train. For $70 round-trip, **Coach Class** passengers sit in 1950s Budd streamliner coach cars with bench seating and air-conditioning. For twice the amount of coach fare, passengers can enjoy **First**

Class treatment—probably not worth the extra money, but it does come with continental breakfast in the morning and appetizers with a cash bar on the trip home—all the while sitting in comfortable recliner chairs. If you really want to savor the views of the high desert, however, I recommend purchasing a seat in the **Deluxe Observation Class,** whose seats are in a glass dome atop the car. Spots here cost $170 round-trip. I even prefer the Deluxe Observation Class to the most expensive ($190 round-trip) service, the **Luxury Parlor Car,** which boasts an open-air rear platform. If you like, you can take one class of seating on the way to the Grand Canyon, and a different class back, allowing you to sample different train experiences. Each car offers a personal service attendant, and while the train chugs across the high desert, musicians wander through the compartments, playing folk and country standards and dishing up some cowboy humor. I'd recommend sitting in a dome car on the way back to Williams, where you can watch a dazzling sunset with a glass of sparkling wine accompanied by live cowboy music.

The trip to the canyon ends at the historic **Grand Canyon Depot** in Grand Canyon Village. From here, passengers can lunch at any of the park lodges and then take a motor coach rim tour as part of a package (p. 51), or they can just go explore on their own. Passengers have just under 4 hours to enjoy the South Rim unless they stay overnight, and rail getaway packages are available. Sign up for lunch and bus tour packages while reserving train tickets.

Williams Depot, 235 N. Grand Canyon Blvd. (take I-40 exit 163, go ½ mile south), Williams. © **800/843-8724.** www.thetrain.com. Round-trip coach tickets $70 adult, $40 youth 11–16, $35 children 2–10, free for children 1 and under; higher classes cost $140–$190 per person, depending on class of service. AE, DC, DISC, MC, V. Daily Wild West Shootout at 9am; train departs at 9:30am and arrives at Grand Canyon at 11:45am. Leaves Grand Canyon at 3:30pm, arriving in Williams at 5:45pm. Advise at time of reservation if a passenger has mobility restrictions.

Western-Style Gun Fights 📷 The same bad guys, sheriffs, and deputies who battle every morning near the Grand Canyon Railway Depot shoot at one another all over again at 7pm on summer nights in downtown Williams (a high school band usually plays before the show starts). The free spectacle, which moves to a different block of Route 66 each night, entertains thousands of visitors every year. If you're in town, don't miss it. These guys act like real gunslingers, only they're funny. To find out where the show will be on a given night, consult one of the schedules available at the **Williams Visitor Information Center** (© **800/863-0546** or 928/635-4061), or ask at any of the town's businesses.

Various locations in Williams. © **800/863-0546.** Free admission. Memorial Day to Labor Day daily 7pm.

Where to Stay
EXPENSIVE

Williams has one moderate-to-expensive chain hotel: **Best Western Inn of Williams** (© 928/635-4400), 2600 Rte. 66, Williams, AZ 86046, with doubles from $130.

Firelight ★ A short walk from the town center in a residential area adjacent to forest land sits Firelight, a Tudor-style B&B with five individually decorated rooms. Named after English counties, they include real or faux fireplaces, jetted tubs, and flatscreen TVs with DVD players. The Yorkshire suite has a four-poster bed, adjacent sitting area, and regal bathroom with a double sink and two-person Jacuzzi, while Somerset features a balcony with sunset views. Gourmet breakfasts are prepared in the open kitchen next to the dining room, and a number of cozy sitting areas are around the house, including an elegant study and an upstairs game room with an original English shuffleboard, 1947 Seeburg jukebox, and a Wii system hooked up to a big screen TV. Numerous walking trails surround the area, and the hosts will gladly help guests with ideas for exploring Northern Arizona.

175 W. Mead Ave., Williams, AZ 86046. www.firelightbedandbreakfast.com. © **888/838-8218** or 928/635-0200. 5 units. $160–$250 double. Rates include full breakfast. AE, DISC, DC, MC, V. No children 16 or under. *In room:* A/C, flatscreen TV w/DVD player, hair dryer, Wi-Fi (free).

Grand Canyon Railway Hotel ★ This sprawling train-lovers' lodge beside the depot replaced the original Fray Marcos Hotel. Today, an array of fun amenities, such as an indoor pool and outdoor sports courts, makes this a great spot for families. In the lobby, oil paintings of the Grand Canyon adorn the walls, and cushy chairs surround a flagstone fireplace. Bellmen carry luggage to the spacious (but somewhat spartan) rooms, all of which come with two queen beds. Suites feature a separate bedroom and living room with a sleeper sofa and kitchenette. **Spenser's Lounge,** which features a beautiful 100-year-old bar imported from Scotland, offers simple dining and top-shelf liquor.

The Grand Canyon Railway, which starts and ends its daily runs at the depot next to the hotel (where there's a gift shop), has become hugely popular with tour groups, many of whom stay at the hotel. The special **Railway Getaway package,** starting at $170 for adults ($49 for children), includes 1 night's accommodation, dinner and breakfast buffets, and round-trip coach travel to the canyon. Additional packages are available for longer stays, including in the canyon.

The all-paved **Grand Canyon Railway RV Park** has opened next door. Since it's under the same ownership as the hotel, patrons of the RV park have access to all of the hotel's amenities, including a fitness trail and a pet resort. Certain packages allow you to combine your RV stay with a ride on the rails.

235 N. Grand Canyon Blvd., Williams, AZ 86046. www.thetrain.com. *©* **800/843-8724** or 928/635-4010. Fax 928/635-2180. 298 units. May 15–Oct 14 $169 and up double, $229 suite; Oct 15–May 14 $109 and up double, $159 suite. AE, DISC, MC, V. **Amenities:** 2 restaurants; lounge; exercise room; Jacuzzi; indoor pool; Wi-Fi in lobby (free). *In room:* A/C, TV.

Grand Living Bed & Breakfast   The most striking element of this Victorian country–style home is the wood: walls of lodgepole pine, bamboo floors, and cherry and oak antiques. Each of the guest rooms on the first floor has large windows, a ceiling fan, a private bath with a claw-foot tub and shower (a Jacuzzi in the **Orchid room**), and a private entrance with a screen door that opens onto the lodge's wraparound veranda. There's another guest room as well as a two-room suite on the second floor that has a 2-night minimum stay and sleeps up to four. The gourmet breakfast includes fresh fruits, baked goods, and a creative egg dish. The owners will help guests arrange horseback riding, rafting, and guided tours. Ask about multinight discounts.

701 Quarterhorse (near Rodeo Rd.), Williams, AZ 86046. www.grandlivingbnb.com. *©* **800/210-5908** or 928/635-4171. Fax 928/635-2920. 6 units. $140–$170 double; $190–$290 suite. Rates include breakfast. AE, DISC, MC, V. No children 9 or under permitted. *In room:* TV w/DVD or VCR, radio/CD player, hair dryer, Wi-Fi (free).

MODERATE

Recommended midpriced chain hotels in Williams include **Quality Inn,** 1029 N. Grand Canyon Blvd. (off I-40 exit 163; *©* **928/635-9888**); **Quality Inn Mountain Ranch Resort,** 6701 E. Mountain Ranch Rd. (6 miles east of Williams on I-40, exit 171; *©* **928/635-2693**); and **Holiday Inn Williams,** 950 N. Grand Canyon Blvd. (off I-40 exit 163; *©* **928/635-4114**). Rates range from $89 to $129 for double occupancy.

Canyon Motel & RV Park 🏊 ☺   Kevin and Shirley Young have lovingly restored their 18 historic flagstone cottages as well as the adorable guest rooms in two **Santa Fe cabooses** and one former **Grand Canyon Railway coach car.** From the outside, the cabooses resemble, well, cabooses, only with private decks. They even sit on segments of train track. They are wonderful for train-loving families of up to six, with a bed for the parents in the larger section, a compact bathroom and shower, and additional beds for the kids in the caboose's cupola. The two largest guest rooms are in the Grand Canyon Railway car. Unlike the cabooses, these rooms have windows that open and enough space to accommodate a queen-size bed and a sleeper sofa. The cottage rooms are a good choice for travelers on a budget. The Youngs operate an adjacent RV park with full hookups, restrooms with showers, and laundry facilities; there are also a handful of tent sites.

1900 E. Rodeo Rd., Williams, AZ 86046-9527. www.thecanyonmotel.com. © 800/482-3955 or 928/635-9371. Fax 928/635-4138. 18 cottage units (10 with shower only), 5 train-car units, 47 RV spaces, 8 tent sites. Cottage unit $44–$78 double; train-car unit $78–$105 double; caboose $160 double; RV space with full hookup $32–$35 for up to 4 people; tent site $25–$28. DISC, MC, V. **Amenities:** Indoor pool (may close seasonally). *In room:* A/C (11 units), TV, fridge (18 units), no phone, Wi-Fi (free).

The Red Garter Bed & Bakery ★★ 🍴
In the early 1900s, this Victorian Romanesque building had a brothel upstairs, a saloon downstairs, and an opium den in the back. The innkeeper, John Holst, has worked hard to preserve the building, built in 1897, and its colorful history. Using early family and city records, he's fleshed out the building's bawdy history, which he gladly shares with visitors. Each of the four guest rooms has custom moldings, a 12-foot-high ceiling, a ceiling fan, and antique furnishings. My favorite guest room, the **Best Gals' Room,** overlooks Route 66 and is the largest and most luxurious of the four. Its two adjoining rooms were once reserved for the brothel's "best gals," who would lean out of the double-hung windows to flag down customers. An evaporative cooler helps keep temperatures down in the house during summer. The first floor bakery and gift shop sells fresh baked goods and kitschy souvenirs.

137 W. Railroad Ave. (P.O. Box 95), Williams, AZ 86046. www.redgarter.com. © 800/328-1484 or 928/635-1484. 4 units, 3 with shower only. $135–$160 double. Rates include continental breakfast. DISC, MC, V. Closed Mon–Fri Dec–Jan. *In room:* TV, no phone.

INEXPENSIVE

Inexpensive chain hotels in Williams include **Travelodge,** 430 E. Rte. 66 (© 928/635-2651); **Motel 6 East,** 710 W. Rte. 66 (© 928/635-4464); and **Motel 6 West,** 831 W. Rte. 66 (© 928/635-9000). Rates range from $66 to $79 for double occupancy.

El Rancho Motel 🔑
It's sure not much from the outside, but this two-story 1966 motel, between the eastbound and westbound lanes of Route 66, is one of the best lodging values in Williams. Guests can swim in the outdoor pool, cook on barbecue grills, or recline in the spotless rooms, which come with a host of amenities. The only drawback is the proximity of certain rooms to the noisy westbound traffic. As for decor, one owner aptly describes it as "blue." In other words, there's just not much to say about it.

617 E. Rte. 66, Williams, AZ 86046. ☏ **928/635-2552.** Fax 928/635-4173. 25 units. Winter $42–$58 double; summer $58–$88 double. AE, DISC, MC, V. 1 small pet allowed per room for $5 extra. **Amenities:** Outdoor pool (seasonal). *In room:* A/C, Direct TV, fridge, Wi-Fi (free).

Where to Eat

Cruisers Cafe 66 ☺ AMERICAN   Built in an old Route 66 gas station, this restaurant is jammed with gas-station memorabilia, including stamped glass, filling-station signs, vintage gas pumps, and photos of classic service stations. It's exactly what you would expect from a family-run cafe along Route 66. Served up with plenty of napkins as well as drinks in unbreakable plastic mugs, the road-house-style food will fuel you for days to come. Start with the appetizer sampler—wings, chicken strips, mozzarella sticks, and fried mushrooms—served on a real automobile hubcap. The grilled burgers are tasty, but the best choice, if you really want to fill up, is the pork-back ribs. Healthier options include vegetarian fajitas, meatless lasagna, and chicken breast sandwiches. Live music is offered nightly in high season, and you may want to accompany your meal with a beer from the Grand Canyon Brewery (located right behind Cruisers Cafe). Free Wi-Fi is available in the restaurant.

233 W. Rte. 66, Williams. ☏ **928/635-2445.** www.cruisers66.com. Reservations not accepted. Lunch and dinner $9–$21. AE, DISC, MC, V. Daily 11am–10pm (may vary seasonally).

Pine Country Restaurant ⚑ AMERICAN   Many locals who dine at this recently expanded restaurant in downtown Williams eat their pie first, *then* order dinner. One taste of any of the almost 50 varieties of fresh-baked pie, including unusual flavors such as banana chocolate peanut butter or cookies n' cream, will convince you that the pie-eaters have their priorities straight. But pie (about $5 a piece) is just a slice of the offerings here. Dinner entrees, such as country-fried steak, grilled shrimp skewers, and rotisserie chicken, are moderately priced and taste home-cooked. The lunch menu mostly consists of burgers, hot sandwiches, and salads. My favorite: the turkey melt with bacon, green chilis, and Swiss cheese on grilled sourdough. A country gift store is attached.

107 N. Grand Canyon Blvd., Williams. ☏ **928/635-9718.** www.pinecountry restaurant.com. Reservations accepted. Breakfast $5–$8; lunch $6–$8; dinner $10–$22. AE, DISC, MC, V. Daily 6am–9pm.

Red Raven ★★ STEAKS/SEAFOOD   This dimly lit dining room, owned by David and Dusty Haines, is the best restaurant in town. The narrow, high-ceilinged room has tables and booths, original art, and decorative plates on the walls. For lunch, the eclectic menu includes wraps and fresh salads; the ginger beef salad includes a thinly sliced charbroiled steak on a bed of lettuce with a homemade ginger-sesame dressing. Among the most creative dinner plates are the basil-butter salmon, 12-ounce Angus steak smothered in a rich mushroom-onion sauce, and charbroiled pork medallions topped with a homemade cilantro pesto. Dinners include soup or salad and fresh bread. Despite the upscale surroundings, most patrons come dressed casually. Wine-lovers will appreciate the thoughtful selections. It's impressive to find a restaurant this good in such a small town.

135 W. Rte. 66. ✆ **928/635-4980.** Reservations accepted. Lunch $8–$10; dinner $11–$22. AE, DISC, MC, V. Summer daily 11am–2pm and 5–9:30pm; winter Tues-Sun 11am–2pm and 5–9pm.

Rod's Steak House ★ STEAKHOUSE   If you're a steak lover, brake for the cow-shaped sign on Route 66 as if it were real livestock. This landmark Route 66 restaurant, which sprawls across a city block between the highway's east- and westbound lanes, has hardly changed since Rodney Graves, an early member of the U.S. Geological Survey, opened it in 1946. It's almost always crowded. Printed on a paper cutout of a cow, the fold-out menu is still only about 6 inches across—more than enough space for its laconic descriptions of the restaurant's offerings. The best steaks include the 16-ounce T-bone, New York strip, and filet mignon (the prime rib, available in different portions, is also terrific). Non–meat eaters should consider the mesquite-broiled mountain trout. Delicious homemade rolls taste like biscuits, and the perennial winner for dessert is mud pie. Expect generous cocktails from the barman.

301 E. Rte. 66, Williams. ✆ **928/635-2671.** Reservations accepted. Entrees $13–$42. AE, DISC, MC, V. Mon-Sat 11am–9:30pm. Closed Sun and first 2 weeks of Jan.

Rosa's Cantina MEXICAN   You might giggle at the sight of inflatable beer bottles hanging from the roof and tableside salt and pepper served in Corona bottles, but don't come to Rosa's for its ambience. Rather, come to feast on traditional Mexican food that, given this is a cowboy town, deserves a high score. Concentrate on the delightful tastes of fajitas, enchiladas, and chiles rellenos; the best dish is the Steak Diablo, a 10-ounce New York strip served with rice, beans, and a devilish jalapeño sauce. Don't forget to order a side of fresh guacamole, or to cool down with one of 11 colorful margaritas. Happy hour is Tuesday through Saturday, 4 to 7pm.

411 N. Grand Canyon Blvd., Williams. ✆ **928/635-0708.** Reservations accepted. Entrees $8–$16. AE, DISC, MC, V. Tues-Thurs 11am–9pm; Fri-Sat 11am–10pm; Sun 11am–8pm. Closed Mon.

CAMERON

54 miles north of Flagstaff on U.S. 89; 30 min. from Desert View and the park's eastern entrance

One of the few authentic trading posts that remain in the Southwest, Cameron is a convenient place to stay if you plan on entering from and exploring the eastern end of the Grand Canyon or visiting destinations in the Navajo Nation.

What to See & Do

The **Cameron Trading Post,** 1 mile north of the crossroads town of Cameron (where Hwy. 64 to Grand Canyon Village branches off U.S. 89 on the Navajo Reservation; ℂ **877/221-0690** or 928/679-2231), merits a stop. Native Americans still sell and trade crafts, livestock, wool, and other goods for merchandise and groceries in the mercantile section of the trading post. When here, be sure to visit the original stone trading post (there's also a small general store attached that sells groceries and sundries). Built in the 1910s, this historic building now houses a Collector's Gallery of museum-quality Native American artifacts, including clothing and jewelry. Even if you don't have $10,000 or $15,000 to drop on an old rug or basket, you can still look around. The main trading post is a more modern building and is Northern Arizona's largest trading post. If you shop here, you will probably pay a little more than you should. You may be able to negotiate up to a 20% discount, especially if you're staying at the motel, but the prices remain high. I prefer taking my chances at the **open-air stands** scattered along highways 64 and 89, where you can sometimes chat with the artists or their families.

Where to Stay

Cameron Trading Post Motel ★   Consider staying here if you want to visit the Canyon's eastern end or are headed between the South and North Rim when the hour's getting late. Each guest room features baby-blue bedding and Southwestern-style furnishings, many of them handmade by the motel's staff. The motel's **Hopi building** borders a terraced garden with stone picnic tables, a fountain, and a large grill. Ask for a room on the second floor of the Hopi or **Apache building** to get the best view. Next to the motel, **Cameron Trading Post RV Park** offers full hookups for $25 per night, but no restrooms or showers.

P.O. Box 339 (54 miles north of Flagstaff on Hwy. 89, and 1 mile north of the east Grand Canyon Desert View access road), Cameron, AZ 86020. www.cameron tradingpost.com. ℂ **877/221-0690** or 928/679-2231. Fax 928/679-2350. 66 units. June 1–Oct 19 $99–$109 double, $149–$179 suite; Oct 20–Dec 31 $69–$79 double; Jan 1–Mar 1 $59–$69 double; Mar 2–May 30 $79–$89 double. AE, DC, DISC, MC, V. Pets accepted for $15 extra. **Amenities:** Restaurant (see below). *In room:* A/C, TV, hair dryer, Wi-Fi (free).

Where to Eat

Cameron Trading Post Dining Room REGIONAL   This tin-ceilinged dining room features a grand fireplace, Native American wall rugs, mahogany wood, and antique Tiffany glass. The eclectic menu draws upon Navajo, Southwest, and Mexican cultures. As one might guess, the Navajo dishes are the tastiest—particularly the hot beef sandwich and the signature Navajo fry bread tacos, which come packed with beef, chili beans, mild green chilis, lettuce, cheese, and tomato (the regular order is enormous, and the so-called "mini" order is still too much for most individuals). Vegetarian fry bread tacos are also available. A taste of the seafood, meanwhile, might remind you that the ocean is far away. The menu states unapologetically that no substitutes are allowed. There's also a children's menu.

On U.S. 89, Cameron. 🕐 **800/338-7385** or 928/679-2231. Reservations not accepted. Breakfast $7–$12; lunch $8–$13; dinner $9–$24. AE, DC, DISC, MC, V. Summer daily 6am–10pm; winter daily 7am–9pm.

TOWNS & OUTPOSTS NEAR THE NORTH RIM

The area surrounding the Grand Canyon north of the Colorado River is one of the most sparsely populated—and scenic—in the continental U.S. Highway 89A crosses the Colorado River at the Grand Canyon's northeastern tip—just 5 miles downstream of **Lees Ferry,** where most canyon river trips begin. Continuing west from the bridge on Highway 89A, you'll pass three lonely lodges—**Marble Canyon Lodge, Lees Ferry Lodge,** and **Cliff Dwellers Lodge**—each separated by a few miles, at the base of the aptly named Vermilion Cliffs.

This eerie desert landscape, featuring balancing rocks and other striking landforms, gives way to forest when you begin the 4,800-foot vertical climb from the Marble Platform to the Kaibab Plateau. Because the area surrounding the park's North Rim is largely national forest, you may have to travel some distance if you fail to find a room inside the park. The closest lodging to the park's northern entrance is at **Kaibab Lodge,** 18 miles north of the North Rim on Highway 67 (see below), and at **Jacob Lake Inn,** 44 miles north of the North Rim (see below). If those two lodges are full, you may have to travel as far north as Fredonia, Arizona, or Kanab, Utah, to find a room.

Where to Stay & Eat
NEAR THE PARK

Jacob Lake Inn   In 1922, Harold and Nina Bowman bought a barrel of gas and opened a gas "stand" near the present-day site of this inn. Seven years later, they built the inn at the junction of highways 67 and 89A, about an hour drive from the closest viewpoint on the North Rim. Today, Jacob Lake Inn is the main hub of activity between the North Rim and Kanab, Utah. To serve the growing summer crowds, the Bowmans' descendants and their friends travel south from their homes in Utah. Together, they run the inn's various businesses: the bakery, which churns out excellent fresh-baked cookies and pies; the soda fountain, which serves milkshakes made from soft-serve ice cream; and the gift shop, which features some high-quality pieces by Native American artists. There's also a restaurant, motel, and full-service gas station.

Lodgers can choose between inn rooms, motel units, and cabins. In 2006, a two-story stone and wood "hotel" building was added; it has country-style rooms with a king or two queen beds and small balconies with views of the surrounding ponderosa pines. Though pleasant inside, the motel rooms in the front building are not nearly as peaceful as the rooms and cabins behind the lodge. The bathrooms have showers but no tubs, and many of them drain onto the same tile floor as the bathroom itself—a curious design. Most people prefer the rustic cabins (closed in winter), which cost less than the motel rooms and have private porches.

The **Jacob Lake restaurant,** with a U-shaped counter and dining room, serves burgers, sandwiches, and steaks, but the most appetizing entree is the fresh trout cooked in the Dutch-style oven. A potent lunch item is the Grand Bull, a thick ground beef sandwich with grilled onions, chilis, cheese, mushrooms, tomatoes, and bacon. Even if you don't need a meal, it's worth stopping at Jacob Lake Inn to buy a few home-baked cookies, a piece of pie, or a milkshake.

Junction of Hwy. 67 and 89A, Jacob Lake, AZ 86022. www.jacoblake.com. ✆ **928/643-7232.** Fax 928/643-7235. 24 hotel units, 12 motel units, 27 cabins (shower only). May 14–Nov 30 $89–$138 double; Dec 1–May 13 $65–$75 double. Pets accepted for $10 extra. **Amenities:** Restaurant; bakery; Wi-Fi (free) in public areas. *In room:* No phone (motels and cabins only).

Kaibab Lodge   Open from mid-May (the opening date is weather-dependent) to November 2, Kaibab Lodge feels as warm and comfortable as a beloved summer camp. It has an open-framed ceiling and enormous pine beams that date from its construction in the 1920s. Guests tend to congregate in front of the 5-foot-wide fireplace (on Adirondack-style chairs), in the small television room, or at the tables across from the counter that doubles as the front desk and the beer bar.

Each cabinlike building houses two to four of the guest rooms, each of which sleep from two to five people. The rooms are spare but clean, with paneling of rough-hewn pine. Most have showers but not tubs, and there are no in-room phones or TVs. Because the older units' walls are very thin, it's best just to share a cabin with friends. Just a short distance from the highway, the rooms open onto the soothing, broad expanse of DeMotte Park, one of the large, naturally occurring meadows on the Kaibab Plateau.

HC 64, Box 30 (26 miles south of Jacob Lake on Hwy. 67, and 5 miles north of North Rim park entrance), Fredonia, AZ 86022. www.kaibablodge.com. ☎ **928/638-2389.** Fax 928/638-9864. 31 units. $95–$180 double. DISC, MC, V. Pets allowed (in some rooms). **Amenities:** Restaurant; bar; Wi-Fi (free) in public areas. *In room:* No phone.

NEAR LEES FERRY

Cliff Dwellers Lodge ★ ▮▮ The pace at this lodge is very relaxing, making it my favorite place to sleep in this area. Cliff Dwellers Lodge sits in the most spectacular setting in the Marble Canyon area. It's just a few hundred yards from an eye-catching area of balancing rocks (formed when boulders, having toppled off the nearby Vermilion Cliffs, "capped" the softer soil directly underneath them, thereby slowing its erosion). In the 1920s, against the side of one of these boulders, two former New Yorkers built a house and began serving dinner and drinks to the occasional passerby. Known simply as **Old Cliff Dwellers,** the house still stands—barely.

The "new" Cliff Dwellers, which dates from the '50s, is set back 50 yards or so from the highway, so the rooms are very quiet. Unless you strongly prefer a bathtub to a shower, ask for a room in one of the older buildings, some of which have carports and recessed patios. My favorite rooms are in the oldest building. They have wood paneling, even on the ceilings and in the bathrooms, which look a bit like saunas. Cliff Dwellers also rents a nearby, three-bedroom house for $200 per night.

The lodge's casual **Cliff Restaurant ★★** (open 6am–9pm in summer; reduced hours in low season) serves what's arguably the best food along this stretch of Highway 89A, with an outstanding chef who prepares creative specials. It's a favorite among rafters and fishers and has an inviting outdoor veranda. The ribs are among the tastiest you'll find anywhere, and I also recommend the wild Alaskan salmon, beef Angus burger, or any of the signature salads. Also on the premises: **Lees Ferry Anglers Fly Shop** and a liquor store.

HC 67-30 (9 miles west of Navajo Bridge on N. Hwy. 89A), Marble Canyon, AZ 86036. www.cliffdwellerslodge.com. ✆ **800/962-9755** or 928/355-2261. Fax 928/355-2271. 20 units. $80–$90 double. AE, DISC, MC, V. **Amenities:** Restaurant. *In room:* A/C (or evaporative cooler), TV, no phone, Wi-Fi (free).

Lees Ferry Lodge ★ Some of the world's best porch-sitting can be enjoyed on the patios outside of this 1929 lodge's low sandstone buildings (a popular stopping place for trout fishers trying their luck above Lees Ferry). The patios, like those at nearby Cliff Dwellers, afford stunning views south across the highway toward the greenish-pink Marble Platform or north to the Vermilion Cliffs. Though the motel sits close to the road, traffic is slow at night. The older rooms, which are small and rustic, have been redecorated in themes ranging from cowboy to—yes—fish. Double rooms in newer, prefab style buildings are available for groups of up to five people.

After rigging boats for trips down the Colorado, many river guides come to the restaurant here, the **Vermilion Cliffs Bar & Grill ★** (open 6:30am–9pm in summer; reduced hours in low season), and not just because it stocks roughly 85 types of domestic and imported beers. The specialty baby back ribs with homemade barbecue sauce taste fabulous, and the chef also prepares excellent hand-cut steaks, including New York strip. The staff provides low-key service in a dining room whose wood walls, tables, chairs, and bar all seem to have been hewn from the same tree. The restaurant can be very crowded at dinnertime during peak fishing periods (generally fall and spring). **Grand Circle Field School** (www.grandcirclefieldschool.org) also runs multiday classes from the lodge about the area's history, flora, fauna, and more.

HC 67-Box 1 (4 miles west of Navajo Bridge on N. Hwy. 89A), Marble Canyon, AZ 86036. www.leesferrylodge.com. ✆ **928/355-2231.** 10 units. $80 double. AE, MC, V. Pets accepted. **Amenities:** Excellent restaurant; bar. *In room:* A/C, no phone.

Marble Canyon Lodge As the closest accommodations to Lees Ferry, this lodge frequently fills up with rafters eagerly awaiting the journey into the canyon or fishermen stocking up for their next excursion. The traffic gives the place a busier, less personal feel than the nearby Cliff Dwellers and Lees Ferry lodges. The rooms here vary, but the ones in the 300 building are brightest and look out at Echo Cliffs. A restaurant and lounge are on the premises, and the lodge also has a selection of unusual books about the region as well as a jewelry store selling handmade silver, copper, and brass designs. Marble Canyon Lodge also rents eight two-bedroom apartments at prices ranging from $134 to $150. Hunting and fishing licenses are sold here. Service is generally so-so.

P.O. Box 6001 (¼ mile west of Navajo Bridge on Hwy. 89A), Marble Canyon, AZ 86036. www.marblecanyoncompany.com. © **800/726-1789** or 928/355-2225. Fax 928/355-2227. 55 units. $75–$85 double. AE (lodge only), DISC, MC, V. **Amenities:** Restaurant; lounge; Wi-Fi in lobby (free). *In room:* A/C, TV, no phone.

KANAB, UTAH ★

78 miles NW of Grand Canyon National Park; 80 miles south of Bryce Canyon National Park; 42 miles east of Zion National Park; 202 miles east of Las Vegas; 312 miles south of Salt Lake City

The Navajo ran off the first Mormon settlers in this area. The second group, who arrived in the 1870s, managed to stick around. Brigham Young himself surveyed Kanab's land and helped lay out its downtown, which remains largely unchanged and has just one streetlight. For years, Kanab survived on ranching alone. Later, in the 1960s, uranium mining boosted the economy. So did film crews who shot Westerns in the spectacular red-rock canyons that surround the town. Each August brings the Western Legends Roundup (www.westernlegendsroundup.com) in which some of the old cowboy stars return to Kanab for a few festival days. Today, tourism drives the economy; travelers stay here while visiting the Grand Canyon (though not in winter, when access to the North Rim is closed), Bryce and Zion parks, Lake Powell, Pipe Spring, Cedar Breaks, and the comparatively new **Grand Staircase–Escalante National Monument** (p. 150)—all within a 90-minutes drive or less from Kanab. The town doesn't have a single bar that serves liquor (although a few restaurants managed to obtain a liquor license), but the people are friendly, the food wholesome, and the nights serene. Seven miles south of Kanab is the smaller town of Fredonia, Arizona. It's not much to look at, but it does have a bar or two.

Caution: Do not speed in Kanab; the police are notorious for giving tickets.

Essentials

GETTING THERE   The only way to reach Kanab easily is by automobile. The nearest car-rental agencies are in St. George, Utah; Cedar City, Utah; and Page, Arizona. The nearest airports are in St. George and Page. Kanab is on U.S. 89 at the junction of U.S. 89A, which crosses into Arizona just 7 miles south of town. To reach Kanab from the North Rim, travel 44 miles north on Highway 67 to Jacob Lake, then go 29 miles northwest on Highway 89A. Allow about 2 hours to get to the first viewpoint on the North Rim from Kanab.

GETTING AROUND   Kanab's center is where Center and Main streets intersect. U.S. 89 comes in from the north on 300

West Street, turns east onto Center Street, south again on 100 East Street, and finally east again on 300 South. U.S. 89A follows 100 East Street south to the airport and, after about 7 miles, to the smaller town of Fredonia, Arizona.

VISITOR INFORMATION The **Kane County Office of Tourism,** 78 S. 100 E., Kanab, UT 84741 (✆ **800/733-5263** or 435/644-5033; www.kaneutah.com), provides information about the surrounding national parks, maps (of highways, hiking trails, and ATV routes), and details (including exhibits) of Kanab's many movie sets. It's open in summer Monday through Friday from 9am to 7pm and Saturday from 9am to 6pm; hours vary in other seasons.

SUPERMARKETS **Glazier's Market,** 264 S. 100 E. (✆ **435/644-5029**), is open Monday through Saturday 7am to 10pm (Sun 8am–8pm). A slightly larger store, **Honey's Marketplace,** 260 E. 300 S. (✆ **435/644-5877**), is open daily 7am to 10pm.

What to See & Do

Kanab's citizens are starting to acknowledge the existence of the sprawling, but still undeveloped, 1.9-million-acre **Grand Staircase–Escalante National Monument** ★★, whose southwest boundary stretches to within just a few miles of town. The monument's western section contains the **Grand Staircase**—formed by spectacular sandstone cliffs stretching between the Bryce and Grand canyons—while the eastern portion includes the **Escalante River,** which cuts through many side canyons on its way from the town of Escalante toward Lake Powell.

Before venturing into this mazelike country, gather maps and information from locals about roads and trails. **Grand Staircase–Escalante National Monument/Kanab Visitor Center,** 745 E. Hwy. 89 (✆ **435/644-4680**), sells USGS and topographic maps of the area, and its friendly staff can help you plan your excursion. It's open daily from 8am to 4:30pm.

If you're considering hiking, stop at **Willow Canyon Outdoor,** 263 S. 100 E. (✆ **435/644-8884**). The shop's friendly staff dispenses advice, maps, outdoor gear, books (including area guidebooks), and a variety of coffees. Hours vary.

So far, few areas are developed for visitors to this rugged desert landscape, where erosion has carved out narrow canyons, broad mesas, amphitheaters, spires, and arches. There are, however, a few bumpy, beautiful roads and many tantalizing places to hike (you'll need a 4WD to access much of the area). Highway 12 between Boulder and Tropic (both in Utah), crosses the north end of Grand Staircase–Escalante National Monument, and Highway 89 between Kanab, Utah, and Page, Arizona, clips the monument's southernmost tip. Linking these highways are a number of gravel roads, which travel through the heart of the monument.

If your aim is simply to cross the monument's boundary, drive 12 miles east of Kanab on Highway 89. To really experience it, however, do one of the following: Eight miles east of Kanab on Highway 89, turn north on Johnson Canyon Road. After 16 miles, turn right onto the gravel **Skutumpah Road,** which leads to some of the best areas for hiking in the area—not to mention incredible scenery. Or, visit the **Toadstools**—an area of hoodoos and balancing rocks near the Paria Contact Station, 43 miles east of Kanab on Highway 89.

A few miles north of the Toadstools is **Cottonwood Road,** which is my favorite drive here, leading north past remarkable geological formations into Grand Staircase–Escalante National Monument. You'll reach **Cannonville** after 56 miles, where there's a visitor center, excellent hiking trails, and picnic spots.

Frontier Movie Town ☺ Come here to see sections of original movie sets from Westerns shot around Kanab, to dress up as a cowboy or cowgirl, and to admire the many autographed photos of actors who visited Kanab while filming their flicks. On nights when groups are visiting, employees dress in period clothing and stage a Wild West drama that culminates in a deafening shootout. Because most of the participants in this drama are pulled from the audience, the acting is as wooden as on the USA Network, but your kids won't care. Best of all, it's free. There's also a Western museum with movie memorabilia and a gift shop, while an outdoor snack shack serves buffalo wings and burgers; an ice cream parlor fulfills dessert cravings.

297 W. Center St., Kanab. ℰ **435/644-5337.** www.frontiermovietown.com. Free admission. Summer daily 8am–10pm; rest of year daily 10am–6pm.

Where to Stay

Kanab has one chain hotel that's very good and slightly more expensive than the others: **Holiday Inn Express and Suites,** 217 S. 100 E. (ℰ **877/320-8454** or 435/644-3100). It also has a number of more inexpensive hotels. Consider **Shilo Inn Kanab,** 296 W. 100 N. (ℰ **800/222-2244** or 435/644-2562), or **Comfort Inn,** 815 E. Hwy. 89 (ℰ **435/644-8888**). For a comfortable, inexpensive campground smack in downtown with tent and RV spaces as well as a few log cabins, try **Hitch N' Post,** 196 E. 300 S. (ℰ **435/644-2142**).

Best Western Red Hills ★ Compared to Kanab's limited and rather aged motel collection, this Best Western stands out as a modern, inviting place to rest your head. The fairly standard rooms are decorated with Southwestern art prints. Choose a room with a king or two queen-size beds; the larger family suites are only slightly more expensive. This property is within easy walking distance of downtown Kanab.

125 W. Center St., Kanab, UT 84741. www.bestwesternredhills.com. © **800/830-2675** or 435/644-2675. Fax 435/644-5919. 75 units. Apr 15–Oct 31 $90–$115 double; Nov 1–Apr 14 $65–$80 double. Price includes breakfast buffet. AE, DC, DISC, MC, V. 1 small pet per room for $10 extra. **Amenities:** Jacuzzi; small heated outdoor pool (seasonal). *In room:* A/C, TV, fridge, hair dryer, Wi-Fi (free).

Parry Lodge   Many of the older rooms (known as "movie units") in this 1929 colonial-style lodge display plaques bearing the names of stars (Dean Martin, Gregory Peck, and Sammy Davis, Jr., among others) who stayed in them while filming Westerns here. One unit (no. 134) was built specially to house Frank Sinatra's mother-in-law while the famed crooner starred in *Sergeants Three* (Sinatra stayed in room no. 127). The movie units are smaller and closer to Center Street than the motel's newer rooms, but they're far more charming. Most have tile floors in the bathroom, feature classic American furnishings, and are shaded by hardwood trees. A buffet breakfast is available, and the restaurant remains a popular dining spot in summer, when old Western films are also played.

89 E. Center St., Kanab, UT 84741. www.parrylodge.com. © **800/748-4104** or 435/644-2601. Fax 435/644-2605. 89 units. May 1–Oct 31 $70–$120 double; Nov 1–Apr 30 $49–$69 double. AE, DISC, MC, V. Pets accepted for $10 extra. **Amenities:** Restaurant (seasonal); heated outdoor pool (seasonal); Wi-Fi (free). *In room:* A/C, TV.

The Victorian Inn ★★   Previously a Clarion hotel, this fully refurbished Victorian-style inn offers the city's most upscale accommodations with 1890s decor and Ethan Allen furniture. There's also an inviting wraparound porch for afternoon relaxation. A friendly staff tends to the inn, offering a full-menu breakfast. Guest rooms include fireplaces and Jacuzzis; the honeymoon suite has a four-poster bed. The Victorian Inn offers convenient access to the North Rim, and also serves as a romantic getaway on its own.

190 N. Hwy. 89, Kanab, UT 84741. www.victorianinn.com. © **435/644-8660.** Fax 435/644-8659. 28 units. $69–$159 double. Rates include full breakfast. AE, DISC, MC, V. Pets accepted for $20 extra. **Amenities:** Fitness center; computer with Internet and printer for guest use (free). *In room:* Flatscreen TV, Wi-Fi (free).

Where to Eat

Escobar's Mexican Restaurant MEXICAN   There's not much to make you feel like you're in Mexico here save for a few shiny sombreros and toy chili peppers dangling from the ceiling. But this ultra-casual Kanab favorite (indeed, sometimes as many kids as adults are in the small dining room) serves Mexican food far more authentic than what you might expect to find in Utah. The best breakfast dishes include *huevos rancheros,* Mexican omelets, and scrambled eggs with *chorizo* (Mexican sausage). For lunch and dinner, big burritos come stuffed with beef, chicken, pork, *carne asada,* or veggies, and a variety of combination dishes let you mix and match tacos, enchiladas, chiles rellenos, or tostados at will. The guacamole is prepared with fresh avocados, and the beer is served as it should be—in a frosty mug. Note that Escobar's is closed Saturday.

373 E. 300 S. ⓒ **435/644-3739.** Reservations not accepted. Breakfast $6-$7; lunch $3-$7; dinner $8-$16. AE, DISC, MC, V. Sun-Fri 11am-9:30pm. Closed mid-Dec to mid-Jan.

Houston's Trails' End Restaurant ★ AMERICAN

Generations of ranchers have eaten in this Old West restaurant, as evidenced by the rifles, branding irons, and spurs hanging on the walls. While country music plays over the stereo, waitresses wearing toy weapons serve up meaty dishes, including the house specialty, chicken-fried steak topped with country gravy. For something a bit more exotic, order the honey-jalapeño pork tenderloin off the newspaper-style menu. The soup is made fresh daily, as are the enormous yeast rolls that come with dinner. Breakfast includes a selection of omelets, while for lunch I find the zesty Southwest chicken salad most delicious. Veggie options include wraps and quesadillas. Domestic and imported beers are available (as they're often not in Utah restaurants), and a small gift shop is attached to the dining room.

32 E. Center St. ⓒ **435/644-2488.** Reservations accepted. Breakfast $4-$12; lunch $9-$12; dinner $10-$23. AE, DISC, MC, V. Daily 7am-10pm. Closed mid-Nov to mid-Mar.

Jakey Leigh's COFFEE

This casual cafe and bakery serves gourmet coffees and homemade cookies and pastries, as well as made-to-order sandwiches. Breakfast items include bagels, muffins, and breakfast burritos. Free Wi-Fi is provided to patrons.

4 E. Center St. ⓒ **435/644-8191.** Coffee $1.75-$4.50; breakfast $2.50-$7; lunch around $6. MC, V. Daily 7am-3pm.

Rewind Diner AMERICAN

Betty Boop, along with a sign that reads, "Here, not everything is black and white," greets you outside of this small, traditional roadside diner, while a morbid-looking mannequin in the shape of a hunchback greets you just inside. The atmosphere is friendly and the cooking dependably good. As you might expect from a '50s-style diner, the entire joint is colored in red, white, and black, and consists of barstools and table booths. The menu features a tempting collection of flavorful sandwiches and gourmet hamburgers (like the surf 'n turf burger with steak and shrimp), along with bigger dishes such as baby back ribs, grilled salmon, and a popcorn shrimp basket. Everything here is made from scratch, except for the all-natural ice cream from Dreyer's. The fries have zero grams of trans fat, and there's a full vegetarian menu. The diner offers free Wi-Fi.

18 E. Center St. 🕿 **435/644-3200.** Reservations not accepted. Lunch and dinner (same menu) $6–$19. AE, DISC, MC, V. Tues–Thurs 11am–8:30pm; Fri 11am–9pm; Sat 5:30–9pm. Closed Sun–Mon.

Rocking V Café ★★ ECLECTIC   In 2000, Vicky Cooper left her stressful job as a TV news reporter to open this eclectic cafe, one of Kanab's best restaurants. The fresh, mostly organic menu might include chicken and mushroom Alfredo, cornmeal-crusted trout, Asian stir-fry, and Thai curry with fresh veggies. My favorite dish is the grilled buffalo tenderloin—free-range buffalo with a burgundy-balsamic reduction served with soup. Finish with the chocolate silk or Key lime pie. The restaurant occupies a glass-fronted 1892 building that has seen duty as a general store, a mortuary, a grocery, and a bank. The wine cellar occupies the old safe, and there's a gallery with local and regional art upstairs.

97 W. Center St. 🕿 **435/644-8001.** Reservations accepted. Dinner $12–$38. MC, V. Wed–Sun 5–10pm (daily in high season). Closed Nov–Feb.

HAVASU CANYON & SUPAI

70 miles north of Hwy. 66; 155 miles NW of Flagstaff; 115 miles NE of Kingman

In the heart of the 185,000-acre Havasupai Indian Reservation, south of the Colorado River in the central Grand Canyon, you'll find the town of Supai. It's nestled between Havasu Canyon's red walls, alongside the spring-fed Havasu Creek. Two miles downstream are some of the prettiest waterfalls on earth, sometimes referred to as "the turquoise waterfalls of the Grand Canyon." Although flash floods in August 2008 slightly altered the composition of some of these iconic blue falls, they remain as beautiful as ever. In order to get here, you must hike, ride a horse or mule, or take a helicopter.

Essentials

Getting There   By Car   You can't drive all the way to Supai or Havasu Canyon. The nearest road, Indian Road 18, ends 8 miles from Supai at Hualapai Hilltop, a barren parking area where the trail into the canyon begins. The turnoff for Indian Road 18 is 6 miles east of Peach Springs and 21 miles west of Seligman on Route 66. Once you're on Indian Road 18, follow it for 60 paved miles to

Hualapai Hilltop. There's no gas or water available anywhere in this area, so be sure to fill up in either Seligman or Kingman.

From Hualapai Hilltop, you can only reach Supai by helicopter, horse, mule, or foot. The helicopter to Supai takes 10 minutes; hiking takes about 4 hours each way. Visitors will then need to pay a $35 entrance fee in order to visit the waterfalls, reached by hiking a bit farther.

By Helicopter   The fastest, most expensive way to reach Havasu Canyon is by helicopter from Hualapai Hilltop (the trail head for Supai and Havasu Canyon). In fair weather conditions, **Air West** (© **623/516-2790**) generally shuttles passengers from here to Supai and back at regular intervals between 10am and 1pm every Sunday, Monday, Thursday, and Friday from March 15 to October 15, and Sunday and Friday only during the rest of the year. The $85 one-way fare (free for children under 2) is paid on the spot with cash or credit card (MC, V only). Seating is first-come, first-served, with tribe members and their goods taking priority over tourists. That means you can't rely on being able to take a helicopter into or out of Supai. Each passenger is allowed to bring one backpack weighing no more than 40 pounds. Although the trip takes only 10 minutes, the views are spectacular.

Note: Given the restricted hours of helicopter service, you should not expect to fly to Supai and back in 1 day unless you're not interested in spending any time in Supai, and even then you may still not be able to get a seat for the trip back.

By Horse or Mule   The most traditional way to get to Havasu Canyon is by horse or mule. You and your luggage can ride either to Havasupai Lodge or to the campground from Hualapai Hilltop (people usually ride horses and then have mules haul their belongings). For the 10-mile trip from Hualapai Hilltop to the campground, pack and saddle horses can be rented through the **Havasupai Tourist Office** (© **928/448-2121** or 928/448-2141), which is based in Supai. The cost is $187 round-trip, or $94 one-way. If you're only taking the 8-mile trip to the **Havasupai Lodge,** call the lodge (© **928/448-2111**) to rent your mule or horse. Round-trip fare between Hualapai Hilltop and the lodge is $135, or $80 for a one-way ride. Make reservations 2 weeks in advance.

Riders must weigh less than 250 pounds, be at least 4 feet, 7 inches tall, be comfortable around large animals, have at least a little riding experience, and be able to mount, dismount, and guide their horse unassisted. It's a good idea to wear jeans, a long-sleeve cotton shirt, and a hat or visor for the ride. Be sure to confirm your horse reservation a day before driving to Hualapai Hilltop. Sometimes no horses are available, and it's a long drive back to the nearest town. Entrance ($35 per person) and camping ($17 per person per night) fees are not included in the mule-trip price. Many people who hike into the canyon decide that it's worth the money to ride out, or at least have their backpacks packed out. Pack mules, which can carry up to four articles weighing up to 130 pounds total, are available for the same price as a mule ride. The campground's gatekeeper can usually help you arrange for a ride out.

On Foot To reach Supai on foot, follow a trail that begins at Hualapai Hilltop and descends 8 miles and about 2,000 feet to the village. It covers a shorter vertical drop than the rim-to-river trails in the canyon, but has no drinking water or restrooms until you reach town. A moderate-level hiker should allow about 3½ to 4 hours to reach Supai (a bit longer on the return). From Supai, it's another 2 miles, mostly downhill, to the campground and the waterfalls. The steepest part of the trail is the first 1.5 miles from Hualapai Hilltop. After this section, it gets relatively gradual. See "Hiking to Supai & the Waterfalls," below, for more information about the hike to Supai.

Fees & Reservations The $35-per-person entry fee to Havasu Canyon is effective year-round and can only be paid in cash.

To make lodging reservations, call **Havasupai Lodge** directly at ℂ **928/448-2111** or 928/448-2201, or send an e-mail with your requested dates to: lodge@havasupaitribe.com. For camping reservations, call ℂ **928/448-2141,** or e-mail your desired dates to touristoffice@havasupaitribe.com. If you show up in Supai without a reservation, you may be asked to hike all the way back to your car, and you may not even be allowed to pay the entrance fee needed to view the waterfalls. Be sure to get an area map and a full trail description before starting your hike. The best is the *Havasu Trail Guide,* written by Scott Thybony and published by the Grand Canyon Natural History Association.

Hiking to Supai & the Waterfalls

Initially, the surroundings on the trail to Supai from Hualapai Hilltop aren't particularly pleasant. Helicopters buzz overhead, bits of paper rot alongside the trail or hang impaled on cacti, and phone lines parallel the path. Unannounced by the wranglers trailing them, horses canter past, startling hikers.

The trail drops in switchbacks down the Coconino Sandstone cliffs below Hualapai Hilltop (this will be the most difficult segment of your hike back), then descends a long slope to the floor of Hualapai Canyon. Most of the hike consists of a descent down the gravelly, gradually sloping creek bed at the bottom of the canyon. Usually dry, this wash is prone to flash floods, so exercise caution during stormy weather. In August 2008, 8 inches of rain fell in a single weekend in the Grand Canyon. When a private dam broke, Supai Canyon was deluged, as an estimated 4,731 cubic feet of water per second rushed into the canyon, sweeping away footbridges and altering the composition of some of the waterfalls. Some 250 residents and tourists had to be evacuated during these floods.

When you reach the confluence with Havasu Canyon, go left, following Havasu Creek's blue-green waters downstream into the town of Supai. Then, when you see the two large hoodoos (rock spires) atop the red-rock walls, you'll know you're near town. The 450 Havasupai tribe members living here believe that if either rock falls, disaster will befall their people. Unconcerned, children chase each other through town, ducking barbed wire strung between sticks, cottonwood trees, and metal poles. Prefabricated wood houses, some with boarded-up windows, line the dirt paths that crisscross this sleepy community, which has a cafe, post office, small general store, church, clinic, school, and a lodge (see "Where to Stay," below).

Roughly 1½ miles past town, you'll find two small falls that have taken the place of Navajo Falls, which ceased to exist following the 2008 floods. Shortly beyond these two small waterfalls, the first significant waterfall you'll see is the 150-foot-high **Havasu Falls,** which features a breathtaking emerald-colored pool, perfect for swimming. Just past the campground, more than 10 miles from the trail head, is 300-foot-high **Mooney Falls,** named for a miner who fell to his death there in 1880. The creek's milky water seems deceptively clear where shallow. It's turquoise at deeper points and emerald at its deepest, under falls so lovely as to make a swimmer laugh with delight. The creek's whitish appearance comes from calcium carbonate, which precipitates around the falls in formations resembling enormous drooping mustaches. These formations are brownish-red because of the mud and iron oxide contained in the runoff.

Three miles past the campground is the smaller **Beaver Falls.** Below it, travertine repeatedly dams the river, forming a series of seductive swimming holes. Getting there requires doing one long, relatively tricky descent down a rock face, using a fixed rope for assistance, and several shorter climbs without ropes. Four miles past these dams, Havasu Creek empties into the Colorado River. The hike downstream from the campground involves numerous river crossings, so bring waterproof sandals in addition to hiking boots.

As you travel, remember that tourists often inundate this village, and that many of the Havasupai have grown weary of outsiders. Don't expect all of them to shout cheerful greetings on the trail.

Other Area Activities

Grand Canyon Caverns ★ ☺ In addition to visiting Havasu Canyon, you may want to tour here, the third largest dry caverns in the world. Discovered by a drunken cowboy in 1927, they are notable less for their pristine limestone formations than for their sheer size. The smallest chamber, **Chapel of the Ages,** reaches 130 yards—longer than a football field, while the second chamber, **Halls of Gold,** extends a whopping 210 yards.

Beyond their grandeur, these caverns are unique for having been dry for more than a million years, and are in fact the largest dry caverns in the U.S. Descending 21 stories (210 ft.) by elevator into the caves, you'll find a mummified bobcat preserved since 1850 by the cool, dry air and bacteria-free environment that naturally replicate the Egyptian mummification process. You'll also see a lifelike replica of a giant ground sloth to give you an idea of what it's like to stand next to an extinct Ice Age creature. While these limestone caverns were shaped by 35 million years of natural history, their recent human history is also interesting: In 1962, they served as the local Cold War fallout shelter. The gift shop here has its share of novelties, including sharks' teeth and Hoover Dam placemats. The cafeteria sells burgers and cold beer. There's also a fun, kitschy motel here, the **Grand Canyon Caverns Inn** (☎ 928/422-3223), which offers simple rooms for around $70 to $100 per night near Peach Springs. Horseback rides and jeep tours to the bottom of the Grand Canyon are now offered, as well. The inn also features a one-of-a-kind suite ($700 for up to six people) located 220 feet down in the caverns and proclaimed the "largest, oldest, darkest, quietest motel room anywhere."

Off Rte. 66 (12 miles east of Peach Springs). ☎ **928/422-3223.** www.grand canyoncaverns.com. Admission $15 adults, $10 kids 5–12, free for children 4 and under. AE, DISC, MC, V. High season daily 9am–5pm (last tour 5pm); low season daily 10am–4pm. Tours every 30 min.

Grand Canyon West ★ Grand Canyon West opened in March 2007, and a visit here requires a full day given the tricky drive to get here: Grand Canyon West is a 5-hour drive from the South Rim, and the final stretch includes 14 miles of slow, unpaved road.

The **Skywalk,** a glass bridge overlooking the western canyon, is Grand Canyon West's lead attraction. (See "Visiting the Skywalk: Is It Worth It?" below.)

Visiting the Skywalk: Is It Worth It?

Visiting the **Skywalk** isn't as easy, or inexpensive, as one might like. First off, you need a full day to come here (it's 242 miles west of the South Rim, and 121 miles east of Las Vegas). Second, you must buy the $44 basic entrance package to Grand Canyon West, plus pay the $32 fee to walk the Skywalk (for a minimum of $76 per person)—unfortunately, it's not possible to just pay for a stroll along the glass bridge. Third, you need to brave long lines at Grand Canyon West's entrance—and services that are sometimes inadequate to cater to the large crowds.

Once you've dealt with these obstacles and actually get to the Skywalk, then yes, what you find is truly remarkable. The horse-shoe-shaped glass bridge extends 70 feet out from the canyon's western edge and more than 4,000 feet above the Colorado River, giving you an eagle's-eye view of one of the world's greatest natural wonders. What you see below the glass floor is breathtaking (although it also gives you a sensation that acrophobes seldom enjoy; expect some visitors to be clinging for dear life to the railing). The bridge, made with more than a million pounds of steel, was engineered to be able to withstand winds in excess of 100 miles an hour from eight different directions, an 8.0 magnitude earthquake from anywhere within 50 miles, and up to 71 million pounds (the equivalent of 71 fully loaded Boeing 747 airplanes). Note that no personal belongings (other than one's clothes minus the shoes; little slippers are provided) are allowed on the Skywalk and must be kept in a locker at the bridge's entrance (the storage fee is included in admission). A photographer is on hand to take photos for around $10 (unfortunately you cannot take your own).

Grand Canyon West encompasses distinct areas of land belonging to the Hualapai Nation, which are connected by a free hop-on, hop-off shuttle bus (no private vehicles are allowed). These areas include **Eagle Point,** where the Skywalk is; **Indian Village,** comprised of dwellings depicting traditional tribal homes; **Guano Point,** with its panoramic views of the canyon and the Colorado River; and **Hualapai Ranch,** where you'll enjoy horse and wagon rides, cowboy demonstrations, a petting zoo, and a touristy trading post.

The required $44 Legacy Package entrance fee includes photo opportunities with Hualapai members in traditional dress and access to the hop-on, hop-off shuttle to all viewpoints. It does not include meals ($15 per person). Customers can add on to the Legacy Package by purchasing options that quickly increase the price. These include the Skywalk, horseback and wagon rides, Hummer off-road tours, helicopter and pontoon tours, whitewater rafting, and overnight accommodations. The **Hualapai Ranch** offers cabins, which accommodate visitors wishing to stay overnight in Grand Canyon West. All-inclusive tour packages from Las Vegas are also available from a variety of operators. Check the website for details regarding these various options.

Off Rte. I-40 (49 miles north of Peach Springs; 70 miles north of Kingman). From Kingman, go north on Stockton Hill Rd. (42 miles), then north on Pierce Ferry Rd. (7 miles), then east on Diamond Bar Rd. to entrance (21 miles). © **888/868-9378.** www.hualapaitourism.com. Basic entrance $44 (including taxes and fees); additional fees for Skywalk and package options. MC, V. High season daily 7:30am–6:30pm; low season daily 8am–4:30pm.

Where to Stay
IN HAVASU CANYON

Havasu Canyon Campground ★★ This riverfront campground allows you to stay up close to Supai's iconic blue waterfalls. The milky creek flows past on one side, a perfect place to cool off. Cottonwood trees and crawling grapevines provide ample shade. The ground, while dusty from heavy use, is soft enough to make for excellent tenting. And then there are the falls.

During monsoon season, pitch your tent in an area high above the creek. If you're seeking solitude, travel farther downstream from the campground's entrance. The camping area is nearly a half-mile long, and few people lug their packs all the way to the end, nearest **Mooney Falls.** However, bear in mind that you may have to walk all the way back to the entrance to find a useable toilet. Bring a water filter, as spring water should be purified before consumption.

A few important drawbacks to this campground: The crowds can be incredibly heavy on weekends. The Havasupai Tourist Enterprise allows 200 campers before cutting off reservations—this is 150 fewer than in the recent past, but still enough to crowd the place. So try to come when it's not so busy. The outhouses seldom—if ever—have paper in them. There are no showers, public phones, fire pits, or grills. Open fires are not allowed, although you can use your own propane stove. Dusty canines nap under picnic tables by day and howl at their own echoes by night. But not far beyond are the sweet sounds of the falls.

10 miles from Hualapai Hilltop on Havasu Canyon Trail. www.havasupaitribe.com. © **928/448-2141.** $35 per person entrance fee, plus $17 per person per night. An extra $5 environmental fee is charged unless you take a garbage sack back to the hilltop with you. MC, V. Year-round.

Havasupai Lodge   For a place halfway to the bottom of the Grand Canyon and 8 miles from the nearest road, this motel is probably about what you'd expect. The rooms, which open onto a grassy courtyard, have two queen beds, private bathrooms, and air-conditioning—a real blessing when the red rock walls surrounding the town begin radiating the midsummer heat. Even if there were televisions, the coolest entertainment would be the waterfalls.

   Havasupai Cafe, across from the general store, serves breakfast, lunch, and dinner. It's a casual place where people fritter away time over french fries and fry bread. The food is relatively inexpensive despite the fact that most ingredients are packed in by horse.

General Delivery, Supai, AZ 86435. www.havasupaitribe.com. © **928/448-2111.** 24 units. $145 double (up to 4 people allowed), plus $35 per person entry fee. MC, V.

NEAR HUALAPAI HILLTOP

Hualapai Lodge   On Historic Route 66 in Peach Springs, this lodge offers the chance to park yourself for the night and learn more about the Hualapai Nation, visit Grand Canyon West and its Skywalk (about a 2-hour drive from the lodge), explore the West Rim's pristine vistas, drive to the Colorado River at Diamond Creek, or take the full-day Hualapai River Runners rafting trip through the western Grand Canyon (p. 89). You'll find a tour operator in the lobby, plus a Native American gift shop and a casual (if not always efficient) restaurant. Spacious guest rooms have rustic wood furnishings, native American artwork, and granite-top bathrooms. Ask for a room on the hotel's east side, which is as far as possible from the noisy train tracks. (The front desk offers free earplugs since trains pass every 15 min.) Half-day jeep tours from the lodge to Diamond Creek are available with an on-line package.

900 Rte. 66, Peach Springs, AZ 86434. www.hualapaitourism.com. © **888/868-9378** or 928/769-2636. Fax 928/769-2372. 55 units. Mar 1–Oct 31 $100–$110 double; Nov 1–Feb 28 $80–$100 double. AE, DISC, MC, V. Continental breakfast included. **Amenities:** Restaurant; fitness center; saltwater pool & spa. *In room:* A/C, flatscreen TV, hair dryer, Wi-Fi (free).

WHERE TO EAT

Delgadillo's Snow Cap ★ 🍴 AMERICAN   I heard about Snow Cap long before I made my way over this part of Historic Route 66, and you just shouldn't miss this slice of Americana unless you are compelled for health reasons to stay away from burgers, shakes, and fries. Open since 1953 and run by the same family, you'll likely recognize this nostalgic open-air root beer stand when you see the '36 Chevy convertible out front. The hilarious owners serve, as they say, cheeseburgers with cheese, dead chickens, and other casual American favorites. When I asked for a straw for my malt, I was literally given a handful of straw. Stop here as you make your way east toward the Grand Canyon, and plan on a good hour of exercise afterward to alleviate your guilt. Be sure to check out the classic cars out back.

Historic Rte. 66, Seligman. ✆ **928/422-3291.** Menu items $2–$7. MC, V. Apr–Oct daily 10am–6pm. Closed Nov–Mar.

GRAND CANYON NATIONAL PARK IN DEPTH

8

Despite the searing summer temperatures, the desolate deserts, and the lack of water, people have been drawn to Arizona and the Grand Canyon for hundreds of years. In the 16th century, the Spanish came looking for gold but settled on saving souls. In the 19th century, despite frightful tales of spiny cactus forests, ranchers drove their cattle into the region and discovered that a few corners of the state actually had lush grasslands.

In the 1920s and 1930s, Arizona struck a new source of gold: sunshine. The railroads had made travel to the state easy, and word of the mild winter climate spread to colder corners of the nation. Today, the golden sun still lures people to Arizona.

But while the weather is a big draw, it's the Grand Canyon that attracts the most visitors to Arizona. A photograph of the Grand Canyon may tell a thousand words, but a thousand words don't even begin to tell the canyon's story, which spans almost 2 billion years.

This chapter's sections tell some of that story. "Looking Back" provides a brief history of Arizona and its Native American culture. "The Lay of the Land" discusses rock layers and how the canyon was carved. "The Flora" describes common plants, ranging from fir trees on the rims to barrel cacti on the canyon floor. "The Fauna" covers the creatures that flourish in the canyon's forbidding climes. Finally, "The Ecosystem" explores a very recent development—humans' effects on the canyon's ecology.

LOOKING BACK

EARLY HISTORY   Arizona is the site of North America's oldest cultures and one of the two longest continuously inhabited settlements in the United States—the Hopi village of Oraibi, which has had inhabitants for roughly 1,000 years. However, the region's human habitation dates back more than 11,000 years, to the time when paleo-Indians known as the Clovis people inhabited southeastern Arizona. Stone tools and arrowheads of the type credited to the Clovis have been found in southeastern Arizona, and a mammoth-kill site has become an important source of information about these people, who were among the earliest inhabitants of North America.

Few records exist of the Desert Culture in Arizona's prehistory which lasted from about 8,000 B.C. to A.D. 100, but by roughly A.D. 200, wandering bands of hunter-gatherers took up residence in Canyon de Chelly in the northern part of the state. Today these early Arizonans are known as the Ancestral Puebloans. The earliest Ancestral Puebloan period, stretching from A.D. 200 to 700, is defined as the Basket Maker period because of the large number of baskets that have been found in ruins from this time. During the Basket Maker period, the Ancestral Puebloans gave up hunting and gathering and took up agriculture, growing corn, beans, squash, and cotton on the canyon floors in northeastern Arizona.

Between 700 and 1300, during what is called the Pueblo period, the Ancestral Puebloans began building multistory pueblos and cliff dwellings. However, despite decades of research, it is still not clear why the Ancestral Puebloans began living in niches and caves high on the cliff walls of the region's canyons. It may have been to conserve farmland as their population grew and required larger harvests or for protection from flash floods. Whatever the reason the cliff dwellings were originally constructed, they were all abandoned by 1300. It's unclear why the villages were abandoned, but a study of tree rings indicates that the region experienced a severe drought between 1276 and 1299, which suggests the Ancestral Puebloans may have left in search of more fertile farmland. Keet Seel and Betatakin, at Navajo National Monument, as well as the many ruins in Canyon de Chelly, are Arizona's best-preserved Ancestral Puebloan sites.

During the Ancestral Puebloan Basket Maker period, the Sinagua culture began to develop in the fertile plateau northeast of present-day Flagstaff and southward into the Verde River valley. The Sinagua, whose name is Spanish for "without water," built their stone pueblos primarily on hills and mesas, such as those at Tuzigoot near Clarkdale and Wupatki near Flagstaff, both now preserved as national monuments. They also built cliff dwellings in such places as Walnut Canyon and Montezuma Castle, both also national monuments. By the mid–13th century, Wupatki had been abandoned, and by the early 15th century, Walnut Canyon and pueblos in the lower Verde Valley region had also been deserted.

As early as A.D. 450, the Hohokam culture, from which the Sinagua most likely learned irrigation, had begun to farm the Gila and Salt river valleys between Phoenix and Casa Grande. Over a period of 1,000 years, they constructed a 600-mile network of irrigation canals, some of which can still be seen today. However, because the Hohokam built their homes of earth, few of their ruins remain. One exception is the Casa Grande ruin, a massive earth-walled structure that has been well preserved and is now a national monument. Many Hohokam petroglyph (rock art) sites serve as a lasting reminder of the people who first made the desert flourish. By the 1450s, however, the Hohokam had abandoned their villages, and today many archaeologists believe that the irrigation of desert soil for hundreds of years may have left a thick crust of alkali in farm fields, which would have made further farming impossible. The disappearance of the Hohokam is commemorated in the tribe's name, which, in the language of today's Tohono O'odham people, means "the people who have vanished."

HISPANIC HERITAGE   The first Europeans to visit the region may have been a motley crew of shipwrecked Spaniards, among whom was a black man named Estévan de Dorantes. This unfortunate group spent 8 years wandering across the Southwest, and when they arrived back in Spanish territory, they told a fantastic story of having seen seven cities so rich that the inhabitants even decorated their doorways with jewels. No one is sure whether they actually passed through Arizona, but in 1539 their story convinced the viceroy of New Spain (Mexico) to send a small expedition, led by Father Marcos de Niza and Estévan de Dorantes, into the region. Father de Niza's report of finding the fabled Seven Cities of Cíbola inspired Don Francisco Vásquez de Coronado to set off in search of wealth in 1540. Instead of fabulously wealthy cities, however, Coronado found only pueblos of stone and mud. A subordinate expedition led by Garcia Lopez de Cárdenas stumbled upon the Grand Canyon, while another group of Coronado's men, led by Don Pedro de Tovar, visited the Hopi mesas.

In the 150 years that followed, only a handful of Spanish explorers, friars, and settlers visited Arizona. In the 1580s and 1600s, Antonio de Espejo and Juan de Oñate explored northern and central Arizona and found indications that mineral riches existed in the region. In the 1670s, the Franciscans founded several missions

A native AMERICAN CRAFTS PRIMER

The Four Corners region is taken up almost entirely by the Navajo and Hopi reservations, so Native American crafts are ubiquitous. You'll see jewelry for sale by the side of desolate roads, Navajo rugs in tiny trading posts, and Hopi kachinas (also spelled katsinas) being sold out of village homes. The information below will help you make an informed purchase.

Hopi Kachina Dolls These elaborately decorated wooden dolls are representations of the spirits of plants, animals, ancestors, and sacred places. Traditionally, they were given to children to initiate them into the pantheon of kachina spirits, which play important roles in ensuring rain and harmony in the universe. Kachinas have long been popular with collectors, and Hopi carvers have changed their style over the years to cater to the collectors' market. Older kachinas were carved from a single piece of cottonwood, sometimes with arms simply painted on. This older style is much simpler and stiffer than the contemporary style that emphasizes action poses and realistic proportions. A great deal of carving and painting goes into each kachina, and prices today are in the hundreds of dollars for even the simplest. The tsuku, or clown kachinas, which are usually painted with bold horizontal black-and-white stripes and are often depicted in humorous situations or carrying slices of watermelon, are popular with tourists and collectors. In the past few years, young carvers have been returning to the traditional style of kachina, so it's now easier to find these simpler images for sale.

Hopi Overlay Silver Work Most Hopi silver work is done in the overlay style, which was introduced to tribal artisans after World War II, when the GI Bill provided funds for former soldiers to study silversmithing at a school founded by Hopi artist Fred Kabotie. The overlay process basically uses two sheets of silver, one with a design cut from it. Heat fuses the two sheets, forming a raised image. Designs often borrow from other Hopi crafts, such as basketry and pottery, and from ancient Ancestral Puebloan pottery. Belt buckles, earrings, bolo ties, and bracelets are all popular.

Hopi Baskets On Third Mesa, wicker plaques and baskets are made from rabbit brush and sumac and colored with bright

among the Hopi pueblos, but the Pueblo Revolt of 1680 obliterated this small Spanish presence.

In 1687, Father Eusebio Francisco Kino, a German-educated Italian Jesuit, began establishing missions in the Sonoran Desert aniline dyes. On Second Mesa, coiled plaques and baskets are created from dyed yucca fibers. Throughout the reservation, yucca-fiber sifters are made by plaiting over a willow ring.

Hopi Pottery Contemporary Hopi pottery tends toward geometric designs and comes in a variety of styles, including yellow-orange ware decorated with black-and-white designs and white pottery with red-and-black designs. Nampeyo, who died in 1942, is the most famous Hopi potter. Today, members of the Nampeyo family are still active as potters. Most pottery is produced on First Mesa.

Navajo Silver Work Whereas the Hopis create overlay silver work from sheets of silver and the Zunis use silver work simply as a base for their skilled lapidary or stone-cutting work, Navajo silversmiths highlight the silver itself. The earliest pieces of Navajo jewelry were replicas of Spanish ornaments, but as the Navajo silversmiths became more proficient, they began to develop their own designs. The squash-blossom necklace, with its horseshoe-shape pendant, is one of the most distinctive Navajo designs.

Navajo Rugs After the Navajos acquired sheep and goats from the Spanish, they learned weaving from the pueblo tribes, and by the early 1800s, their weavings were widely recognized as being the finest in the Southwest. Women were the weavers among the Navajos, and they primarily wove blankets. However, by the end of the 19th century, the craft was beginning to die out as it became more economical to purchase ready-made blankets. Although today the cost of Navajo rugs, which take hundreds of hours to make, has become almost prohibitively expensive, enough women still practice the craft to keep it alive.

The best rugs are those made with homespun yarn and natural vegetal dyes. However, commercially manufactured yarns and dyes are increasingly used to keep costs down. More than 15 regional styles of rugs exist, and quite a bit of overlapping and borrowing occurs. Bigger and bolder patterns are likely to cost quite a bit less than very complex and highly detailed patterns.

region of northern New Spain. In 1691, he visited the Pima village of Tumacácori. Father Kino taught the inhabitants European farming techniques, planted fruit trees, and gave the Natives cattle, sheep, and goats to raise. However, it was not until 1751, in response to a Pima rebellion, that the permanent mission of Tumacácori and the nearby presidio (military post) of Tubac were built. Together these two Spanish outposts became the first permanent European settlements in what is today Arizona.

In 1775, a group of settlers led by Juan Bautista de Anza set out from Tubac to find an overland route to California, and in 1776, this group founded the city of San Francisco. That same year, the Tubac presidio was moved to Tucson. As early as 1692, Father Kino had visited the Tucson area and by 1700 had laid out the foundations for the first church at the mission of San Xavier del Bac. However, it was not until some time around 1783 that construction of the present church, known as the White Dove of the Desert, began.

In 1821, Mexico won its independence from Spain, and Tucson, with only 65 inhabitants, became part of Mexico. Mexico at that time extended all the way to Northern California, but in 1848, most of this land, except for a small section of southern Arizona that included Tucson, became U.S. territory in the wake of the Mexican-American War. Five years later, in 1853, Mexico sold the remainder of what is today southern Arizona to the United States in a transaction known as the Gadsden Purchase.

INDIAN CONFLICTS   At the time the Spanish arrived in Arizona, the tribes living in the southern lowland deserts were peaceful farmers, but in the mountains of the east lived the Apache, a hunting-and-gathering tribe that frequently raided neighboring tribes. In the north, the Navajos, relatively recent immigrants to the region, fought over land with the neighboring Utes and Hopis (who were also fighting among themselves).

Coronado's expedition through Arizona and into New Mexico and Kansas was to seek gold. To that end he attacked one pueblo, killed the inhabitants of another, and forced still others to abandon their villages. Spanish-Indian relations were never to improve, and the Spanish were forced to occupy their new lands with a strong military presence. Around 1600, 300 Spanish settlers moved into the Four Corners region (where Arizona, Colorado, Utah and New Mexico intersect), which at the time supported a large population of Navajos. The Spanish raided Navajo villages to take slaves, and angry Navajos responded by stealing Spanish horses and cattle.

For several decades in the mid-1600s, missionaries were tolerated in the Hopi pueblos, but the Pueblo tribes revolted in 1680, killing the missionaries and destroying the missions. Encroachment by farmers and miners moving into the Santa Cruz Valley in the south caused the Pima people to stage a similar uprising in 1751, attacking and burning the mission at Tubac. This revolt led to the establishment of the presidio at Tubac that same year. When the military garrison moved to Tucson, Tubac was quickly abandoned because of frequent raids by Apaches. In 1781, the Yuman tribe, whose land at the confluence of the Colorado and Gila rivers had become a Spanish settlement, staged a similar rebellion that wiped out the settlement at Yuma.

By the time Arizona became part of the United States, it was the Navajos and Apaches who were proving most resistant to white settlers. In 1863, the U.S. Army, under the leadership of Col. Kit Carson, forced the Navajos to surrender by destroying their winter food supplies. The survivors were marched to an internment camp in New Mexico; the Navajos refer to this as the Long Walk. Conditions at the camp in New Mexico were deplorable, and within 5 years the Navajos were returned to their land, although they were forced to live on a reservation.

The Apaches resisted white settlement 20 years longer than the Navajos did. Skillful guerrilla fighters, the Apaches, under the leadership of Geronimo and Cochise, attacked settlers, forts, and towns despite the presence of U.S. Army troops sent to protect the settlers. Geronimo and Cochise were the leaders of the last resistant bands of rebellious Apaches. Cochise eventually died in his Chiricahua Mountains homeland. Geronimo finally surrendered in 1886, and he and many of his followers were relocated to Florida by the U.S. government. Open conflicts between whites and Indians finally came to an end.

TERRITORIAL DAYS In 1846, the United States went to war with Mexico, which at the time extended all the way to Northern California and included parts of Colorado, Wyoming, and New Mexico. When the war ended, the United States claimed almost all the land extending from Texas to Northern California. This newly acquired land, called the New Mexico Territory, had its capital at Santa Fe. The land south of the Gila River, which included Tucson, was still part of Mexico, but when surveys determined that this land was the best route for a railroad from southern Mississippi to Southern California, the U.S. government negotiated the Gadsden Purchase. In 1853, this land purchase established the current Arizona-Mexico border.

When the California gold rush began in 1849, many hopeful miners from the east crossed Arizona en route to the gold fields, and some stayed to seek mineral riches in Arizona. However, despite the ever-increasing numbers of settlers, the U.S. Congress refused to create a separate Arizona Territory. When the Civil War broke out, Arizonans, angered by Congress's inaction on their request to become a separate territory, sided with the Confederacy, and in 1862, Arizona was proclaimed the Confederate Territory of Arizona. Although Union troops easily defeated the Confederate troops who had occupied Tucson, this dissension convinced Congress, in 1863, to create the Arizona Territory.

The capital of the new territory was temporarily established at Fort Whipple near Prescott, but later the same year was moved to Prescott itself. In 1867, the capital moved again, this time to Tucson. Ten years later, Prescott again became the capital, which it remained for another 12 years before the seat of government finally moved to Phoenix, Arizona's capital to this day.

During this period, mining flourished, and although small amounts of gold and silver were discovered, copper became the source of Arizona's economic wealth. With each mineral strike, a new mining town would boom, and when the ore ran out, the town would be abandoned. These towns were infamous for their gambling halls, bordellos, saloons, and shootouts. Tombstone and Bisbee became the largest towns in the state and were known as the wildest towns between New Orleans and San Francisco.

In 1867, farmers in the newly founded town of Phoenix began irrigating their fields using canals that had been dug centuries earlier by the Hohokam. In the 1870s, ranching became another important source of revenue in the territory, particularly in the southeastern and northwestern parts of the state. In the 1880s, the railroads finally arrived, and life in Arizona changed drastically. Suddenly the region's mineral resources and cattle were accessible to the east.

STATEHOOD & THE 20TH CENTURY   By the beginning of the 20th century, Arizonans were trying to convince Congress to make the territory a state. Congress balked at the requests but finally in 1910 allowed the territorial government to draw up a state constitution. Territorial legislators were progressive thinkers, and the draft of Arizona's state constitution included clauses for the recall of elected officials. President William Howard Taft vetoed the bill that would have made Arizona a state, because he opposed the recall of judges. Arizona politicians removed the controversial clause, and on February 14, 1912, Arizona became the 48th state. One of the new state legislature's first acts was to reinstate the clause providing for the recall of judges.

Much of Washington's opposition to Arizona's statehood had been based on the belief that Arizona could never support economic development. This belief was changed in 1911 by one of the most important events in state history—the completion of the Salt River's Roosevelt Dam (later to be renamed the Theodore Roosevelt Dam). The dam provided irrigation water to the Phoenix area and tamed the violent floods of the river. The introduction of water to the heart of Arizona's vast desert enabled large-scale agriculture and industry. Over the next decades, more dams were built throughout Arizona, and, in 1936, the Hoover Dam on the Colorado River became the largest concrete dam in the Western Hemisphere. This dam also created the largest man-made reservoir in North America. Arizona's dams would eventually provide not only water and electricity but also the state's most popular recreation areas.

Despite labor problems, copper mining increased throughout the 1920s and 1930s, and with the onset of World War II, the mines boomed as military munitions manufacturing increased the demand for copper. However, within a few years after the war, many mines were shut down. Today, Arizona is littered with old mining ghost towns that boomed and then went bust. A few towns, such as Jerome and Bisbee, managed to hang on after the mines shut down and were eventually rediscovered by artists, writers, and retirees. Bisbee and Jerome are now major tourist attractions known for their many art galleries.

World War II created a demand for beef, leather, and cotton (which became the state's most important crop), and Arizona farmers and ranchers stepped in to meet the need. During the war, Arizona's clear desert skies also provided ideal conditions for training pilots, and several military bases were established in the state. Phoenix's population doubled during the war years, and, when peace finally arrived, many veterans returned with their families. However, it would take the invention of air-conditioning to truly open up the desert to major population growth.

During the postwar years, Arizona attracted a number of large manufacturing industries and slowly moved away from its agricultural economic base. Agriculture and mining, as well as cattle ranching, remain important contributors to the economy. Yet today, electronics manufacturing, aerospace engineering, and other high-tech industries provide significant employment for Arizonans. The largest economic segment, however, is now the service industries, with tourism and retirement playing crucial roles.

Even by the 1920s, Arizona had become a winter destination for the wealthy, and the Grand Canyon, declared a national park in 1919, was luring visitors even when they had to get there by stagecoach. The clear, dry air also attracted people suffering from allergies and lung ailments, and Arizona became known as a healthful place. With Hollywood Westerns enjoying immense popularity, dude ranches began to spring up across the state. Eventually the rustic guest ranches of the 1930s gave way to luxurious golf resorts. Today, Scottsdale, Phoenix, and Tucson boast dozens of luxury

GET YOUR KICKS ON route 66

It was the Mother Road, the Main Street of America, and for thousands of Midwesterners devastated by the Dust Bowl days of the 1930s, the road to a better life. On the last leg of its journey from Chicago to California, Route 66 meandered across the vast empty landscape of northern Arizona, and today, much of this road is still visible.

Officially dedicated in 1926, Route 66 was the first highway in America to be uniformly signed from one state to the next. Less than half the highway's 2,200-mile route was paved, and in those days, the stretch between Winslow and Ash Fork was so muddy in winter that drivers had their cars shipped by railroad between the two points. By the 1930s, however, the entire length of Route 66 had been paved, and the westward migration was underway.

The years following World War II saw Americans take to Route 66 in unprecedented numbers for a different reason. A new prosperity and reliable cars made travel a pleasure, and Americans set out to discover the West. Motor courts, cafes, and tourist traps sprang up along the highway's length, and these businesses increasingly turned to eye-catching signs and billboards to lure passing motorists. Neon lit up the once-lonely stretches of highway.

By the 1950s, Route 66 just couldn't handle the traffic. After President Dwight Eisenhower initiated the National Interstate Highway System, Route 66 was slowly replaced by a four-lane divided highway. Many of the towns along the old highway were bypassed, and motorists stopped frequenting such roadside establishments as Pope's General Store and the Oatman Hotel. Many closed, while others were replaced by their more modern equivalents. Some, however, managed to survive, and they appear along the road like strange time capsules from another era, vestiges of Route 66's legendary past.

resorts. In addition, tens of thousands of retirees from as far north as Canada make Arizona their winter home and play a substantial role in the state's economy.

Continued population growth throughout the 20th century resulted in an ever-increasing demand for water. Yet, despite the damming of nearly all of Arizona's rivers, the state still suffered from insufficient water supplies in the south-central population centers of Phoenix and Tucson. It took the construction of the controversial and expensive Central Arizona Project (CAP) aqueduct to carry water from the Colorado River over mountains and

Flagstaff, the largest town along the Arizona stretch of Route 66, became a major layover spot. Motor courts flourished on the road leading into town from the east. Today, this road has been officially renamed Route 66 by the city of Flagstaff, and a few of the old motor courts remain. Although you probably wouldn't want to stay in most of these old motels, their neon signs were once beacons in the night for tired drivers. Downtown Flagstaff has quite a few shops where you can pick up Route 66 memorabilia.

About 65 miles west of Flagstaff begins the longest remaining stretch of old Route 66. Extending for 160 miles from Ash Fork to Topock, this lonely blacktop passes through some of the most remote country in Arizona (and goes right through the town of Kingman). After leaving Seligman, the highway passes through such waysides as Peach Springs, Truxton, Valentine, and Hack-berry. At Valle Vista, near Kingman, the highway goes into a 7-mile-long curve. Some claim it's the longest continuous curve on a U.S. highway.

After the drive through the wilderness west of Seligman, King-man feels like a veritable metropolis; its bold neon signs once brought a sigh of relief to the tired and the hungry. Today, it boasts dozens of modern motels and is still primarily a resting spot for the road weary.

The last stretch of Route 66 in Arizona heads southwest out of Kingman through the rugged Sacramento Mountains. It passes through Oatman, which almost became a ghost town after the local gold-mining industry shut down and the new interstate high-way pulled money out of town. After dropping down out of the mountains, the road once crossed the Colorado River on a narrow metal bridge. Although the bridge is still there, it now carries a pipeline instead of traffic; cars must now return to the bland I-40 to continue their journey into the promised land of California.

deserts and to deliver it where it was wanted. Construction on the CAP began in 1974, and in 1985 water from the project finally began irrigating fields near Phoenix. In 1992, the CAP reached Tucson. However, recent years of drought in the Southwest have left Phoenix and Tucson once again pondering where they will come up with the water to fuel future growth.

By the 1960s, Arizona had become an urban state with all the problems confronting other areas around the nation. The once-healthful air of Phoenix now rivals that of Los Angeles for the thickness of its smog. Allergy sufferers are plagued by pollen from the nondesert plants that have been introduced to make this desert region look more lush and inviting. However, until the recent economic downturn, the state's economy was still growing quite rapidly. High-tech companies had been locating within Arizona, and a steady influx of retirees as well as Californians fleeing earthquakes and urban problems had given the state new energy and new ideas. Things slowed considerably during the economic downturn, but, of course, the sun still shines here, even in January and February when much of the rest of the country is locked in a deep freeze, and that remains a powerful lure.

THE LAY OF THE LAND

If you could observe 2 billion years pass in a single hour, you'd see the land from which the Grand Canyon is carved wander across the globe, traveling as far south as the equator—perhaps even farther. You'd see it dip below sea level, rise as mountains, dry into dunes, and get smothered under swamps. You'd watch as water deposited different sediments—such as silt, mud, and sand—atop it. Out of sight, compacted from above and cemented together by minerals, these sediments would eventually form *sedimentary* rocks such as sandstone, siltstone, limestone, and shale. Some of these rocks would resurface later, only to be eroded by wind and water. Others would remain buried. Because the canyon itself may be as little as 6 million years old, you probably wouldn't recognize it until the last 11 seconds of the hour, when two or more rivers began to cut down through the Colorado Plateau's rocks. As a frame of reference, keep in mind that all of human history would take up only a quarter of a second at the end of the hour.

Although you can't personally experience the canyon's 2-billion-year history, the layers of rock in the Grand Canyon record much of what happened. Because the rocks are both well preserved and exposed down to very deep layers, the canyon is one of the world's best places for geologists to learn about the Paleozoic era, and eras even earlier. For an illustration of these layers, see p. 175.

The record starts with the **Vishnu Schist** and other basement rocks, which consists of schist, gneiss, and granite (layer 12 in the illustration on p. 175). The canyon's oldest and deepest layer, it's the black rock draped like a wizard's robe directly above the Colorado River. Originally laid down as sedimentary rock, the layer was driven deep into the earth, and underneath a mountain range, more than 1.7 billion years ago. There, it got to temperatures so extreme (1,100°F/593°C) and was under pressure so great that its chemical composition altered, changing it to *metamorphic* rock, which is much harder and glossier than the others.

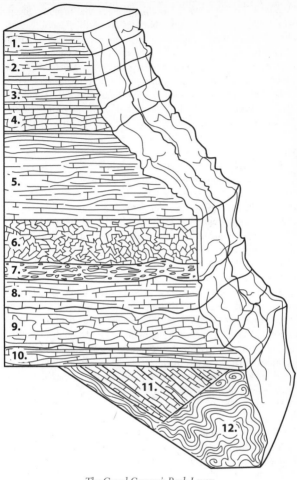

The Grand Canyon's Rock Layers

The **Grand Canyon Supergroup** (layer 11), a group of sedimentary and *igneous* (volcanic) rocks laid down between 1.2 billion and 800 million years ago, appears directly above the schist in numerous canyon locations. These pastel-colored layers stand out because they're tilted at about 20 degrees. **Desert View** is one good place to see them. Once part of a series of small mountain ranges, erosion shaved off the Supergroup, so that it disappeared from many parts of the canyon.

Where the Supergroup has disappeared, the **Tapeats Sandstone layer** (layer 10) sits right on top of the Vishnu Schist, although more than a billion years separate the two layers. Erosion created this huge gap, commonly referred to as the **Great Unconformity.** Because of it, the layers have little in common. While the Vishnu Formation predates atmospheric oxygen, Tapeats Sandstone contains fossils of sponges and trilobites from the Cambrian era's explosion of life. It also tells of the beginnings of the Tapeats Sea's incursion 525 million years ago. At that time, the water was so shallow and so turbulent that only the heaviest particles—sand—could sink. That sand eventually formed the sandstone.

The **Bright Angel Shale** (layer 9) forms the gently sloping blue-gray layer (known as the Tonto Platform) above the Tapeats Sandstone. It tells of a Tapeats Sea that had become deeper and considerably calmer in this area. Some 515 million years ago, the water was calm enough to let fine-grained sediment settle to the bottom. The sediment formed a muck that eventually became the shale. Above it is the **Muav Limestone** (layer 8), which dates back 505 million years. The Muav layer recalls a Tapeats Sea that was deeper still in this area—so deep that feathery bits of shell from tiny marine creatures sank. These bits of shell, together with other calcium carbonate that precipitated naturally out of the water, created the limestone. Where not stained by the layers above, the Muav appears as a yellowish cliff underneath an obvious layer known as the Redwall Limestone (see next paragraph). The **Temple Butte Formation** (layer 7), averaging 385 million years old, is made of purplish-colored dolostone in the east deposited from former tidal channels that aren't coastal and were laid down in the intertidal environment (marine or brackish). The Temple Butte is easier to distinguish in the western regions, where the cliffs extend hundreds of feet and marine fossils are prevalent.

About halfway between rim and river, the **Redwall Limestone** (layer 6) forms some of the canyon's steepest cliffs—800 feet high in places. This imposing rock layer reveals a Mississippian-age sea that deposited calcium carbonate layers across all of what is now North America about 340 million years ago. Silvery-gray under the surface, the Redwall is stained red by iron oxide from the rocks above. To see the Redwall's true color, look for places where pieces have recently broken off.

Just above the Redwall is the **Supai Group** (layer 5). Formed about 300 million years ago, these layers of sandstone, shale, and siltstone were deposited in tidal flats along shorelines. They usually form a series of red ledges just above the Redwall cliffs. Right above them, and even deeper red, is the **Hermit Formation** (layer 4), deposited in the flood plain of one or more great rivers around

280 million years ago. This soft shale usually forms a gentle slope or platform directly below the **Coconino Sandstone** (layer 3), which is the easiest layer in the canyon to identify. The third layer from the top, it's the color of desert sand and forms cliffs that are nearly as sheer as those of the Redwall. The Coconino was laid down as dunes in a Sahara-like desert that covered this land about 275 million years ago. Everywhere in this layer, you'll see slanted lines caused by cross-bedding—where new dunes blew in atop old ones. While the other layers display fossils that become increasingly complex through time (the Supai contains fossils of insects and ferns, and marine invertebrates are common in the Redwall), the Coconino's only imprints are lizard and arthropod tracks that always go uphill. (This seems odd until you watch a lizard on sand. It digs in while going up, making firm marks in the process, then smears its tracks coming down.) Some of these fossils are visible along the South Kaibab Trail.

On the top are the canyon's youngest rocks—the yellow-gray **Toroweap Formation** (layer 2) and the cream-colored **Kaibab Formation/Limestone** (layer 1), which forms the rim rock. Both were deposited by the same warm, shallow sea at the end of the Paleozoic era (270–273 million years ago), when this land was roughly 350 feet below sea level. Younger layers once lay atop the Kaibab Formation, but they have eroded away in most areas of the canyon. To see examples of this, look east from Desert View to nearby Cedar Mountain or northeast to the Vermilion and Echo cliffs.

Moving Mountains

Today, the ancient rocks are part of the **Colorado Plateau.** Between roughly 65 and 38 million years ago, this land was lifted by a process known as *subduction* (some observers believe that uplifting is still occurring). When a continental plate butts up against an oceanic plate, the heavier, denser oceanic plate is forced underneath it. Like an arm reaching under a mattress, this slipping—or subduction—can elevate land on the upper plate that's far inland from continental margins.

This happened in the Four Corners area (a region on the Colorado Plateau) during an event known as the **Laramide Orogeny,** which involved the Pacific plate subducting under the North American plate, pushing 130,000 square miles of land that was in the Four Corners area up to elevations ranging from 5,000 to 13,000 feet. This area, which consists of many smaller landforms, has six individual plateaus—the Coconino and Hualapai on the South Rim; and the Kaibab, Kanab, Uinkaret, and Shivwits on the North Rim—that are all part of the larger Colorado Plateau. The

Laramide Orogeny also marked the beginning of the uplift of the Rocky Mountains.

Because the earth's crust is very thick under the Grand Canyon and its surrounding area, the layers of rock here rose without doing much collapsing or shearing. Where significant faulting did take place, the rocks sometimes folded instead of breaking. *Monoclines* are places where rocks bend in a single fold. As you drive up the 4,800-foot climb from Lees Ferry to Jacob Lake on the North Rim, you'll ascend the East Kaibab monocline. Driving east from Grandview Point, you'll descend the Grandview monocline. In both cases, you'll remain on the same rock layer, the Kaibab Formation, the whole time.

The Colorado Plateau is an ideal place for canyon formation for three reasons. First, it sits at a minimum of 5,000 feet above sea level, so water has a strong pull to saw through the land. This makes the rivers here more active than, say, the Mississippi, which descends just 1,670 feet over 2,350 miles. With an average drop of 8 feet per mile, the Colorado River in the Grand Canyon is 11 times steeper than the Mississippi. Second, the Colorado Plateau's desert terrain has little vegetation to hold it in place, so rain quickly erodes it. Third, rain often comes in monsoons that fall hard and fast, cutting deep grooves instead of eroding the land evenly, as softer, more frequent rains would.

The different layers and rock types make the resulting canyons more spectacular, perhaps, than any in the world. In addition to being different colors, the rocks vary in hardness and erode at different rates. Known as *differential erosion*, this phenomenon is responsible for the *stair-step effect* at the Grand Canyon.

Here's how it works: The softer rocks—usually shales—erode fastest, undercutting the cliffs above them, which are made of harder rock. During winter's melt-freeze cycles, water seeps into cracks in these now-vulnerable cliffs, freezes, and expands, chiseling off boulders that collapse onto the layers below. These collapsed rocks tumble down into boulder fields such as those at the bases of the canyon's temples. The biggest rock slides sometimes pile up in ramps that make foot descents possible through cliff areas. Where soft rock has eroded off of hard rock underneath it, platforms form. One such platform, known as the **Esplanade,** is obvious in the western canyon. The end result is a series of platforms and cliffs.

Runoff drives the process, and more of it comes from the North Rim. This happens for two reasons. First, the land through which the canyon is cut slopes gently from north to south. So runoff from the North Rim drains into the canyon while runoff from the South Rim drains away from it. And more precipitation falls at the higher elevations on the North Rim—25 inches, as opposed to 16 inches for the South Rim. As this water makes its way—often along fault lines—to the Colorado River, it cuts side canyons that drain into the main one.

These side canyons tend to become longer and more gradual through time. Since the runoff can't cut any lower than the Colorado River, it eats away the land near the top of each side canyon. As this happens, each canyon's head slowly moves closer to its water source—a process known as *headward erosion.*

Standing at Grand Canyon Village looking down the Bright Angel fault, you may notice that the gorge formed along it is longer on the Colorado River's north side. This is typical of the Grand Canyon's side canyons. Because more water comes off the North Rim, more erosion has taken place on that side of the river, and longer canyons have been formed.

Then Came the Floods

Eroded material has to go somewhere. The rocks that fall into the side canyons are swept into the Colorado River, usually by flash floods during the August monsoon season. While it may be hard to imagine a current this strong in what is usually a nearly dry side canyon, look again at how thousands of tiny drainages converge like capillaries into a single significant creek bed. In most cases, the water over several square miles of hard land drains into one relatively narrow rock chute. A downpour, then, can generate floods that are immensely powerful and very dangerous.

Below each significant side canyon are boulders, which are swept into the Colorado River by these floods. These boulders form dams in the larger river, creating rapids where the water spills over them. The water above each set of rapids usually looks as smooth as a reservoir. Below the first rocks, however, it cascades downstream, crashing backward in standing waves against large boulders. Before Glen Canyon dam began blocking the river flow in 1963, the Colorado River broke up many of the biggest rocks during its enormous spring floods. These floods, which commonly reached levels five times higher than an average flow today, swept along small rocks, which would in turn chip away and break apart boulders, eventually moving *them* downstream. For the canyon to have reached its present size, the river had to have swept away more than 1,000 cubic miles of debris. Now, with the sizable spring floods a thing of the past, less debris moves, and the rapids have become steeper and rockier.

While it's fairly easy to explain how the side canyons cut down to the Colorado River's level, it's much harder to say how the Colorado cut through the plateaus that form the sides of the Grand

Canyon. Unless the river was already in place when these adjoining plateaus started rising roughly 60 million years ago, it would have had to first climb 3,000 feet uphill before it could begin cutting down. The explorer John Wesley Powell, who mapped the Colorado River in 1869, assumed that the river had cut down through the land as the land rose. The river in the eastern canyon may indeed be old enough to have accomplished this. The western canyon, however, is much younger. In fact, there's no evidence of a through-flowing Colorado River in the western Grand Canyon before about 5 million years ago.

Geologists have proposed a number of theories about how the river assumed its present course, none of which is supported by a strong body of evidence. The difficulty is that only scattered pieces of evidence can be used to date the canyon precisely. Most theories center on the idea of an ancestral Colorado River that flowed through the eastern canyon, exiting the canyon via a channel different from its current one. This ancestral river would have been diverted onto its present course by another, smaller river that probably reached it via headward erosion. One theory holds that this "pirate" river cut headward all the way from the Gulf of California, while another maintains that it may have originated on the Kaibab Plateau during a period when the climate was wetter than it is today. No one is sure what happened, and the debate is still open.

THE FLORA

C. Hart Merriam, an American zoologist and ethnographer who studied the plant life around the canyon in 1889, grouped the species here into geographical ranges that he called "life zones." According to Merriam, different life zones resulted from "laws of temperature control" that corresponded to elevation change. Each life zone began and ended at a particular elevation, much like the rock layers that ring the canyon walls.

Merriam's theory was a good one at the time, but he didn't immediately recognize the significance of other variables. Today, naturalists understand that the Grand Canyon's flora is strongly affected by factors such as air currents, water flows, soil types, slope degree, and slope aspect (the orientation of the earth's surface in relation to the sun). Most naturalists now prefer to talk about "biological communities," avoiding the mistake of fixing species in any particular zone.

However, if your goal is to identify a few major plant species and the general areas in which to find them, life zones still work fairly well. So we'll use them, with thanks to Dr. Merriam. The canyon's five life zones are: **boreal,** from 8,000 to 9,100 feet; **transition,** from 7,000 to 8,000 feet; **upper sonoran,** from 4,000 to 7,500 feet; **lower sonoran,** from the bottom of the canyon to 4,000 feet; and **riparian,** along the Colorado River's banks and tributaries. Some of the more common or unusual plants in each zone are as follows:

Boreal Zone

Blue spruce The magnificent blue spruce, sometimes called the Colorado spruce, is native to the Western U.S. and grows at elevations of 5,900 to 10,000 feet. It is one of the most popular evergreens, even showcased as the national Christmas tree each year in Washington, D.C. It has silvery to blue-green needles, blooms in April and May with 3-inch cones, and grows 50 to 75 feet high, with a full spread of 25 feet at maturity.

Douglas fir Found on the North Rim (most often close to the rim itself) and on isolated north-facing slopes below the South Rim, this tree grows up to 130 feet high and 6 feet in diameter. Its hanging cones, which grow to about 3 inches long, have three-pronged bracts between their scales. Each of its soft needles is about 1 inch long. The Douglas fir is built for cold weather; its branches, while cupped, are flexible enough to slough off snow.

White fir You'll know you've moved into spruce-fir forest when you start tripping over deadfall and running into low

Blue spruce

Douglas fir

White fir

branches. One of the more common trees in this high-alpine forest, the white fir has smooth, gray bark. Its cones grow upright to about 4 inches long, and its 2-inch-long needles curve on two sides. The white fir closely resembles the subalpine fir. But the subalpine fir's branches, unlike those of the white fir, grow to ground level, and its needles are about an inch shorter.

Transition Zone

Big sagebrush

Big sagebrush More common on the rims than in the canyons, this fuzzy gray-green shrub grows to 4 feet high on thick wood stalks. To make sure you haven't misidentified it as rabbit brush (another gray-green plant of comparable size), look at a leaf—it should have three tiny teeth at the end. Or simply break off a sprig (outside the park) and smell it. If it doesn't smell divine, it's not sagebrush. Some Native American tribes burned sage bundles during purification rituals.

Gambel oak

Gambel oak To find Gambel (or scrub) oak on the South Rim in winter, look for the bare trees. The only deciduous tree in the South Rim's immediate vicinity, its leaves turn orange before falling. To find Gambel oak in summer, look for its acorns, its long (up to 6 in.), lobed leaves, and its gray trunk. It grows in thick clumps that clutter the ponderosa pine forest's otherwise open floor. A plant with a similar name, shrub oak, grows lower in the canyon and has sharp, hollylike leaves.

Indian paintbrush

Indian paintbrush You should be able to identify this rare plant from the name alone. Many of its flower-like bracts are colored red or orange at their tips, making them look as if they've been dipped in paint.

Lupine Common on both rims, this flower blooms from spring to late summer. You can spot lupine by its palmate leaves and tiny purple flowers growing in clusters at the top of its main stem.

Ponderosa pine Found on both rims and in isolated places in the canyon, this is the park's only long-needled pine. It dominates the forest at elevations between 6,000 and 9,000 feet, can live 120 years, and reaches heights of 100-plus feet. The ponderosa pine can also withstand forest fires (provided the fires come often enough to keep flammable brush on the forest floor to a minimum); its thick bark shields the inside of the tree from the heat. And once the tree's low branches have burned off, fire can no longer climb to the crown. So the trees that survive grow stronger. When the fires are over, they thrive on the nutrients in the ash-covered soil. Mature ponderosa pines have thick red-orange bark (younger ones have blackish bark), 6-inch-long needles in groups of three, and no low branches. Once you've identified one, smell its bark—you'll be rewarded with a rich vanilla-like scent. This tree provides shelter for the Kaibab and Abert squirrels.

Quaking aspen The ponderosa pine may smell better, but tree-huggers should save the last dance for the quaking aspen, which grows alongside it in many North Rim forests. Its cool, dusty white bark feels great against your cheek on a hot day. Its green, shimmering leaves—on long, twisted stems—shudder at the very idea of a breeze, creating the impression of a tree that's "quaking" in the wind. If you hug one

Lupine

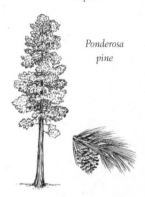

Ponderosa pine

Quaking aspen

aspen, you're probably hugging many: Dozens and sometimes hundreds of these trees have been known to sprout from a common root system, meaning they're technically one plant. In fact, one of the world's largest organisms is a quaking aspen in Utah.

Upper Sonoran

Cliff rose & Apache plume These flowering shrubs, which grow on both the rims and in the canyon, have much in common.

Cliff rose

Apache plume

Both are members of the rose family, grow tiny five-lobed leaves, and send up numerous delicate flowers from which feathery plumes sometimes protrude. However, a few differences do exist: Cliff rose is larger, growing up to 25 feet, compared to 5 feet for the Apache plume. The cliff rose's blossoms give way to seeds whose white plumes allow the wind to scatter them some distance. The flowers are a creamy yellow, as opposed to white for the Apache plume. And its leaves, unlike those of the Apache plume, are hairless. The Apache plume blooms a few weeks longer—from early spring into October.

Mormon tea Common throughout the park, this virtually leafless plant has hundreds of jointed, needlelike stems that point skyward. Once the plants are full-grown, they remain largely unchanged for as long as 500 years. Photos of desert scenes taken more than 50 years apart show the same Mormon tea plants with every stem still in place. The only difference between young and old plants is their color—the more ancient plants are yellow-green or even yellow-gray; younger ones are light green. The early Mormon pioneers and the Native Americans used the stems, which contain pseudo-ephedrine and tannin, for medicinal purposes.

Mormon tea

Piñon pine

Piñon pine Wherever a new juniper tree sprouts, a piñon pine usually takes root in its shade (junipers are more heat-tolerant), growing to about the same size (30 ft.) as the juniper. Shorter and rounder than most pines, the piñon grows 1-inch-long needles, usually in pairs, and often lives more than 2 centuries. Together, the piñon pine and the Utah juniper (see listing below) dominate much of the Southwest's high desert. Piñon (or pine) nuts, packing 2,500 calories per pound, have always been a staple for Native Americans in this area. Now they're also popular in Italian restaurants, where they're used to make pesto.

Utah agave & banana yucca The plants consisting of 3-foot-long spikes are most often agave or yucca. Agave leaves have serrated edges, while yucca leaves have rough, sandpaper-like sides. Native Americans used these plants' fibers and leaves to make sandals, baskets, and rope. If you were to break off a particularly sharp leaf and peel away the fibers from its edge, you would eventually end up with just a thread with a needlelike tip. The agave blooms only once every 15 to 25 years. When it does, it's easy to spot—its spiky base sends up a wooden stalk, about 14 feet high, atop which yellow flowers grow. Because this flourish occurs so rarely, the agave is often referred to as the century plant. After

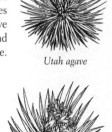

Utah agave

Banana yucca

flowering, it dies. Some naturalists theorize that the agave, whose leaves become rich in nutrients just before it flowers, evolved to bloom rarely so that animals would not grow accustomed to eating it. This trick didn't fool the Ancestral Puebloans, who discovered that the roasted hearts of the plant were always nutritious. Unlike the agave, the banana yucca, one of the Southwest's most common and useful plants, blooms every 2 to 3 years, sending up 4-foot-high stalks off which yellow flowers hang. Its fruit, which tastes a bit like banana, ripens in late summer.

Utah juniper This tree, which seldom grows higher than 30 feet, *looks* as though it belongs in the desert. Its scraggy bark is as dry as straw, its tiny leaves are tight and scalelike, and its gnarled branches appear to have endured forever. Burned in campfires

Utah juniper

since the dawn of time, juniper wood releases a fragrant smoke that evokes the desert as much as the yipping of coyotes. Its dusty-looking blue berries are actually cones, each with one or two small seeds inside. Juniper is a traditional flavoring for game meats and for gin.

Lower Sonoran

Barrel cactus

Barrel cactus The barrel cactus does indeed resemble a small, green barrel. One of the more efficient desert plants, it can survive for years without water. Contrary to the popular myth, however, there's no reservoir of drinking water inside.

Blackbrush The Tonto Platform's blue-gray color doesn't derive solely from the Bright Angel Shale. It also comes from blackbrush, a gray, spiny, 3-foot-high bush that dominates the flora atop the platform. Blackbrush grows leathery, half-inch-long leaves on tangled branches that turn black when wet. Because the plant's root system is considerably larger than the plant itself, each one commands plenty of area; there are usually 10 to 15 feet between blackbrush plants.

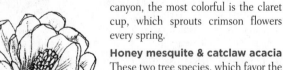
Blackbrush

Hedgehog cactus The hedgehog cactus looks like a cluster of prickly cucumbers standing on end. Of the four species in the canyon, the most colorful is the claret cup, which sprouts crimson flowers every spring.

Hedgehog cactus

Honey mesquite & catclaw acacia These two tree species, which favor the walls above rivers or creek beds, show us the heights reached by the Colorado River's predam floods. After a flood recedes, mesquite and acacia seedlings take root in the moist soil. Later, the maturing trees send pipelike roots down to the river or creek bed. Both species, which have dark branches and leaves with small paired leaflets, reach heights of about 20 feet, and grow seedpods several inches long. The mesquite's leaflets, however, are longer and narrower than the acacia's. And while the acacia has tiny barbs like cat claws for protection, the mesquite grows paired inch-long thorns where leaves meet the stems. Mesquite beans were a staple for the Ancestral Puebloans.

Honey mesquite

Opuntia cactus Most members of this family are known as prickly pear. Although prickly pears do grow on the South Rim, the most impressive are lower in the canyon. There, the prickly pear's flat oval pads link up in formations that occasionally sprawl across 40 or more square feet of ground. Look closely at each pad and you'll notice that, even in the most contorted formations, the narrow side always points up, reducing the amount of sunlight received. Because this cactus tends to hybridize, it produces a variety of yellow, pink, and magenta flowers from April to June. Put a finger inside one of these flowers, and the stamens will curl around it, a reflex designed to coat bees with pollen. This plant's cactus pads can be roasted and eaten (once its spikes are removed), and the fruit, which ripens in late summer, is edible, too; it's often used to make

Catclaw acacia

Opuntia cactus/ prickly pear

jelly. There are several opuntia species, ranging from very prickly (grizzly bear) to spineless (beavertail).

Riparian

Fremont cottonwood To cool off in the shade, look for this tree's bright green canopy, which grows near many of the Colorado River's tributaries but seldom by the large river itself. The tree's spreading branches and wide, shimmering leaves shade many of the canyon's springs. Its trunk, covered with grooved, ropelike bark, can grow as wide as a refrigerator. Its flowers, which bloom in

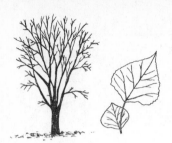

Fremont cottonwood

spring, drop tiny seeds that look like cotton and can ride breezes to distant water sources. A nice grove of these trees shelters the picnic area at Indian Garden.

Tamarisk The CCC once used this exotic species for flood-bank control. Today, it is the plant that boaters and hikers love to hate. Before Glen Canyon dam was built, the Colorado River's annual spring floods thinned or wiped out most of the tamarisk along its banks. Now, tamarisk and coyote willow have taken over many beaches, creating thickets that can make hiking miserable. Other animals don't mind the thickets; they're home to a diverse population of birds, lizards, and insects. Soft as ostrich feathers, the plant's stems grow tiny, scalelike leaves and sprout small, white flowers in spring. While young tamarisk consists of skinny, flexible stalks, older plants have wood trunks.

Tamarisk

THE FAUNA

To view wildlife at the Grand Canyon, bring a flashlight. Most desert animals are either *nocturnal* (active at night) or *crepuscular* (active at dawn and dusk). Lying low during the day allows them to avoid the powerful sun, thus cutting their water needs and enabling them to forage or hunt without overheating. All have specialized mechanisms to survive this harsh environment, and many, if provoked, can be as prickly as the plants around them.

Mammals

Bat

Bats The **western pipestral** is the Grand Canyon's most common bat. At sunset, you'll see them flutter above the rim, rising and falling as if on strings. Gray with black wings, they emit ultrasonic sounds that echo differently off of different objects. The bats then "read" the echoes to determine what they're approaching. If it's an insect, they know what to do. A single bat can eat 500 bugs in an hour.

Bighorn sheep If there's a hint of a foothold, a bighorn sheep will find it. Its hooves are hard and durable on the outside but soft and grippy underneath, a perfect design for steep, rocky terrain. You'll often hear them clattering before you spot their stocky, gray-brown bodies and white rumps. Six feet long, males can weigh 300 pounds. Their horns are coiled; females' are straight. Look for bighorn sheep in side canyons that have water, and sometimes on the rims.

Bighorn sheep

Coyotes Coyotes will eat almost anything—bugs, carrion, plants, rodents, and bird eggs included. Their versatile diet has helped them flourish, and you'll find them all around the canyon, but you must be alert in order to spot one. They look like lanky midsize dogs. But their noses are more sharply pointed, and their tails hang between their legs when they run. During summer, their bodies are tan, their bellies white, and their legs rust-colored. In winter, the ones on the rims turn mostly gray. If you camp during your visit, you'll probably hear their squeaky yips and howls at sunset. Look for them at dusk in North Rim meadows or at daybreak around the Tusayan garbage dumpsters.

Coyote

Desert cottontails Common even in the canyon's most populated areas, these oval-eared rabbits feed on grasses, twigs, juniper berries, and leaves. Their bodies are mostly tan, but sometimes all you'll see is their white tails as they dash away from coyotes and bobcats.

Desert cottontail

Elk **Merriam's elk,** which were native to this area, were killed off by human hunters in the 1920s. Transplanted from Yellowstone, **Roosevelt elk** have flourished on the South Rim. Their bodies are tan, their heads and necks dark brown and shaggy. These long-legged, thick-bodied animals grow to enormous sizes: Bulls weigh as much as 1,000 pounds and stand up to

Elk

5 feet high at the shoulders; cows average 550 pounds. Unlike deer, which prefer bushes and shrubs, elk feed primarily on forest-floor grasses. Rather than migrate far, they'll dig through snow for forage. Every year, the bulls grow large racks of antlers, used to battle one another for cows. In fall, during mating season, bulls can be dangerously aggressive. At this time, you may hear their high-pitched "bugling." Herds of elk often roam the National Forest on the South Rim near Grandview Point. Elk are uncommon on the North Rim.

Mountain lions These solitary cats, whose legs act like powerful springs, will probably see you before you see them. Sightings around the canyon are rare, even among people who have spent

Mountain lion

their lives studying them. This isn't because the animals are small—they grow up to 6 feet long and weigh 200 pounds, with cylindrical tails as long as 3 feet. Their coats are tawny everywhere except the chest and muzzle, which are white. Retractable claws let these graceful animals sprint across rocks and dig in on softer slopes—bad news for deer and elk. Hunted almost to extinction in this area in the early 1900s, the mountain lion has recovered of late, especially on the North Rim, where more than 100 are believed to live.

Mule deer

Mule deer Mule deer are among the South Rim's most readily seen mammals. These tan or gray ungulates, which get as heavy as 200 pounds, are common everywhere in the park, including developed areas. They often summer on the rims, then move into the canyon or lower on the plateaus in winter, when their fur turns grayish-white. Every year, the bucks grow antlers, then shed them in March after battling other males during mating season. Mule deer feed on bushes and shrubs, but they especially like cliff rose. Active at night, they frequently dart in front of cars, making night driving risky.

Raccoons Recognizable by their black "bandit" masks, gray bodies, and black-striped tails, raccoons are fairly rare here because of the lack of water. Still, you may spot one.

Raccoon

Ringtails Ringtails, which are raccoon relatives, frequently raid campsites near the Colorado River. Their tails are rung with luminous white bands. Their ears are pink and mouse-like, their bodies gray-brown. Ringtails are smart enough and dexterous enough to untie knots. If cornered, they may, like a skunk, spray foul-smelling mist. When not infiltrating campsites, they feed on mice and other small animals. Look for ringtails at night on the rafters in El Tovar Restaurant. (The hotel has tried unsuccessfully to move them.)

Ringtail

Squirrels The Kaibab and Aberts squirrels were once the same species sharing the same ponderosa pine forest. After the canyon separated the squirrels, subtle genetic differences between the groups took hold. Though both still have tufts of fur above their ears, the **Kaibab squirrel,** which lives only on the North Rim, is gray with a black underbelly and a white tail. The **Aberts squirrel,** on the South Rim, has a gray body, a reddish back, and a dark tail with white sides. Both still nest in and feed on the bark of ponderosa pines, and both are notoriously clueless (even by squirrel standards)

Kaibab squirrel

Aberts squirrel

around cars. Other squirrel species around here are the golden-mantled ground squirrels that look like oversize chipmunks, and the grayish-brown rock squirrels that have lost their natural fear of humans and often beg for handouts. Do not give them food.

Birds

Bald eagle

Bald eagles It's hard to mistake a mature bald eagle for any other bird. Dark plumage, a white head and tail, and a yellow beak combine to give this bird, with its 6-foot wingspan, a look as distinctive as America itself. In winter, bald eagles often sit in trees along the river in the eastern canyon, where they like to fish for trout.

Common ravens These shiny blue-black birds soar like raptors above the rims—when not walking like people around the campgrounds. They're big—up to 27 inches long—and smart. They've been known to unzip packs, open food containers, and team up to take trout from bald eagles. The common raven lives year-round on the South Rim and is the most frequently sighted large bird there.

Common raven

Golden eagles Golden-brown from head to talon, this bird is commonly spotted soaring above the rims, its wings spanning 6 feet or more. Wings tucked, the golden eagle can dive at speeds approaching 100 mph. Although known to have killed fawns, they usually prefer smaller mammals. A golden eagle sometimes can be mistaken for an immature bald eagle.

Great horned owls This bird often perches in trees along the rims. Look for black circles around its eyes, puffy white feathers on its chest, and feathery tufts that resemble horns above its ears.

Golden eagle

Great horned owl

Peregrine falcons Identifiable by its gray back, black-and-white head, and pointed, sickle-shaped wings, this bird frequently preys on waterfowl, sometimes knocking them out of the air. Once endangered, the peregrine has benefited from the outlawing of the harmful pesticide DDT. The Grand Canyon is now home to the largest population of peregrines in the continental U.S.

Peregrine falcon

Red-tailed hawks One of the more commonly seen raptors, the red-tailed hawk flies with its wings on a plane the way an eagle does, but has a smaller (4-ft.) wingspan. Identifiable by its white underside, reddish tail, brown head, and brown back, the red-tailed hawk will sometimes drop a snake from great heights to kill it.

Red-tailed hawk

Swifts and swallows Two small birds—**white-throated swifts** and **violet-green swallows**—commonly slice through the air above the rims, picking off bugs. The swift's black-and-white body is uniformly narrow from head to tail. Its wings, which curve back toward its tail, seem to alternate strokes as it flies. The swallow, which has a rounder body and green feathers on its back and head, flies more steadily than the swift.

Violet-green swallow

White-throated swift

Turkey vulture *Wild turkey*

Turkey vultures If you see a group of birds circling, their wings held in a "V" shape, rocking in the wind like unskilled hang-glider pilots, you're watching a group of turkey vultures. Up close, look for the dark plumage and bald red head. California condors sometimes follow turkey vultures because the vultures have a better sense of smell and can more easily locate carrion.

Wild turkeys Growing to 4 feet long, the males of this species are easiest to spot. They have bare blue heads, red wattles, and 6-inch-long feathered "beards" on their chests. The females are smaller and less colorful. They're common on both rims, but seen most often in North Rim meadows. Ancestral Puebloans once raised wild turkeys in pens.

Invertebrates

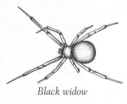

Black widow

Black widows These spiders often spin their irregularly shaped, sticky webs in crevices in the Redwall Limestone (you'll only find them down in the warmer areas of the canyon, and not on the rims). Although they're most active at night, you can occasionally spy one in the shadows. Their large, round abdomens give them a unique appearance. Only the females, recognizable by the red hourglass shape under the abdomen, are poisonous, with bites that are extremely painful but seldom fatal.

Scorpion

Scorpions Like a crayfish, each scorpion has two pincers and a long tail that curls toward its head like a whip. At the end of the tail is a stinger. Of the two species commonly found in the canyon, the most numerous by far is the **giant hairy scorpion.** Three to four inches long, this tan-colored scorpion inflicts a bite that's usually no worse than a bee sting. The **bark (or sculptured) scorpion** is more dangerous. Up to 2 inches long and straw colored, it injects a neurotoxic venom much stronger than that of its larger counterpart. These bites are very painful and can be deadly in rare cases. The best way to see scorpions is to shine an ultraviolet light on the canyon floor at night—in this light, they glow.

Reptiles

Chuckwallas Common in the lower parts of the canyon, chuckwallas look as if they've just completed a crash diet, leaving them with skin that's three sizes too big. When threatened, they inflate that loose skin, wedging themselves into rock crevices. From 11 to 16 inches long, chuckwallas have blackish heads and forelegs.

Collared lizards At the canyon's middle and lower elevations, you'll see a variety of collared lizards, which grow to 14 inches long and have big heads, long tails, and two black bands across their shoulders. Usually tan, **black-collared lizards** change shades when the temperature shifts. **Western collared lizards** are among the more colorful in the park, with blue, green, and yellow markings supplementing the black bands. These lizards are not the least bit shy around people, and are not dangerous. Sometimes, they'll stare you down for hours.

Chuckwalla

Collared lizard

Rattlesnakes If something rattles at you below the rim, it's probably the **Grand Canyon rattlesnake,** the most common rattler here. Its pinkish skin with dark blotches blends well with the canyon's soil. Like other rattlers, it has a triangular head, heat-sensing pits between its eyes, and a rattle used to

Rattlesnake

warn larger animals to stay away. To maintain an acceptable body temperature, this snake becomes active only when the ground temperature approaches 78°F (26°C). At other times, it's sluggish, perhaps sunning itself on a ledge or curling up under a rock pile or log.

Though it's venomous, the Grand Canyon rattlesnake is more reluctant to bite than other rattlesnakes (other rattlesnake species are seldom seen here). They're often near water, where they prey on small rodents. Human bites are extremely rare in the canyon; nevertheless, avoid getting close and seek help immediately if bitten.

Short-horned lizards These lizards can be found sunning themselves or scurrying across the forest floors on the canyon rims. With horizontal spines on their heads and rows of barbs on their

backs, these short, stout lizards look like tiny dinosaurs—or "horny toads," as they're commonly called. They can squirt blood from their eyes at attackers from up to 3 feet away.

Short-horned lizard

THE ECOSYSTEM

Grand Canyon National Park is part of an amazingly varied ecosystem responsible for an immense wealth of flora and fauna. But all is not perfect in paradise, and the park is a continuation of the land around it, which has been affected by human use. The air is compromised by distant industry and not-so-distant automobiles, the Colorado River constricted by dams, and the silence broken by high-flying jets and low-flying sightseeing planes. Theodore Roosevelt's dictum—to "leave it as it is"—now seems oversimplified. In the new millennium, the canyon's ecology depends nearly as much on far-reaching public policy as it does on nature.

Effects of the Glen Canyon Dam

Some of the most significant changes in the Grand Canyon's ecology result from the Glen Canyon Dam, which constricts the Colorado River just northeast of the Grand Canyon. Finished in 1963, the dam provides large amounts of subsidized hydroelectric power to cities such as Phoenix. It also provides recreational opportunities for a couple million visitors to Lake Powell every year.

In addition to inundating the once majestic Glen Canyon area with water, the dam has altered the biological communities in and around the Colorado River. Water temperatures in the canyon used to fluctuate from near freezing in winter to 80°F (27°C) or warmer in summer. The river, a mere trickle in winter, surged during the spring snowmelt to levels five times higher than the biggest floods today. Now, penstocks 230 feet below Lake Powell's surface take in water that varies only slightly from 48°F (9°C) year-round, at a rate that hardly changes. And the water has been sanitized. In predam days, the Colorado carried tons of reddish silt that had washed into it from the canyons of the Four Corners area (thus the name Rio Colorado, Spanish for "red river"). Today, that silt settles to the bottom of Lake Powell's torpid waters, and the river emerges from the dam as clear as snowmelt.

These changes (along with the Hoover Dam's impact and the introduction of new fish species) undermined the canyon's native fish population, which had evolved to survive in extreme temperatures, powerful flows, and heavy silt. Four of the eight native fish species died off, and one—the humpback chub—is breeding only where warmer tributaries enter the Colorado. In their places, rainbow trout, which were introduced below the dam for sport fishing, have flourished. Along the shores, tamarisk and coyote willow choke riverbanks that predam floods once purged of vegetation. This plant life is home to small lizards, mammals, and waterfowl, which, in turn, attract birds of prey such as the peregrine falcon.

Another effect of the dam has been the loss of an estimated 45% of sand from the beaches along the Colorado River. Before the dam was built, the canyon's huge floods lifted sand off the bottom of the river and deposited it in large beaches and sandbars. The postdam flows are too weak to accomplish this. There's also a shortage of sand: The reservoir captures about 95% of the sand headed into the canyon from upstream.

In 1996, the Bureau of Reclamation, the National Park Service, and a group of concerned environmental groups sought to find out whether a manmade flood released from the dam would restore some of the beaches. For 7 days in March and April 1996, the dam unloosed a sustained flow of 45,000 cubic feet per second—the maximum it could safely release. Although the flood packed only a fraction of the force of predam deluges, it did temporarily restore parts of 80 canyon beaches. Most scientists initially deemed the experiment—known as the Beach Habitat Restoration Flood—a success.

However, the beaches created during the 1996 flood eroded faster than expected—85% of them had washed away within 6 months. Additional experimental flows were performed in 2000, 2004, and 2008 designed to mitigate the erosion.

Effects of Air Traffic

While the dams encroach on the river, airplanes and helicopters encroach on the natural silence. For years, planes and helicopters were free to fly anywhere over the canyon and below the rims. Then, after a collision between sightseeing aircraft killed 25 people in 1986, the FAA established strict flight corridors and forced helicopters and planes to fly at different altitudes.

Though sightseeing flights have long been forbidden over Grand Canyon Village, their droning is still audible at popular destinations, and public opinion supports noise reductions. In 2000, the FAA implemented new regulations for sightseeing flights over Grand Canyon: These froze the maximum number of air-tour flights per year at the number between May 1997 and April 1998, tightened requirements for reporting flights, and replaced one meandering flight route in the western canyon with two straighter ones.

Unfortunately, most visitors won't notice any changes. The busiest flight corridors still thrive, and only a small part of the canyon is out of earshot of aircraft noise. The sounds travel an average of 16 miles laterally from aircraft in the eastern canyon and even farther in the west. However, the cap on flights does ensure that, at the very least, the problem shouldn't worsen much in the future.

By keeping the number of flights relatively constant, the FAA made it easier for researchers to monitor acoustics in the park. The Park Service and FAA may use this data to help achieve Congress's goal of restoring "natural quiet" to at least half of the park during the majority of daylight hours.

The Park Service believes this goal can be safely achieved through a combination of smaller flight corridors, quieter aircraft, and fewer (or shorter) flights. But many obstacles loom. For starters, the Park Service and FAA must agree on exactly what Congress meant. They must decide what constitutes "audible" and what "quiet technology" is. The safety of air traffic over the canyon cannot be compromised. And, while environmental groups press for quiet, representatives from the area's air tour industry seek to avoid limits on their operations.

Air Quality

Northern Arizona enjoys some of America's best-quality air. But it's not perfect, and air pollution does impact the canyon's ecology. In summer, air pollution comes from urban areas in Southern California, Southern Arizona, Nevada, and northern Mexico. In winter, during periods of calm weather, nearby pollution sources can play a more significant role. Overall, ozone levels in the park have been steadily rising; visibility has declined.

The federal Clean Air Act mandates that natural visibility eventually be restored to all national parks and wilderness areas. Seeking to accomplish this goal at the Grand Canyon by 2065, the National Park Service regularly takes part in a commission that includes state and federal EPA regulators, Native American tribal leaders, industry representatives, and other interested parties.

Efforts to improve air quality passed successfully in 1999 when scrubbers (air-pollution control devices) were installed at the Navajo Generating Station in Page, Arizona. This coal-burning station may have been responsible for as much as half of the canyon's air pollution in winter.

Yet the problem extends far past obvious polluters in the immediate area. For natural visibility to be restored, pollution sources ranging from automobile emissions in Los Angeles to factories in Mexico must be addressed. WRAP (the Western Regional Air Partnership) targeted at least a few of these distant polluters in 2001, when it proposed a declining cap on sulfur dioxide emissions throughout the western states. Utah, Arizona, Wyoming, and New Mexico are the four participating states and are meeting the declining cap and successfully implementing the recommendations.

Forest Fires

Even as National Park Service scientists fret over air quality, they know that more forest fires are needed in the ponderosa pine forest on the canyon rims. Before humans began suppressing forest fires, these areas experienced low-intensity blazes every 7 to 10 years. These fires made the forest healthier by burning excess undergrowth and deadfall, thinning tree stands, and returning nutrients to the soil. After fire suppression began, however, flammable material again accumulated on the forest floors, and trees grew too close together. With so much "fuel" available, the fires that did occur burned much hotter than before—hot enough, even, to kill old-growth ponderosas, which tend to be fire-resistant. These grand old trees, once gone, can not be replaced for centuries and changes in climate may preclude them from ever returning.

Today, fire suppression is no longer an automatic response. Land management agencies try to manage fire for ecological benefits. New policies enable the National Park Service to burn more areas more often, improving the forest health. Taking into account factors such as air quality, weather, location, fire-danger level, and available manpower, Grand Canyon National Park hopes to carry out prescribed burns on a few thousand acres per year. Prescribed fires are ignited and monitored under scientific conditions in order to achieve specific objectives, such as reducing forest fuels. Fires caused by lighting may be allowed to burn within an identified, undeveloped area for the same purpose as prescribed fires. Of course, fire use is not an exact science; in May 2000, a prescribed burn named the Outlet Fire spread faster and farther than expected, blackening more than 14,000 acres near Point Imperial on the North Rim, and closing parts of the park for weeks. Another forest service fire in 2006, called the Warm Fire, jumped over Highway 67 and scorched an area south of Jacob's Lake.

In the face of climate change, we remain unsure about the impact of stand-replacing fires. Our models still aren't effective at predicting future precipitation, although longer droughts followed by heavy downpours seem to be the new pattern.

Index

See also Accommodations and Restaurant indexes, below.

General Index

A

3X 4/14 (9/14)

5 × 3/18 (5/19)

6X 5/19 (4/29)